Grace, Faith, Free Will

Contrasting Views of Salvation:
Calvinism and Arminianism

Other books by Robert E. Picirilli

Paul the Apostle

Romans

Galatians

The Randall House Bible Commentary (general editor of series)
    Commentator on the following books:
        1, 2 Corinthians
        1, 2 Thessalonians
        Ephesians
        Philippians
        1, 2 Peter

Selected titles available from—

Randall House Publications
114 Bush Road • P.O. Box 17306
Nashville, Tennessee 37217 USA
phone 615-361-1221 • 1-800-877-7030
fax 615-367-0535 • www.randallhouse.com

Grace
Faith
Free Will

Contrasting Views of Salvation:
Calvinism and Arminianism

Robert E. Picirilli

randall house

Published by Randall House
114 Bush Road
Nashville, TN 37217
www.randallhouse.com

Grace, Faith, Free Will
Contrasting Views of Salvation: Calvinism and Arminianism

by Robert E. Picirilli

ISBN: 0-89265-648-4

Table of Contents

Foreword

I have in mind several purposes for this work. The first two are most important.

First, I wish to contribute to the contemporary renewal of discussion about the issues that have divided Calvinism and Arminianism since the Reformation. I do not deceive myself to think that I can bring about a rapprochement between the two, but I know that each new generation of Christian believers finds it next to impossible to avoid revisiting these issues. My goal is to present both sides, so that the reader will know exactly what those issues are: to clarify understanding of both positions and help readers intelligently decide for themselves.

Second, I intend to urge a very specific form of Arminianism as the best resolution of the tensions, and in this respect I am not impartial. The trouble with "Arminianism" is that it means different things to different people. My aim is to present what I call "Reformation Arminianism," by which I mean the views of Arminius himself and his original defenders. This is an Arminianism that has too often been lost sight of by friend and foe alike, and it is eminently virile and defensible.

Some readers may be surprised to learn that there is an Arminianism that defends:

- total depravity,
- the sovereignty of God to control all things for the certain accomplishment of His will,
- God's perfect foreknowledge of, and the certainty of, all future events—including the free, moral choices of human beings,
- the penal satisfaction view of the atonement,
- salvation by grace through faith and not by works, from beginning to end,
- and that apostasy cannot be remedied.

They may also be surprised to learn that this was essentially the Arminianism of Arminius himself. As Alan P. F. Sell has observed, "In important respects, Arminius was not an Arminian."[1]

---

[1] Alan P. F. Sell, *The Great Debate* (Grand Rapids: Baker, 1983), 97.

i

Though the original Arminianism did not continue in the Dutch Remonstrant Church, there have been proponents of Reformation Arminianism at various times and places. The Anabaptist Balthasar Hubmaier held similar views. Thomas Grantham, an important theologian among the early English General Baptists, set forth much the same soteriology as Arminius in his *Christianismus Primitivus, or the Ancient Christian Religion,* published in London in 1678.[2] Wesley recaptured much of the essence of Arminius' views.

Calling this "Reformation Arminianism" may result in criticism.[3] But I am convinced both that Arminius' theology was thought out in conscious consideration of the beliefs of the Reformers; and that Arminius succeeded in maintaining the Reformation insistence on salvation *sola gratia, sola fide,* and *solo Christo.* Sell reminds us that "Arminianism arose as a genuine option *within,* and not as a parasite upon, the Reformed Church in Holland."[4] Hence by "Reformation Arminianism" I mean both to distinguish the thinking of Arminius and the original Remonstrants from some of the forms Arminianism has taken since, and to identify it with the chief emphases of the Reformation.

In carrying out the two major purposes mentioned above, my method has been to pursue historical, systematic, and Biblical theology. In the first chapter I have reviewed the historical setting as it involved the struggle of Arminius and the original Remonstrants. Then each of four sections, in turn, is devoted to one of the four key issues: Predestination, Atonement, Salvation by Faith, and Perseverance. In each of these four sections there are three chapters: the first sets forth the Calvinistic view, the next the Arminian view, and the last some Biblical theology studies in support of the Arminian view. The exact procedure within each section varies, depending on the nature of the material. For the most part, I have concentrated on the traditional expressions. Consequently, the primary focus is on the classic Calvinistic theologians for that side, and on Arminius himself for that

---

[2] I have Matthew Pinson to thank for calling my attention to Grantham and will cite his (as yet unpublished) paper occasionally in this work.

[3] I do not claim that Arminius belongs among the magisterial Reformers. But I felt the need to give this species of Arminian soteriology some name; "evangelical Arminianism" is too broad, "Wesleyan Arminianism" already in use with another meaning, and "Remonstrance Arminianism" too likely to mean the Dutch Remonstrant Church, which is very different from the original Remonstrants. I considered and finally decided against "proto-Arminianism" as too clinical.

[4] Sell, 5.

side. Space does not allow for much attention to variations on the theme.

Some may ask, since I am urging a form of Arminianism, why I have taken the time to set forth both sides in each section. For two reasons. First, I once heard Dr. Roger Nicole observe that we should always make sure we can state an opponent's position in such a way that he will agree that we have expressed it correctly. I think he is right, and I have made a conscientious attempt to do that. It does no good to argue against another view if you have first misrepresented it. Straw men go down all too easily.

Second, I want those on each side to understand the other view from inside. Experience has taught me both that my Arminian friends often do not understand what Calvinism really is, and that Calvinists often misunderstand Arminianism. The resulting arguments are often emotional rather than based on careful understanding of each other. I would like to rectify that defect.

My third purpose for this work, while not primary, is nonetheless important. On the current scene we are witnessing a neo-Arminianism that takes some strange turns along the way. Those in this movement—sometimes called "openness theism"—deny the omniscience of God, for example, or tell us that God saves all who would become believers if they had a chance. As I see it, neither evangelical Christianity in general, nor Arminianism in particular, is any better off for that. Instead, the differences between Calvinism and Arminianism become confused and cloudy. By presenting the issues in the traditional terms—with a fresh perspective, I hope—I want to draw the debate back to the fundamental issues.

I offer now not so much a dedication as special appreciation for two teachers who helped shape my thinking long ago: first to L. C. Johnson who taught me Reformation Arminianism (although he did not call it that) straight from Arminius; and second to Wayne Witte who taught me classic Calvinism straight from Berkhof and Shedd and their kin, and did so with grace.

I also owe thanks to two distinguished friends who have read the text at my request and offered helpful suggestions: Leroy Forlines, a colleague who has read it for the Arminian side, and Bob Reymond, a well-known Reformed thinker who has read it for the Calvinist side. I do not lay at the feet of either of them the responsibility, however, for the views I present.

I close with the words of Arminius, written at the end of his own foreword to "An Examination of the Treatise of William Perkins concerning the Order and Mode of Predestination":

> May God grant that we all may fully agree, in those things which are necessary to His glory, and to the salvation of the church; and that, in other things, if there can not be harmony of opinions, there may at least be harmony of feelings, and that we may "keep the unity of the Spirit in the bond of peace."

PART ONE

Historical Setting

One who calls himself "Arminian" does so with considerable risk. The name means different things to different people. Many automatically think of Arminians as liberal, differing little from Universalists, at least holding to salvation by works and possibly holding Arian views on the Trinity or Pelagian views on the goodness of man. In truth, some "Arminians" have held or now hold some such things.

Not so Arminius himself or his original followers. Charles Cameron has written, perceptively, that "Arminius is a largely misunderstood theologian. He is frequently assessed according to superficial hearsay."[1] Therein lies the importance of going back to the beginning. Only by retracing the story can we put into its proper setting that movement I am calling Reformation Arminianism. And only then can we evaluate the possibilities for such a brand of Arminianism today.

---

[1]Charles M. Cameron, "Arminius—Hero or Heretic?" (*Evangelical Quarterly,* 64:3 [1992], 213-227), 213.

PART ONE

CHAPTER ONE

Arminius and the Revolt Against Calvinism

This chapter represents a "historical theology" treatment of the issues that divide Calvinists and Arminians, which should serve as a proper introduction to the systematic and Biblical explorations that will make up the major share of this work.The following account, while important to an understanding of the issues, is necessarily brief. Those who wish more detailed information are urged to read the 1971 work of Carl Bangs, *Arminius: A Study in the Dutch Reformation,* indicated in the bibliography. It is by far the best work on Arminius, and I will be summarizing from it often in this chapter.

Arminius' Rearing and Education

Jacobus Arminius was a name he took later. He was born Jacob Harmenszoon—a good Dutch name meaning "Harmen's son"—in Oudewater, Holland, probably in 1559.[2] His father, a smith who made swords and armor, apparently died before his birth, leaving the widowed mother to care for several children.

As a child, Arminius was educated through others' support. First, a local priest with Protestant leanings, Theodore Aemilius, became his patron and teacher. During his early teens, Arminius lived with Aemilius in Utrecht. When Aemilius died in 1575, a new benefactor involved himself—Rudolphus Snellius, a professor in the University of Marburg. Arminius studied there for about a year; during that time, all his family was massacred in the destruction of Oudewater in August 1575. Spanish forces had retaliated when Oudewater joined with those seeking independence from Spain.

Meanwhile, a university had been established at Leiden, in his homeland, and the maturing Arminius enrolled there on October 23, 1576. This is the first record of his use of "Jacobus Arminius," a latinized version of his name. The custom of the time called for the adop-

---

[2]The traditional date is 1560. A better argument for 1559 has been made by Carl Bangs, *Arminius: A Study in the Dutch Reformation* (Nashville: Abingdon, 1971), 25, 26.

tion of such a Latin name in scholarly pursuits. ("Jacobus" translates into English as "James," and so he is often referred to by that name.) He distinguished himself in the study of such subjects as mathematics, logic, theology, and the Biblical languages.

While at Leiden, Arminius experienced his first taste of controversy within the Reformed churches, where there were differences of opinion about the relationship between church and state. Arminius was sympathetic with a Leiden pastor by name of Caspar Coolhaes, who held, against Calvin, that the civil authorities did have certain powers in church affairs.

In Leiden, the city burgomasters exercised such powers; not so in Calvin's Geneva. Bangs thinks that Coolhaes, with his more tolerant spirit and independence from Calvin, "took essentially the same positions which were later to be known by the name of Arminianism."[3] If so, Coolhaes was probably an important influence on Arminius.

When Arminius completed his studies at Leiden in 1581, still too young for assignment as a pastor, the clergy and magistrates in Amsterdam offered him opportunity for further education. Upon his agreement to devote himself to serve the Amsterdam church, they arranged to support him at Calvin's academy in Geneva.

At the time, the chair of theology there was occupied by Theodore Beza, Calvin's successor. Beza represented what many call "hyper-Calvinism"; others say he simply took the teachings of his master and gave them logical consistency. At any rate, Jewett calls Arminius "Beza's best known student."[4]

We cannot be sure how much Arminius agreed or disagreed with Beza's "high Calvinism" at the time. He was involved in controversy in Geneva, but over logic rather than predestination, and not directly with Beza. As a result, he left to study at Basel, being there for about a year in 1583-84. Even so, he returned to study again at Geneva until some time in 1586.

While at Basel, Arminius was a favorite of professor J. J. Grynaeus, a Lutheran with Zwinglian views, and thus another important influence in a direction other than strict Calvinism. Under him, Arminius expounded parts of Romans, thus perhaps laying the groundwork for the controversial sermons on Romans 7 and 9 that would come later. Some of Arminius' contemporaries reported that he was offered the

    [3]Bangs, 52.
    [4]Paul K. Jewett, *Election and Predestination* (Grand Rapids: Eerdmans, 1985), 63.

title of Doctor at Basel, only to refuse on grounds of his youth. He was about 24 at the time.

So far as we know, Arminius' second stay at Geneva was not characterized by tension. Even Beza, in response to an inquiry from the Amsterdam authorities who were supporting Arminius, said:

> Let it be known to you that from the time Arminius returned to us from Basel, his life and learning both have so approved themselves to us, that we hope the best of him in every respect, if he steadily persist in the same course, which, by the blessing of God, we doubt not he will.[5]

Whether Arminius agreed with Beza's predestinarian views or not, Arminius openly expressed admiration for Beza's brilliance.

There were other professors at Geneva: Charles Perrot was one who may have influenced him. Perrot argued for tolerance in theological matters, and is reported to have said, "Justification by faith only has been preached up too much; it is time to speak of works."[6] Among Arminius' peers at Geneva was his life-long friend, Johannes Uitenbogaert,[7] who was to play an important role in the later controversies.

By mid-1586, the burgomasters in Amsterdam had decided that Arminius should soon leave the university and return to take up duties as pastor. First, Arminius and a friend decided to make a trip to Italy, which included a hasty trip to Rome. Later, Arminius' critics would say that he had kissed the pope's slipper and consorted with Cardinal Bellarmine—never mind that there was no truth in this or that Arminius never had a good word to say of popes.

Arminius as a Pastor

In late 1587, then, Arminius arrived in Amsterdam. After obtaining the necessary approvals by church and civil authorities, he was finally ordained on August 27, 1588. As a pastor, he would serve both church and city in that period of history when the lines between church and state were not so strongly drawn. Bangs is confident that the attitude of the city council at the time was mild and broad, for lib-

---

[5]Bangs, 73, 74.

[6]Bangs, 76.

[7]Uitenbogaert is but one of many personal or place names, in this story, that are spelled in various ways in the sources. Throughout, I have adopted Bangs' spellings.

erty of conscience, and that Arminius was regarded by them as a kindred spirit.[8]

Arminius was a popular preacher. The several ministers organized the preaching schedule at the various churches in the city, and he was soon taking his turn. "He consistently drew large crowds whenever it was known that he would be the preacher of the day."[9] He preached often from Romans, although no controversy was occasioned until he reached chapter 7 in 1591. Meanwhile he carried out his pastoral duties and managed at the same time to court Lijsbet Reael, daughter of a member of the city council and thus part of the upper crust of Amsterdam society. They were married in September 1590.

By this time, Arminius was beginning to be embroiled in controversy. He did not originate it; there were disputes already, among the Reformed churches, in regard to some of Calvin's and Beza's teachings. Arminius' involvement came about as follows. One of the severe critics of "Calvinism" was a humanist named Dirck Coornhert. Two Reformed ministers of Delft, under the pressure of Coornhert's arguments, had expressed modifications of Beza's high Calvinism in a pamphlet published in 1589. Arminius was asked to enter the fray, either to refute the Delft ministers' modifications, or to refute Coornhert himself, or both—there is some confusion on that point.

Regardless, the story usually goes that Arminius, while studying to defend Beza's Calvinism against its critics or modifiers, found that the Scriptures would not support Calvinism at all.[10] Bangs makes a good case for doubting this popular version. He is convinced that Arminius never had accepted Beza's formulation of the doctrine of predestination.[11] In that case, the controversy was inevitable, given the wide influence of Calvin and of Beza as his interpreter.

The first episode came when Arminius preached on Romans 7 in 1591. The high Calvinists maintained that the person described in verses 14-24 is a regenerate man. Arminius preached that this person must be a sinner, else God's power is ineffective. He was roundly criticized, a fellow minister named Petrus Plancius taking the lead. At a

---

[8]Bangs, 123,124.

[9]Donald M. Lake, "Jacob Arminius' Contribution to a Theology of Grace," *Grace Unlimited*, ed. Clark H. Pinnock (Minneapolis: Bethany Fellowship, 1975), 226.

[10]For the usual view of Arminius' "conversion" from Calvinistic predestinarianism, see another member of the Bangs family, Mildred Bangs Wynkoop, *Foundations of Wesleyan-Arminian Theology* (Kansas City: Beacon Hill Press, 1967), 47-49.

[11]Bangs, 138-141.

meeting of the ministers in January 1592, Plancius accused Arminius of teaching Pelagianism, of being overly dependent on the early church fathers, of deviating from the Belgic Confession and Heidelberg Catechism (creedal statements influential in the Reformed church at the time), and of holding incorrect views on predestination and the perfection of man in this life.

Discussions were not fruitful. Finally, the city burgomasters involved themselves, over the objections of the church consistory. Arminius insisted that he was within the bounds of the creeds. The burgomasters supported him and admonished his critics to forbear, at least until the disputed points should at some time be decided in a general church council of the Netherlands.

Arminius' sermons have not survived, but we may assume that his later (c. 1599) treatise on Romans 7 (published in 1612 by "The Nine Orphan Children" of Arminius) contains the essence of what he preached. In the introduction to that treatise, he insisted that Romans 7:14 (and following) refers to "a man living under the law," otherwise called unregenerate. He acknowledged that those who held his view were "charged with holding a doctrine which has some affinity to the two-fold heresy of Pelagius, and are said to ascribe to man, without the grace of Christ, some true and saving good, and, taking away the contest between the flesh and the spirit which is carried on in the regenerate, are said to maintain a perfection of righteousness in the present life." He hastens to "confess that I detest, from my heart, the consequences which are here deduced"—apparently meaning all the views just named—and to assert that he will "make it evident that neither these heresies, nor any other, are derived from this opinion." He adds, specifically, that his view "refutes the grand falsehood of Pelagius."[12]

The second episode occurred about a year later, when Arminius reached Romans 9 in his preaching. Plancius brought charges: (1) that Arminius had taught that no one is condemned except by his own sin—which would imperil Beza's doctrine of predestination and exclude infants from condemnation; (2) that he had made too much of the role of good works; (3) that he had taught that angels are not immortal.[13]

---

[12]James Arminius, *The Writings of James Arminius,* tr. James Nichols and W. R. Bagnall (Grand Rapids; Baker, 1956), II:219, 220. The entire treatise occupies pages 196-452.

[13]Again, in the absence of the sermon, we must rely on Arminius' subsequent written analysis of Rom. 9. See Arminius, III:527-565.

Arminius answered the first accusation by replying that Plancius was overlooking original sin—thus sidestepping the issue of predestination. As for the second, Arminius insisted that he had nothing to recant since he had attributed no merit to good works. The third charge was explained as resulting from his insistence that only God possesses immortality of Himself. Arminius concluded his defense by restating his assent to the two creeds, adding that his only hesitation would be a matter of the interpretation, not the wording, of the Belgic Confession, Article 16. That article refers to the elect as: "all whom he, in his eternal and unchangeable counsel, of mere goodness hath elected in Jesus Christ our Lord." Arminius raised the question whether the "all" means all believers, as he interpreted it, or implies an arbitrary decree on God's part to bestow faith, as others believed. In other words, Arminius apparently felt that the article could very well mean conditional election. At any rate, the church consistory found Arminius' statement acceptable and urged all to maintain peace until such time as a general synod of the churches might determine the proper interpretation. Perhaps they feared to do more, lest the city burgomasters again involve themselves.

From this point in May 1593 until May 1603, Arminius' life and ministry were relatively peaceful. After his first two children had died in infancy, a daughter and four sons were born and survived to bring Arminius and Lijsbet much joy. His pastoral ministry was typical of the times, and he was active in ecclesiastical matters in and beyond Amsterdam. He was often involved in opposing heresies, although he kept postponing a request that he refute the Anabaptists—perhaps because their doctrine of predestination was closer to his own. Probably the hardest time of his ministry came when bubonic plague invaded Amsterdam in 1601 and claimed some 20,000 victims. On one occasion, in a slum, Arminius took water into a home where no one else would enter to relieve a family with all members afflicted by the scourge.

During these years in Amsterdam, Arminius wrote many theological treatises, although they were not published until after his death. These included the extensive essays on Romans 7 and 9 (referred to above) and a lengthy correspondence with Franciscus Junius.

Most of these writings dealt primarily with sin, grace, predestination, and the freedom of the will. The essay on Romans 7 concludes that "Nothing can be imagined more noxious to true morality than to assert that 'it is a property of the regenerate *not to do the good which they would, and to do the evil which they would not'.*"[14]

The treatment of Romans 9 took the form of a lengthy letter to one Gellius Snecanus, a Reformed minister in Friesland, who had written in favor of conditional predestination and had published, in 1596, an *Introduction to the Ninth Chapter of Romans.* Arminius recognized views similar to his own and wrote to tell Snecanus how he personally dealt with Romans 9 and its implications of an arbitrary predestination. Beza had interpreted the "lump" (Rom. 9:21) to be "the human race, as not yet created, and not yet corrupt"; Arminius, citing Augustine, understood it to be mankind as already fallen, so that the objects both of God's mercy and of His judgment are sinners.[15] The message of Romans 9, according to Arminius, was "the freedom of God's mercy, whereby he alone determines who shall be saved, namely, the believer."[16]

Correspondence with Junius, a Calvinist professor in Leiden more moderate than Beza, was meant to be confidential. Arminius wrote a lengthy statement of his views about Junius' position; Junius responded by expressing Arminius' position as 27 propositions and writing a lengthy reply to each. Arminius responded—after learning that one of Junius' students had copied the correspondence and shown it to fellow students—with even longer discussion of each of Junius' replies.

Arminius' main point was to insist that all of God's saving works deal with men as *sinners,* and that God must not be made the author of sin. He understood unconditional predestination to do that. He also felt constrained to insist that election is "Christocentric"; salvation is by the redemptive work of Christ and not by an arbitrary decree.

Arminius the Controversial Professor

On August 28, 1602, the plague took the life of Lucas Trelcatius, a professor of theology at the university at Leiden. Arminius' friends began immediately to seek his appointment in Trelcatius' place. Opposition began just as quickly, led by Franciscus Gomarus, an influential professor of theology there.

Finally, after many consultations, Gomarus reluctantly approved and the curators and Leiden burgomasters officially appointed Arminius as professor of theology on May 8, 1603. Shortly afterward,

---

[14]Arminius, II:423.

[15]Arminius, III:554.

[16]The wording is a summary by Bangs, 198; see Arminius, III:554-559.

he was granted a doctorate, perhaps the first that Leiden had award-ed. He would spend the last six years of his life there, almost always in a storm of theological controversy. He was also suffering from tuberculosis. At the same time, his family grew to include seven sons and two daughters. As Bangs put it, during this period he was "blessed with family and friends but cursed with illness and con-flict."[17]

At the heart of the conflict was predestination. Even among the Calvinists there was not agreement on all details. The more severe ones, like Beza and Gomarus, held that God *first* decreed to save and damn certain individuals and *then* decreed the fall as a step necessary toward accomplishing this—a position often called "supralapsarian-ism." Others reversed the order, holding that God *first* decreed to cre-ate and to permit the fall, and *then* decreed to save or damn fallen individuals—a position often called "sublapsarianism" or "infralap-sarianism."[18]

But all of them agreed that the decrees to save or damn were *unconditional,* and that God foreknows all future events because He has first ordained them. Arminius believed that all the Calvinists final-ly made sin necessary and therefore caused by God. Most important-ly, he held that election to salvation was election of *believers,* which means that election is *conditioned on faith.* He also insisted that God's foreknowledge of man's choices did not cause or make those choices necessary.

By early 1605 the lines of conflict were clearly drawn and the ten-sion persistent. Arminius was by no means alone. The differences were widespread and included both political and theological implica-tions. The issue of church-state separation continued to affect the debate. So did the wearying, half-hearted war for independence from Spain, and the vying for political power that went along with that.

At the risk of oversimplification, we may say that there were two parties. On one side was the war party, refusing any peace with Spain short of total independence, led by Prince Maurice, who as military commander desired to achieve greater power. The staunch Calvinists inclined to this side, and it was their hope to get the church's gov-erning authority free of any kind of answerability to the state.

On the other side was a peace party, ready for a truce with Spain, led by Jan van Oldenbarnevelt, who as grand pensionary of Holland

---

[17]Bangs, 251.

[18]For further discussion on this subject, see the following chapter.

personified and exercised the civil power. Those who supported this side were inclined to greater theological tolerance and approved the traditional structure that provided for civil authorities to exercise some controls over church officials. Arminius and those associated with him were on this side.

One of the practical issues that kept arising throughout the theological controversy was whether and how to convene a national synod that might rule on the disputed points. Arminius and his friends kept insisting that such a synod should be convened, and that it should have the power to revise the confessions. His opponents preferred to use the influence of their local synods against the Arminians.

In 1607 the States General notified the several states to send deputies to confer about preparation for calling a synod. At the conference Arminius lost a bid to have the proposed synod left open to revise the confessions. From that point on, although he and his followers continued to press for the national synod as their best hope, he must have realized that there was little chance of winning tolerance of his views. He was under attack from all quarters, accused of everything that could be imagined. Most of his efforts to have his accusers present formal charges went for nothing. A synod was not convened during his lifetime.

In 1608, as a result of Arminius' petition to the States General for a legal inquiry into his situation, a meeting was held before the High Court, with Arminius and Gomarus as the principals. At the end, the two men were ordered to put their sentiments into writing, to be submitted to the States General. The result, on Arminius' part, was his *Declaration of Sentiments,* which "represents the mature views of Arminus."[19] Before, he had usually tried to sidestep the debated points. Now, even though not in a national synod as he had desired, he had at least the opportunity of making this official declaration before the proper governing officials of the country.

In the *Declaration of Sentiments,* after countering the Calvinists' views, Arminius proceeded to set forth his own: in essence, that God's decree of election was to save those sinners who repent and believe in Christ. The decree to save and damn particular persons was based on God's foreknowledge of their faith or unbelief. On the matter of perseverance—which had not been so crucial an issue as predestination—Arminius was cautious: "I never taught that *a true believer can*

---

[19]Bangs, 307.

either totally or finally fall away from the faith and perish, yet I will not conceal that there are passages of Scripture which seem to me to wear this aspect."[20] He concluded with another appeal for a national synod, one that would be open to the possibility of revisions in the confessions.

From that point events moved swiftly. Gomarus asked and received permission to appear before the States of Holland. His presentation was vitriolic. Arminius was guilty, he said, of errors on predestination, original sin, foreknowledge, the possibility of falling from grace, the Trinity, the authority of Scripture, regeneration, works, and several more things; he was also two-faced and inconsistent, saying one thing at one time and a different thing at another, one thing in public and something else in private or to his students at home. The governors did not sustain Gomarus' accusations. Even so, throughout the country a vicious campaign was on, and pamphlets flew back and forth on both sides. "An entire population [became] passionately involved in theological controversy."[21]

In August 1609, the States General asked Arminius and Gomarus to come for a "friendly conference," each to be sided by four ministers of his choice. As grand pensionary, Oldenbarnevelt presided. Arminius' counselors included Uitenbogaert. After meetings on Thursday and Friday, August 13, 14, the sessions were recessed for the weekend. Arminius, whose condition had been growing worse for some time, became too ill to continue and had to return home to Leiden. The conference was dismissed. The States officials directed that Arminius and Gomarus should submit their views in writing within 14 days. Gomarus turned in his work on time. Arminius never finished his; he was on his sickbed for the last time. On Monday, October 19, 1609, he died. His body was laid to rest on Thursday, beneath the paving slabs of the church called Pieterskerk in Leiden.

The Remonstrants and the Synod of Dort

In one sense, the controversy was just beginning. Before Arminius' death, some of the local synods had demanded that all their ministers submit statements about their views on the confessions. The States General recognized that this represented resistance

---

[20] Arminius, I:254.

[21] Gerrit Jan Hoenderdaal, "The Life and Struggle of Arminius in the Dutch Republic," *Man's Faith and Freedom,* ed. Gerald O. McCulloh (Nashville: Abingdon, 1962), 20.

to his authority. The order was countermanded and aggrieved parties were directed instead to forward statements to the States General.

Consequently, in 1610, with tensions still building, the followers of Arminius presented a petition to the States, called a "Remonstrance" (so that those who supported it were called "Remonstrants" and the opposing Calvinists "Contra-Remonstrants"). Among the leaders of the Arminian side were Uitenbogaert, a scholar named Simon Episcopius, and an influential lawyer named Hugo Grotius; Oldenbarnevelt gave them his support.

The Remonstrance expressed the Arminians' main points briefly in five articles. These are as follows:

> *Art. 1.* That God, by an eternal, unchangeable purpose in Jesus Christ his Son, before the foundation of the world, hath determined, out of the fallen, sinful race of men, to save in Christ, for Christ's sake, and through Christ, those who, through the grace of the Holy Ghost, shall believe on this his Son Jesus, and shall persevere in this faith and obedience of faith, through this grace, even to the end; and, on the other hand, to leave the incorrigible and unbelieving in sin and under wrath, and to condemn them as alienate from Christ.

This article presents the main point at issue. It accepts predestination as including both election to salvation and reprobation to condemnation. But it puts both of these decrees *after* man's voluntary (not necessitated) fall into sin, and it makes both of these decrees *conditional* upon the respective faith or unbelief of the individuals who are the objects of election or reprobation. That is in opposition to the Calvinistic view of unconditional election.

> *Art. 2.* That, agreeably thereto, Jesus Christ, the Saviour of the world, died for all men and for every man, so that he has obtained for them all, by his death on the cross, redemption and the forgiveness of sins; yet that no one actually enjoys this forgiveness of sins except the believer.

This article emphasizes unlimited or universal atonement, and yet makes clear that not all are actually saved by that atonement; only believers experience its redemptive effects. This opposes the Calvinistic view that the atonement provided redemption only for the elect.

> *Art. 3.* That man has not saving grace of himself, nor of the energy of his free will, inasmuch as he, in the state of apostasy and sin, can of and by

himself neither think, will, nor do any thing that is truly good (such as saving Faith eminently is); but that it is needful that he be born again of God in Christ, through his Holy Spirit, and renewed in understanding, inclination, or will, and all his powers, in order that he may rightly understand, think, will, and effect what is truly good.

This article emphasizes that everything involved both in salvation and in Christian living is by God's grace. Not even man's free will can initiate a positive response to God apart from enabling grace. Thus even saving faith is not effected by man "of himself." The Arminians were always accused of attributing too much to man and thus depreciating grace. This article was meant to counteract that false accusation and show that they were at one with their opponents in attributing all good to God's grace.

Art. 4. That this grace of God is the beginning, continuance, and accomplishment of all good, even to this extent, that the regenerate man himself, without prevenient or assisting, awakening, following and co-operative grace, can neither think, will, nor do good, nor withstand any temptations to evil; so that all good deeds or movements, that can be conceived, must be ascribed to the grace of God in Christ. But as represents the mode of the operation of this grace, it is not irresistible, inasmuch as it is written concerning many, that they have resisted the Holy Ghost.

The fourth article continues the emphasis of the third, but adds an important provision: God's grace operates in such a way that man can successfully resist it. No one is overpowered by it, man's freedom is not taken away by its work. This was meant to oppose the Calvinistic view that saving grace is irresistible.

Art. 5. That those who are incorporated into Christ by a true faith, and have thereby become partakers of his life-giving Spirit, have thereby full power to strive against Satan, sin, the world, and their own flesh, and to win the victory; it being well understood that it is ever through the assisting grace of the Holy Ghost; and that Jesus Christ assists them through his Spirit in all temptations, extends to them his hand, and if only they are ready for the conflict, and desire his help, and are not inactive, keeps them from falling, so that they, by no craft of power of Satan, can be misled nor plucked out of Christ's hands. . . . But whether they are capable, through negligence, of forsaking again the first beginnings of their life in Christ, of again returning to this present evil world, of turning away from the holy doctrine which was delivered them, of losing a good conscience, of becoming devoid of grace, that must be more particularly determined out of the Holy Scriptures, before we ourselves can teach it with the full persuasion of our minds.[22]

This final article is the longest. It shows that the early Arminians, although they had not fully made up their minds, were open to the view that one may be lost after being saved. This had not been one of the key issues in the controversy, although it had been raised. The statement represents a cautious and early feeling on the subject. Ultimately the Arminians would come to express this view without such hesitation, standing in opposition to the Calvinistic belief in necessary perseverance.

The ensuing years were stormy. Various attempts were made by the States General to bring peace. For awhile, with the aid of the magistrates, Remonstrants remained in office in many cities and continued to call for a general synod, one that would involve all of the Protestant churches in the states. By 1618 however, Maurice, growing in power, used the militia to forcibly replace Remonstrant magistrates with Calvinists in city after city. He convinced many that Oldenbarnevelt and the Arminians were sympathizers with the Catholics and would inevitably deliver the country up to Spain. In this way he succeeded in preparing the way for a national synod that would be thoroughly anti-Arminian. The States General issued a call for such a synod to take place beginning May 1, 1618. Oldenbarnevelt and Grotius were arrested, and the way was paved for a synod whose outcome was already pre-determined (not to say predestined).

After delays, the synod convened November 13, 1618, and held sessions until May 9, 1619, in Dordrecht—ever after known as the Synod of Dort. Although mostly a Dutch national synod, representatives of Reformed churches attended from Great Britain, Switzerland, the Palatinate, Hesse, Wetterau, Emden, and Bremen. The deck was stacked from the start: directions for the selection of delegates were such that Arminians were ruled out by definition.

Three Arminian delegates from Utrecht managed to get seated anyway, but early in the proceedings they were forced to yield their seats to Calvinistic alternates. All Arminians were regarded as charged with heresy rather than participants in the synod.

---

[22]These articles may be found in several places. The English translation given here, along with Dutch and Latin versions, is found in Philip Schaff, _The Creeds of Christendom_ (Grand Rapids: Baker, 1966), III:545-549.

Episcopius, as the leading Arminian spokesman, and twelve other Remonstrants were cited to appear and answer charges.

On January 14, 1619, the Remonstrant defenders were dismissed, their views condemned as heresy. Ultimately, the Belgic Confession and Heidelberg Catechism were adopted as orthodox statements of the doctrine of the Reformed churches. In addition, five "canons" in opposition to the Remonstrance were written and adopted. To this day, the "Canons of Dort" stand as part of the official doctrinal basis of many of the Reformed Churches. And, as opposed to the five Articles of the Remonstrance, they are sometimes called the "five points of Calvinism."

Punishment for the Remonstrants, now officially condemned as heretics and therefore under the judgment of both church and state, was severe. All Arminian pastors—some 200 of them—were deprived of office; any who would not agree to be silent were banished from the country. "Spies were paid to hunt down those suspected of returning to their homeland."[23] Some were imprisoned, among them Grotius; but he escaped and fled the country. Five days after the synod was over, Oldenbarnevelt was beheaded. The controversy was settled.

A postscript is in order. After Maurice's death in 1625, the Remonstrants were accorded toleration—by the country, not in the Reformed Church. In 1630 they were granted the freedom to follow their religion in peace, to build churches and schools. In 1795, the Remonstrant Church was officially recognized and remains to this day. A Remonstrant Theological Seminary was instituted at Amsterdam, with Episcopius and Grotius among its first professors. That seminary also still exists. I regret to say that the Dutch Remonstrant Church represents an Arminianism today that is little different from humanistic liberalism:

> The inclination towards freedom of speculation, the rejection of all creeds and confessions, a preference of moral to doctrinal teaching, Arian views respecting the Trinity, the virtual rejection of the doctrines of Original Sin and imputed righteousness, and the depreciation of the spiritual value of the Sacraments, have resulted in the gradual reduction of Arminianism in Holland to a negligible theological quantity, and

---

[23]Roy S. Nicholson, "A Historical Survey of the Rise of Wesleyan-Arminian Theology," *The Word and the Doctrine,* ed. Kenneth E. Geiger (Kansas City: Beacon Hill Press, 1965), 30.

to the dimensions of an insignificant sect, numbering only some twenty congregations.[24]

As I have noted in the Foreword, the distinctive doctrines of Arminius, and of most of his earliest supporters, have appeared elsewhere from time to time. The views of the (somewhat) Anabaptist Balthazar Hubmaier were close to those of Arminius and will repay study. Wesley and the theologians who developed the early Methodist teachings had much in common. So did the English General Baptists, under the influence of Thomas Grantham, while they were yet sound in the faith.[25]

These are just examples: each of them, in part at least, has served to "rescue" Arminianism from its sickness and restore it to evangelical health and to the emphasis on the grace of God that Arminius and the original Remonstrants gave. But that story is beyond the scope of this work. It is sufficient to observe, here, that there is available to us even today a kind of Arminianism that takes its lead from Arminius himself and his first followers, a truly Reformation Arminianism. It is the purpose of the rest of this work to indicate what such an Arminian viewpoint really is.

---

[24]Frederic Platt, "Arminianism," *Encyclopaedia of Religion and Ethics,* ed. James Hastings (New York: Charles Scribner's Sons, n.d.), I:811. An interesting (and approving) explanation of the development "From Arminius to Arminianism" is found in chapter 2 of *Man's Faith and Freedom,* cited above.

[25]There are families of Baptists today in the tradition of Grantham's *1660 Confession.*

For Further Reading on the History of Arminius and the Remonstrants

Bangs, Carl. *Arminius: A Study in the Dutch Reformation.* Nashville: Abingdon, 1971.

Bagnall, W. R. "A Sketch of the Life of James Arminius" in *The Writings of James Arminius,* tr. James Nichols and W. R. Bagnall. Grand Rapids: Baker, 1956 (vol. I, pp. 9-15).

Lake, Donald M. "Jacob Arminius' Contribution to a Theology of Grace," *Grace Unlimited,* ed. Clark H. Pinnock. Minneapolis; Bethany Fellowship, 1975.

McCulloh,Gerald O. ed., *Man's Faith and Freedom.* Nashville: Abingdon, 1962.

Nicholson, Roy S. "A Historical Survey of the Rise of Wesleyan-Arminian Theology," *The Word and the Doctrine,* ed. Kenneth E. Geiger. Kansas City: Beacon Hill Press, 1965.

O'Malley, J. S. "Arminianism," *Dictionary of Christianity in America,* ed. Reid, Linder, Shelley, and Stout. Downers Grove: InterVarsity, 1990.

Platt, Frederic. "Arminianism," *Encyclopaedia of Religion and Ethics,* ed. James Hastings. New York: Charles Scribner's Sons, n.d. (vol. I).

Sell, Alan P. F. *The Great Debate.* Grand Rapids: Baker, 1983. [An account of the struggle between Calvinism and Arminianism throughout church history]

The Plan of Salvation

A study of the theology of salvation typically begins with the decisions of God made before creation. When we do that, we are dealing with what is technically called the decrees of God, or—to borrow Warfield's title—*The Plan of Salvation.* [1]

Systematic theologians usually treat this subject under the heading of predestination. In turn they subdivide predestination into two parts, election and reprobation. The specific definitions of these terms depend, more or less, on the theological position of those defining them.

We will first examine the Calvinistic view of predestination (chapter 2), then the Arminian view (chapter 3). In each case, a "systematic theology" approach will be somewhat briefly outlined, with such comments as seem necessary for understanding.

Then will follow (chapter 4) the pursuit of some "biblical theology" investigations that appear helpful for the issues involved. This methodology will be used throughout the rest of the book, with some variations that reflect the nature of the material.

---

[1] Benjamin B. Warfield, *The Plan of Salvation* (Grand Rapids: Eerdmans, 1942).

PART TWO

CHAPTER TWO

The Classical Calvinistic Doctrine of Predestination

Theological Background

If one is to understand any theologian's views about predestination, he must first consider that theologian's basic assumptions about the nature of God, man, and salvation.

The Concept of God

• *God is sovereign,* the absolute monarch of the created universe. In brief, God's sovereignty means that He is absolutely free to act as He wills and in accord with His own nature. To put this another way, His actions are not "conditioned" by any considerations other than being true to Himself. There are no obligations, on God's part, to anyone or anything outside Himself. There are no limitations imposed on Him or His actions by anyone or anything other than His own will and attributes.

• *God is creator and preserver of everything that is not Him.* Among other things, this means that all that exists does so by His will. And what is includes what happens: the whole course of history, all the actions of all created beings.

Nothing, in other words, is out of control. There are no surprises for God. Nothing that transpires is outside His plan: "The counsel of the Lord is His eternal good pleasure, according to which He willed and conceived all things that are ever realized or occur in time."[2]

To say again: nothing ever happens that is uncertain, accidental, or by chance. Nothing really can develop in either of two ways, indeterminately. If He did not certainly know all that will transpire, He could not include everything in His plan and maintain absolute control over all events.

Furthermore, nothing can happen apart from God's providential control, His preservation and upholding of all things. Even the atoms of energy in the bullet of the murderer's gun are sustained for their grisly work by Him.

• *God is omniscient, and His knowledge manifests His will.* He knows perfectly and certainly all that will happen. He knew it all

---

[2]Herman Hoeksema, *Reformed Dogmatics* (Grand Rapids: Reformed Free Publishing Association, 1966), 155.

before creating. He knew all that *could* be: all contingencies, in other words. Looking at all possible consequences of the decisions He might make for the universe and man, He chose that course of events (out of all possible courses of events) that He set in motion by His creative decisions. Thus He willed what is and therefore knew all that *would* be. In a real sense, then, His knowledge equals His will. He knows all that will be as certain to be because He willed it to be.

• *Nor can His will be thwarted.* This follows from His absolute sovereignty. There is no force in the universe that can thwart the will of God, else that force would be superior to God and would therefore be God. All forces in the universe other than God owe their existence to His creative actions and are therefore subordinate to Him and under His governing control. Nothing and no one can overthrow God or prevent Him from accomplishing all that He wills.

• *God is good and He alone is to be glorified.* God is the source of all that is good and is therefore deserving of all the glory for anything good. No other being can take credit for anything good. "God is all, and we are in ourselves nothing. . . . He only is the overflowing fountain . . . the creature is always at the receiving end."[3]

The Concept of Man

Equally essential to understanding God's plan for man's salvation is a Biblical concept of man as the object of God's grace.

• *Man is God's creature.* Since this is true, man is wholly subordinate to and absolutely governed by God. God owes nothing to man and is answerable in no way to man for His plan or actions. Man has no claim on God that God must take into account when He acts.

• *Man is fallen and wholly sinful.* As a result of the fall, man is bad, not good. He is therefore capable of doing nothing good that merits anything from God. As already noted, all good must be attributed to God and is for His own glory.

This is the doctrine of total depravity. Man, as fallen, is not free. His will is bound to a darkened intellect as a result of the sinfulness of his own nature. He is therefore not capable of any good, and this would certainly include responding, before regeneration, to the offer of salvation for all who believe. As a sinner, he cannot put faith in God.

The Concept of Salvation

This follows naturally from the preceding.

---

[3]Hoeksema, 154.

• *Salvation is **altogether** the work of God.* Not even a small amount of credit can go to man: "Soteriology is strictly theology. The emphasis must not be laid on man, but on the work of God. Soteriology emphasizes not the acceptance, but . . . the application of salvation by the Holy Spirit."[4]

• *Salvation is **entirely** gracious.* Grace is the favor of God that is bestowed entirely apart from considerations of deserving. Since man is totally depraved there can be no deserving anyway; there is no merit for one who has no good. Even faith must therefore be seen not as something good man does but as a gracious work of God.

As Augustine, the "first true predestinarian," concluded, "Not only Christ's objective work of salvation but the human response to that work as well were of God. In other words, salvation is wholly of grace."[5]

In conclusion, the Calvinist is sure that this background can hardly lead to any conclusions about God's Plan of Salvation except the following:

    —all that happens is by His plan and will;

    —whoever is saved is saved simply because God willed it;

    —those who are lost are also in that condition by His plan.

This background should prepare us for a discussion of the major elements of the Calvinistic system of doctrine on the subject of predestination.

The Doctrine of the Decrees of God in General

Another important part of the background for the theology of salvation is the theology of God's decrees. The Calvinistic theologians call this subject, variously, "The Divine Decrees in General" (Berkhof); "God's Eternal Counsel" (Hoeksema); "The Divine Decrees" (Shedd).

Definition

The decrees of God refer to "His eternal purpose according to the counsel of His will, whereby, for His own glory, He has foreordained whatsoever comes to pass" (*Westminster Shorter Catechism*). The doctrine of the decrees is "that God has sovereignly determined from all eternity whatsoever will come to pass, and works His sovereign will

---

[4]Hoeksema, 442, 443.

[5]Paul K. Jewett, *Election and Predestination* (Grand Rapids: Eerdmans, 1985), 5, 6.

in His entire creation, both natural and spiritual, according to His pre-determined plan."[6]

The purpose of such discussion is to say what I have already said, above, in the Theological Background: namely, that nothing that exists or occurs is contrary to the pre-determined, all-encompassing plan (decision, will, counsel, decree, ordainment) of God.

Description

The characteristics of the decrees are as follows.

• *They are not recorded, as such, in Scripture.* They are in the cate-gory referred to in Deuteronomy 29:29: "The secret things belong unto the LORD our God." He *has* revealed that He has such an all-inclusive plan, but we learn what it includes only as we see what actu-ally happens, especially as interpreted by Scripture. (This point does not mean, of course, that God has revealed nothing of His will in the Scriptures.)

• *They are founded in the Divine wisdom* (Ps. 104:24). God's coun-sel (Greek *boulē*) is in essence the same as His wisdom. Shedd speaks of "God's wise insight and knowledge, in the light of which he forms his determination."[7]

• *They manifest one plan.* This "follows from God's oneness and simplicity. . . . We may never separate the counsel of God into various parts."[8] Any distinctions we make between "decrees"—even using the plural—is strictly (albeit appropriately) to enable us, in our finite logic, to look at the various details of God's one purpose (Greek *proth-esis*). Technically, then, even a so-called "order of decrees" is invalid and is merely for our convenience.

• *They are comprehensive.* This means that God's one plan is all inclusive, incorporating whatever comes to pass:

—so-called "accidental" things,

—all that is "mechanical" (cause-effect laws, etc.),

—all the moral decisions/actions of "free" beings, whether good or bad. Proverbs 21:1 puts in this category "the heart of the king." Acts 2:23; 4:28 include even the evil act of crucifixion. "Unless this is strictly maintained, the sovereignty and Lordship of God can-not be confessed according to Scripture."[9] Otherwise there would be another force in the universe, besides God, whose will must be taken

---

[6]Louis Berkhof, *Systematic Theology* (Grand Rapids: Eerdmans, 1949), 100.

[7]W. G. T. Shedd, *Dogmatic Theology* (Grand Rapids: Zondervan reprint, n.d.), I:399.

[8]Hoeksema, 159.

[9]Hoeksema, 157.

into account before we—or even God—could know what is accomplished. In that case what is actually the outcome might not be what God willed!

• *They include men's free acts.* This reiterates what has been made clear, in general, in the preceding point: God's decrees encompass *the voluntary acts* of free creatures, rendering all such acts equally certain.

Two types of such "free" actions exist:

1. for sinful acts, the decree is *permissive;* man is left alone to bring sin to pass;
2. for good acts, the decree is *efficacious;* God works immediately on man's will to incline it.

In both types, the action is *free*—in the sense of "voluntary" (unforced), and man is a free, moral agent.

For both types, the "how" is a mystery to us: both how the permissive decree can render certain without causing, and how God's positive influence on the human will can work effectively and yet the man remain truly free.

God's decree includes not only the action or outcome itself, but *all the antecedents, circumstances, and influences* (including direct influence on the will, in the case of good actions) of the action, yet in a manner consistent with the nature of man as a free, moral agent. In other words, man's actions in such cases are rationally self-determined and are not aspects of the law of necessity that governs the cause-effect movements of material things in the cosmos. But the decree does make the actions necessary.

Since the Bible presents both sides of these truths (that God has decreed them and yet that man performs freely) without noting any contradiction between them, there must not be any contradiction—regardless of our inability to explain how this is so.

• *They include sin and evil.* This follows from the preceding. God's decrees render the fall of man and acts of sin *certain,* but such decrees are *permissive* rather than actively causal. God does not act immediately on man's will to influence or incline him toward sin; He is therefore not responsible for (not the efficient cause of) sin.

How God's decree renders sin certain without causing it is a *mystery:* that is, it is unrevealed. But He permits sin for good reasons sufficient to Himself, including the manifestation of attributes that would otherwise be undemonstrable—like mercy and compassion. And we can be sure that He ultimately overrules sin for good and for His own glory.

• *They are eternal.* If God is eternal, His *will* is. His will is, after all, God Himself, an aspect of His being. There never was a "time" when, following consideration, God settled on a plan. The carrying out of His plan (purpose or counsel) may be in time, but the purpose itself is as eternal as God is.

• *They are immutable.* This is implied by the preceding, as well as by Scriptures that say, "I am the LORD, I change not" (Mal. 3:6). If He does not change, His will does not change. With Him there is no variableness or shadow of turning (Jas. 1:17). God never changes His mind or alters His purpose. He suffers from none of the failings of men—fickleness, ignorance, impotence—that lead to changes of mind.

• *They are unconditional, absolute.* God's decrees are conditioned by nothing outside His own good pleasure (Greek *eudokia*) or counsel. Whatever the decree contains, its success is not dependent on anything outside the decree itself. "The *execution* of the plan may require means or be dependent on certain conditions, but then these means or conditions have also been determined in the decree."[10]

• *They provide the basis for God's foreknowledge.* He knows, from eternity, all that will transpire. This foreknowledge is based on His decrees. The decrees make all things certain. Certainty precedes knowledge. God eternally and necessarily possesses knowledge of all possibilities. Out of that knowledge of all possibilities, He decreed what "set of possibilities" to actualize. From that decree He therefore knows all actualities. "So long as anything remains undecreed, it is contingent and fortuitous. It may or may not happen"[11]—by which Shedd means to deny that there are any such things in the universe.

In fact, "foreknowledge," in the Bible, generally means more than merely knowing in advance ("prescience"), carrying with it the idea of loving selection to a personal relationship. Thus foreknowledge, in this sense, is essentially the equivalent of election (and therefore cannot be the "basis" of election). Further, this foreknowledge is of *persons* and not of their actions or qualities (including faith).

In the sense of pre-cognition (prescience), foreknowledge would not be possible for God if He had not already made all events certain by foreordination. Thus foreknowledge follows from foreordination or predestination, not vice versa, and is essentially the same thing.

• *They are efficacious.* This means that the effect of the decree, by virtue of its existence, is to render certain to come to pass everything decreed. God's decrees, therefore, are exactly equivalent to whatever

---

[10]Berkhof, 105.
[11]Shedd, I:397.

actually comes to pass. As noted above, no force can thwart the will of God. "He hath done whatsoever he hath pleased" (Ps. 115:3), and since everything that is equals what He has done, then everything that comes to pass is identical with what He has pleased.

Viewing God's decrees as efficacious makes it advisable to subdivide them into two types:

1. Those that are *positively* efficacious: that is, directly and actively causal, including

    a. all "events" in the physical/material realm, and

    b. the "immediate spiritual agency of God upon the finite will" of man for good (moral) actions[12] (Phil. 2:13). In other words, then, God is *the author* of all that is good.

2. Those that are *permissively* efficacious: that is, indirectly and not actively causal, but rendering certain nevertheless. This includes only the sinful acts of moral beings. It means that God does not immediately act on the human will to produce evil. He *is not the author* of evil.

This wording is my own way of expressing the more common view of Calvinists, like Berkhof[13] and Shedd.[14] But not all appreciate this distinction. Hoeksema, for example, insists that there is only one point to be made: namely, that *all* the decrees are efficacious. He then argues against the artificial distinction between efficacious and permissive.[15] In fact, however, all agree on the main point of this characteristic: namely, God's decrees are perfectly *successful.* Everything that comes to pass is the decreed will of God, and His will cannot ever be overturned.

The decrees include the means of accomplishing purposes as well as the ends themselves. This follows from the fact that they are all-encompassing. If proclamation of the gospel, for example, is required for faith and conversion, then that proclamation is ordained just as certainly as the faith and conversion.

Predestination: The Divine Decrees Respecting Salvation

Definition of Terms[16]

    • *Predestination* is the overall subject, defined as: "the counsel of God concerning fallen men, including the sovereign election of some

---

[12]Shedd, I:406.

[13]Berkhof, 103, 105.

[14]Shedd, 405-412.

[15]Hoeksema, 158, 159.

[16]For the purposes of this work, the definitions are limited in reference to the plan of salvation for human beings.

and the righteous reprobation of the rest."[17] This definition makes clear that predestination involves two sides, the foreordination of the destinies of the saved and of the lost, sometimes called "double pre-destination."

- *Election* is the predestination of the saved: "that eternal act of God whereby He, in His sovereign good pleasure, and on account of no foreseen merit in them, chooses a certain number of men to be the recipients of special grace and of eternal salvation."[18]

- *Reprobation* is the predestination of the damned: "that eternal decree of God whereby He has determined to pass some men by with the operation of His special grace, and to punish them for their sins, to the manifestation of His justice."[19]

Election to Salvation:[20] The Positive Predestination

- *Basis or source of election to salvation* (how or why it originates):

1. Election is an expression of the sovereign will of God, by and for His good pleasure. Therefore, its basis *is not* (a) anything in man, nei-ther merit nor so-called "foreseen faith"; *nor is it* (b) Christ Himself as though He were the impelling or moving or meritorious cause of elec-tion. "The electing love of God precedes the sending of the Son."[21]

2. Election originates in the Divine compassion, in pity for the sin-ner.

   a. Reasons: because man is His handiwork, and because man has capacity for holiness and worship.

   b. The difference between "all" and "the elect": In fact, God *has* compassion on all, but He *expresses* saving compassion only on the elect. The reason for this remains unrevealed: "reasons sufficient for God, and unknown to the creature."[22]

- *Characteristics of this election:* these are basically the same as of the decrees in general.

---

[17]Berkhof, 109.

[18]Berkhof, 114.

[19]Berkhof, 116.

[20]Most theologians distinguish between election to salvation and other kinds, such as the corporate election of Israel or the election of persons to fill certain offices or serv-ice roles. Only the former needs discussion here.

[21]Berkhof, 114.

[22]Shedd, I:424.

1. Election is immutable.

2. Election is eternal (not "election in time").

3. Election is not chargeable with injustice or partiality, since He owes nothing to anyone, and since all have forfeited His blessings and have no claim or right to them.

4. Election is irresistible. God's purpose cannot be thwarted by man.

> a. Men do resist, of course—*all* do—but the resistance of the elect does not prevail over the purpose of God to save them.
>
> b. God secures success "by the immediate operation of the Holy Spirit, upon the human will as spirit."[23] He "does exert such an influence on the human spirit as to make it willing."[24]
>
> c. Still, this is *not* an "overpowering" that is inconsistent with free agency;[25] it is "not compulsory."[26] "God is the creator of the will, and never works in a manner contrary to its created qualities."[27]

5. Election is unconditional. Not even "foreseen faith" can be a condition for election; it depends solely on the sovereign good pleasure of God:

> a. Since all sinners are alike helpless, there is no basis for distinction.
>
> b. Since all good—even faith—is a fruit of the grace of God, man cannot be credited with meeting any condition and thus, in part, determining his own salvation.

• *The purpose of election:*

1. The *proximate* or immediate purpose is the salvation of the elect.

2. The *ultimate* purpose is the glory of God.

• *Objects of election:* some secondary questions.

1. Will a greater number be saved than lost? Not all Calvinists agree; many would say yes.

---

[23]Shedd, I:428.
[24]Berkhof, 115.
[25]Berkhof, 115.
[26]Shedd, I:428.
[27]Shedd, I:428.

2. Will some unevangelized heathen be regenerated? Again, not all agree, but some—probably not many these days—would say *yes.* Shedd speaks of this possibility, referring to "such of the pagan world as God pleases to regenerate without the written word." He observes, "The Divine Spirit does not invariably . . . wait for the tardy action of the unfaithful church in preaching the written word, before he exerts his omnipotent grace in regeneration."[28]

Even for Shedd, however, this is not to be thought of as the ordinary method of God, but an extraordinary one. Furthermore, even when this extraordinary method is effected, one should understand that the work of Christ is still the basis for the regeneration of the unevangelized person.

3. Will *all* who die in infancy be saved? Once more, not all Calvinists agree, but the general tendency is to answer *yes.* This is, in part, the reason Charles Hodge can say that "The number of the finally lost in comparison with the whole number of the saved will be very inconsiderable."[29]

Reprobation: The Negative Predestination
• *Two main parts in the doctrine:*

1. *Preterition* is the decree to by-pass some in bestowing regenerating (not "common") grace. This aspect of the decree is:
> • sovereign—man's demerit *not* the basis;
> • for reasons known only to God Himself;
> • permissive or passive, not acting on man (that is, not influencing his will, as in election).

2. *Condemnation* is the decree to punish, to assign the sinner to dishonor and wrath. This aspect of the decree is:
> • judicial—visiting sin with punishment;
> • has a known reason: sin;
> • is positive, active, efficient (not just permissive, passive).

The three bullet points under these two aspects of the decree of reprobation are directly comparable and are intentionally opposite to each other.

---

[28]Shedd, I:436, 439.

[29]Charles Hodge, *Systematic Theology* (Grand Rapids: Eerdmans reprint, n.d.), III:879, 880.

• *Comparison with election.* Election and reprobation are not completely parallel.

1. They are alike in being eternal, unconditional, immutable, and not chargeable with injustice or partiality.

2. They are different in two ways:
>   (a) election is, reprobation is not, effected by direct action of God on the will;
>   (b) election is actively efficacious, while reprobation (at least the preterition aspect) is permissive.

All this means, therefore, that God is the author or cause of good, of righteousness and salvation, and responsible for this. He is not the author or cause of sin, of the fall or damnation, and is not responsible for this. The decree of election is the efficient cause of salvation; but the decree of reprobation is not the efficient cause of perdition. "The efficient cause of perdition is the self-determination of the human will."[30] Although He is the decretal cause of the fall, sin, and evil, He forces no one to sin against his will.

• *Other issues involved in reprobation*

Because reprobation tends to sound harsh, the doctrine is somewhat controversial and involves points of difference even among Calvinists. Some of these issues are as follows:

1. The doctrine is logically necessary as an antithesis to election. If some are elect, others are not: "The rejection implied in the concept of election is also a part of the purpose of him who accomplishes all things according to the course of his will."[31] As Shedd observes, to all transgressors God must show either mercy (election) or justice (reprobation).[32] Thus the rejection by God of the reprobate is not left in Scripture as mere implication (see Rom. 9:13, "Esau I have hated").

2. Shedd treats extensively, and answers, the objection that the doctrine of reprobation would make God's universal offer of salvation insincere. This argument need not be pursued at length here, but can be briefly summarized as follows:[33]

a. Sincerity depends on the nature of the desire, not on results.

---

[30]Shedd, I:445.
[31]Jewett, 27.
[32]Shedd, I:430.
[33]Shedd, I:451-457.

   b. The *decree* of God is not necessarily equal to His desire. His natural, spontaneous desire (for example, Ezek. 33:11) is "constitutional," a sincere, abiding desire that manifests compassion
for all, but one that does not require a decree to gratify that
desire. In other words, God's "will" is capable of more than one
meaning: (1) His revealed will equals His desire, which does not
delight in the death of the sinner; this may also be called His
legislative will, or the will of complacency. (2) His secret will
equals His decree, which justly ordains the death of the sinner;
this may also be called His decretive will, or the will of His good
pleasure.

   c. Thus reprobation is consistent with a sincere desire that all be
saved. For one thing, the atonement is sufficient for all. For
another, God sincerely desires that all to whom salvation is
offered—thus all men—would put faith in Christ and be saved.
In fact, however, He knows that none will do so, and so He goes
a step further and effectively secures the salvation of some by
a gracious election. Why He by-passes the rest, and indeed
ordains their damnation, remains a matter that He has not
revealed—except for the reason given in Romans 9:22: namely,
to show His wrath and make His power known by means of ves-
sels of wrath prepared for destruction.

3. Calvinists debate among themselves the order of the decrees
respecting election and reprobation. At this point, it is sufficient to
observe that Berkhof and Shedd represent the more typical position of
modern Calvinists when they insist that reprobation presupposes the
fall. This is what is sometimes called an "infralapsarian" (or "sublapsarian") position, regarding the decree of damnation as flowing logically
from the decree to permit the fall. Some Calvinists hold to a "supralap-
sarian" position, regarding the fall as a decreed means of accomplishing
the decree of condemnation. Hoeksema is among these.[34]

Originally the difference between supralapsarians and infralap-
sarians simply involved whether God (efficaciously) decreed the fall,
but it has come to be more complicated (and often confusing). The
chief difference lies in the logical (not chronological) order of the
decrees, as follows:[35]

---

   [34]Hoeksema, 161-165.
   [35]The statement of order given here, including the wording, is from Robert L.
Reymond, *A New Systematic Theology of the Christian Faith* (Nashville: Thomas Nelson,
1998), 488, 480. See there for further discussion of variations.

Supralapsarianism

- The election of some men to salvation in Christ (and the repro-bation of the others),
- The decree to create the world and both kinds of men,
- The decree that all men would fall,
- The decree to redeem the elect, who are now sinners, by the cross work of Christ,
- The decree to apply Christ's redemptive benefits to these elect sinners.

Infralapsarianism (or sublapsarianism)

- The decree to create the world and (all) men,
- The decree that (all) men would fall,
- The election of some fallen men to salvation in Christ (and the reprobation of the others),
- The decree to redeem the elect by the cross work of Christ,
- The decree to apply Christ's redemptive benefits to the elect.

4. Shedd is more or less typical in observing that the decree of reprobation does not prevent the active work of the Spirit of God in striving with the non-elect.[36] He does, in fact, strive with them, convicting of sin. But they—like the elect—resist, and the Spirit goes no further. In this respect, reprobation is the by-passing of the next step. With the elect, the Spirit takes the next step and regenerates. The universal "striving" is part of common grace. Every sinner is stronger than common grace; no one can resist regenerating grace.

5. Shedd may not be typical of Calvinists in general when he discusses the relationship between reprobation and certainty. Reprobation makes certain perdition (because the bondage of the sinner's will precludes recovery apart from regeneration), but it does not render perdition necessary. Shedd insists that the decree of reprobation has no effect on the sinner until after sin is freely chosen.[37] Other Calvinists would insist that he is ignoring Rom. 5:12-14 in making this distinction. The argument is not essential to our purposes in this work.

6. The end of reprobation, as of election, is the glory of God.

---

[36]Shedd, I:435.
[37]Shedd, I:444-446.

For Further Reading on the
Calvinistic Doctrine of Predestination

Berkhof, Louis. *Systematic Theology*. Grand Rapids: Eerdmans, 1949 (pp. 100-125).

Berkouwer, G. C. *Divine Election*. Grand Rapids: Eerdmans, 1960. [A more contemporary reading of Calvinism with a somewhat Barthian flavor, not always representative of classic Reformed theology]

Boettner, Loraine. *The Reformed Doctrine of Predestination*. Grand Rapids: Eerdmans, 1954.

Clark, Gordon. *Biblical Predestination*. Philadelphia: Presbyterian and Reformed, 1969.

Custance, Arthur. *The Sovereignty of Grace*. Grand Rapids: Baker, 1979.

Hoeksema, Herman. *Reformed Dogmatics*. Grand Rapids: Reformed Free Publishing Association, 1966 (ch. V). [Many Calvinists regard Hoeksema as too extreme to be truly representative of the Reformed faith.]

Pink, A. W. *The Sovereignty of God*. Grand Rapids: Baker, 1963.

Shedd, William G. T. *Dogmatic Theology*. Grand Rapids: Zondervan, n.d., (vol. I, pp. 393-462). [Some Calvinists regard Shedd as too speculative in some matters.]

CHAPTER THREE

The Classical Arminian
Doctrine of Predestination

Introduction: Theological Background

In the preceding chapter we have surveyed the theological background for the Calvinistic doctrine of predestination. There we dealt with:

1. the concept of God, as sovereign, creator-preserver, omniscient, and alone good and worthy of glorification;
2. the concept of man, as subordinate creature, fallen and depraved;
3. the concept of salvation, as wholly of God and entirely gracious.

That same material also provides the background for the Arminian doctrine of predestination. The question before us, then, is two-fold: To what extent will the Arminian agree with the picture of God, man, and salvation sketched there? And in what ways will he differ?

Areas of Agreement

For the most part, the Arminian will agree with the theological background outlined in the introduction to Calvinism:

• *God is sovereign.* I cannot improve on the description of sovereignty presented in the previous chapter. No conditions can be imposed on God from outside Himself. Nothing other than His own nature limits His freedom to act according to His own good pleasure.

• *God is creator and preserver of all that exists outside himself,* so that all that is—including all that happens—is in accord with His will, His plan for the history of the created, subordinate, sustained universe.

• *God is omniscient,* and the implications include: (1) that He knew all possible contingencies; and (2) that from all these He decided or willed what is.

• *No force exists except that which is subordinate to God* and cannot thwart His will.

• *God is the source of all good* and is alone deserving of glory.

• *Man is created and wholly governed by God.*

• *Man is fallen and thoroughly depraved,* and therefore capable of no good apart from the work of God to enable him. One may add (although I think the Calvinist will not disagree) that this needs some clarification. Fallen man is not capable of any good that would justify him before God, nor is he capable of any absolute good. Even so, fallen man continues to be in the image of God and the recipient of common grace and general revelation. This means that he is capable of relative good, of doing and thinking things that are relatively worthwhile and noble. He exists, in other words, in a state of contradiction and painful conflict, always falling short of the glory of God (Rom. 3:23).

• *Salvation is wholly the gracious work of God,* thus yielding no credit or merit to man. There is no room for "synergism" (the view that God and man work together to accomplish salvation).

I suggest, therefore, that one should begin with a careful review of the theological background of Calvinism outlined in the previous chapter. The Arminian builds on the same foundation.

Areas of disagreement

If Arminians share, in large measure, the Calvinists' concepts of God, man, and salvation, where do they part ways? There are at least three differences, as much matters of emphasis as outright disagreement.

• *The relationship between certainty, contingency, and necessity.* Arminians agree that God knows all things that will be as certain and as in accord with His plan. But they insist that many of these certainties are truly contingent. To Arminians, Calvinists at least appear to deny that there really are true contingencies, things that can transpire in either of two (or more) ways.

The Arminian insists that there are things that actually can go either of two ways, and yet God knows which way they will go. He knows all future events perfectly. This means that they are all certain, else He would not know what will be. Furthermore, it means that all future events are in accord with His overall plan and purpose: nothing ever happens in His universe that is outside His knowledge or control or that thwarts His ultimate plan.

This is *not* contradicted by the fact that there are events that really can go in more than one way. The Arminian insists that there is no conflict between "certainty" and true "contingency," although explanation of this requires a careful and technical discussion of three important terms: certainty, contingency, and necessity.[1] The distinction between these plays an important role in the issues related to predestination. I would venture that, in this matter alone, there is more room for misunderstanding and more to be gained from clarity than from almost any other point in dispute.

All things that occur are certainly foreknown by God. Every happening is certain and known as such by God from all eternity.

Does this mean "What will be will be" (Spanish, *Que sera, sera*)? Indeed, but the meaning of that set of words requires closer examination. The sentence is, in fact, like a mathematical equation with two equal sides. If I were to say that 4 = 4, for example, I might well be accused of saying nothing.

The proposition "What will be will be" is exactly the same, nothing more than "what will be = what will be." Everything that will happen will happen; and if I add "certainly" to the statement—"everything that will happen will certainly happen"—I have added nothing. The so-called "certainty" of an event means nothing more than its "eventness," the simple fact that it will occur—and God knows it will.

The free acts of morally responsible persons are *contingent.* A contingency is anything that really can take place in more than one way. This freedom to choose does not contradict certainty. Certainty relates to the "factness" of an event, to *whether* it will be or not; contingency relates to its *nature* as free or necessary. The same event can be both certain and contingent at the same time.

Events that can transpire in just one way, that must inevitably be the way they are, are said to be *necessary.* For such events there were causes leading to the event that allowed no freedom of choice, causes that necessarily produced the event. Whenever God, for example, "makes" something happen the way it does without allowing for any other eventuality, that event is a necessity.

An event can be certain without being necessary: "shall be" (certain) is not the same as "must be" (necessary). Some events are "necessary"; that is, they are inevitably caused by a prior influence. Others are "contingent"; that is, they are free, capable of more than one possibility depending on an unforced choice. Both kinds are equally certain, as known to God.

---

[1]Should someone finally say that he cannot comprehend how an event can be both certain and contingent at the same time, the Arminian can always respond in the same way the Calvinist responds to similar "apparent" contradictions: The Bible teaches both without being conscious of any contradiction; therefore there must be no contradiction.

How then does *knowledge* of an event relate to the factness of an event? Human knowledge illustrates: while we cannot know the future, we can know past events, and know them as certain. At the same time, the certainty lies in their factness, and our knowledge of them affects that factness in no way at all. The knowledge issues from our awareness of the facts.

Just so, God foreknows everything future as certain. That certainty of future events does not lie in their necessity but in their simple factness. They will be the way they will be, and God knows what they will be because He has perfect awareness, in advance, of all facts. But that knowledge *per se,* even though it is *fore*knowledge, has no more causal effect on the facts than our knowledge of certain past facts has on them.

To provide a simple illustration, let us suppose that tomorrow I will come to a fork in a road and need to make a choice about which way to travel. The fact is that I will choose one or the other, and the one that I will choose is the one that I will certainly choose. (Once again, the "certainly" adds nothing.) But this is *not at all* to say that I *must* choose it. In fact, I will be free to choose either route, considering whatever I wish to consider at that time. That God knows which I will choose, and incorporates it in His plan, does not limit my choice; He also knows what would happen if I should make the other choice— and how to incorporate that very real possibility in His plan.

To clarify: If I will choose the right fork tomorrow, it is certain that I will choose it. But it is equally true that if I will choose the left fork tomorrow, it is certain that I will choose it and He knows I will choose it. The choice will be freely made, by *me,* tomorrow. The future is both certain and open; it will not be closed until it occurs. The action is, therefore, truly contingent and actually can go either way, even though the way it will go is (to speak tautology again) the way it will go.

These points Arminius presented with convincing clarity. He said, for example, "If [God] resolve to use a force that . . . can be resisted by the creature, then that thing is said to be done, not *necessarily* but *contingently,* although its actual occurrence was certainly foreknown by God."[2] Thus even what was divinely prophesied might take place contingently and not by necessity, if produced by a resistible cause. Arminius used the case of Jesus' bones as an illustration, denying that

---

[2]James Arminius, *The Writings of James Arminius* (three vols.), tr. James Nichols and W. R. Bagnall (Grand Rapids: Baker, 1956), I:291. The entire discussion makes a strong case that one event cannot be both a necessity and a contingency at the same time.

they could not have been broken but affirming the certainty that they *would* not.[3]

In another place Arminius observes, "Because God, in His infinite wisdom, saw, from eternity, that man would fall at a certain time, that fall occurred infallibly, only in respect to His prescience, not in respect to any act of the divine will." He goes on to distinguish "between what is done *infallibly* [meaning "certainly"] and what is done *necessarily.* The former depends on the infinity of the knowledge of God, the latter on the act of His will." The former, he says, "has respect only to the knowledge of God, to which it pertains to know, infallibly and with certainty, contingent things."[4]

One of the best of the Wesleyan theologians was Richard Watson. While his style is that of the old divines, and somewhat cumbersome, I recommend highly his treatment of this difference between certainty, contingency, and necessity. I quote here just a few lines:

> The position, that *certain* prescience destroys contingency, is a mere sophism. . . .
>
> The great fallacy in the argument . . . lies in supposing that contingency and certainty are the opposites of each other. . . . Contingency in moral actions is, therefore, their freedom, and is opposed, not to certainty, but to necessity. . . . The question is not . . . about the certainty of moral actions, that is, whether they will happen or not; but about the nature of them, whether free or constrained, whether they must happen or not. . . .
>
> The foreknowledge of God has then no influence upon either the freedom or the certainty of actions, for this plain reason, that it is knowledge and not influence; and actions may be certainly foreknown, without their being rendered necessary by that foreknowledge. . . .
>
> But if a contingency will have a given result, to that result it must be determined. Not in the least.[5]

He goes on to cite S. Clarke, to the effect that, even if the future were not foreknown, it would still be certain! Precisely, because "certainty" is simply futurity.

The Calvinist errs, on this subject, in suggesting that God knows the future certainly only because He first unconditionally fore-

---

[3]Arminius, I:289-292.

[4]Arminius, III:197.

[5]Richard Watson, *Theological Institutes* (New York: Nelson and Phillips, 1850), I:378-381.

ordained (predestined) it. But that is to confuse knowledge with an active cause and so in effect to take away contingency. God's foreknowledge, in the sense of prescience,[6] is part of His omniscience and includes all things as certain, both good and evil, contingent and necessary. It is not in itself causal.

Furthermore, God's foreordination of events is not necessary for His foreknowledge of them, at least not in the limited way such a statement implies. In fact, He eternally knows all the possibilities, the things that will *not* be as perfectly as the things that *will* be. As Arminius put it, "God foreknows future things through the infinity of his essence, and through the pre-eminent perfection of his understanding and prescience, not as he willed or decreed that they should necessarily be done, though he would not foreknow them except as they were future, and they would not be future unless God had decreed either to perform or to permit them."[7]

Furthermore, *from* His knowledge of all possibilities, he chose and ordained the course of action that He willed to set in motion—a course of events that includes contingencies which He did not and does not make necessary one way or the other. Applied to election and reprobation, then, predestination is not the basis of foreknowledge; the Biblical order is foreknowledge, then predestination (Rom. 8:29).

I pause here to make passing comments on a deformed Arminianism that denies God's foreknowledge either of all "free" human decisions or at least of man's sinful decisions.[8] Clark Pinnock has led the way in this innovation. For the theory I cite Pinnock's summary of the position of Richard Rice:

> Just as there are things God cannot do though omnipotent, Rice argues, so there are things God cannot know though omniscient, namely future free choices that are not properly objects of knowledge. If human choices are truly free, he reasons, they do not exist to be known in advance by any knower, not even God.[9]

---

[6]It may be that "foreknowledge," in the Scripture, sometimes involves more than prescience. That possibility will come up again below.

[7]Arminius, II:480.

[8]See, for example, T. W. Brents, *The Gospel Plan of Salvation* (Nashville: Gospel Advocate, 1966), 92ff.

[9]Clark H. Pinnock, ed., *The Grace of God, The Will of Man* (Grand Rapids: Zondervan, 1989), xii.

In other words, "Decisions not yet made do not exist anywhere to be known even by God."[10]

At the end of this chapter I will devote a longer note to the issues involved in this; for now it is enough to observe that this is not Reformation Arminianism. When Pinnock observes that this is a form of theism midway between the traditional form and process theism, one wonders if he does not betray the influence of process theology. He is correct in insisting that God is not static and impassive, but neither is God a Hegelian "Becoming." Jack Cottrell is correct when he observes, "To say that God could not foreknow truly free human decisions is either to exalt man too highly or to reduce God to a creaturely status."[11] As Norman Geisler has trenchantly observed, "If Pinnock's view of God is right, then he cannot even be an Arminian!"[12]

• *An emphasis on the nature of man as personal,* not only as creature and fallen. As Clark Pinnock has correctly said, "God's dealings with his human creation are dynamic and personal and the responses that we make to him have far-reaching consequences."[13] This involves several truths.

1. Man is in the image of God, thus having—among other things—a *will* of his own. There is a will in the universe other than God's: subordinate to Him, yes, but a true will nevertheless. Were that not true, man would not be truly personal.

2. Man is free, as possessing a true will, to make real choices and decisions between two (or more) courses of action (true contingency, again). A choice that actually can go but one way is not a choice, and without this "freedom" there is not personality.

This is not *absolute* freedom. It is not unlimited, unconditioned, or sovereign, like God's freedom. In that sense, God is the only free being that exists.

This freedom is therefore a limited, conditioned, "governed" freedom. For one thing, all the parameters of the choices have been given by God. For another thing, the freedom has been further affected by the fall, and what man can *theoretically* do he often *practically* can not. The sinner, for example, is not "free" not to sin. Apart from the

---

[10]Ibid., 25.

[11]Jack W. Cottrell, "Conditional Election," in *Grace Unlimited,* ed. Clark H. Pinnock (Minneapolis: Bethany Fellowship, 1975), 69.

[12]Norman Geisler, *Predestination and Free Will,* ed D. and R. Basinger (Downers Grove: InterVarsity, 1986), 170.

[13]Clark H. Pinnock, "Responsible Freedom and the Flow of Biblical History," in *Grace Unlimited,* ed. Clark H. Pinnock (Minneapolis: Bethany Fellowship, 1975), 97.

enabling grace of God, no sinner is "free" to accept the offer of salvation and put faith in Christ. Depraved man's will is bound by sin. Arminius confessed this: "The will is, indeed, free, but not in respect to that act which can not be performed or omitted without supernatural grace."[14] And he consistently insisted that "Nothing good can be performed by any rational creature without this special aid of His grace."[15]

But this depravity does not take away man's endowment. Depraved man is still personal, and this endowment is part of personality. As Jewett put this, from a Calvinist perspective, "Since he has made us as *persons* . . . his will for us is not realized in the form of 'destiny.'. . . He does not compel the Yes of his elect to the offer of his grace; rather, he *wins* it."[16] I can only wish that he, and other Calvinists when they say similar things, did not contradict this by saying that God "makes willing" the human will (as noted in the previous chapter). No wonder Jewett adds, typically: "How this can be we cannot say."[17]

3. Man is therefore an *actor* in the universe. His endowment with a will plus his moral freedom equals the fact that he is an actor. God is not the only actor in the universe, and the more enthusiastic statements of some Calvinists sometimes make it sound as if He were. To cite Pinnock again, "God is a person and men are personal, made in his image. Therefore, he deals with man as a person. . . . The world is not simply a pure function of the Deity."[18]

And man acts for evil or for good. Nor does this "for good" contradict (1) that God is the source of all good and the only worthy object of glory; or (2) that man is fallen and incapable of good. After all, God created the free will, so that even this endowment is gracious. Beyond that, God's gracious work is necessary for man, especially fallen man, to perform any good. Consequently, the Bible everywhere holds man responsible to act for evil and for good.

• *An understanding of the tension between God's sovereignty and man's freedom.* Both Calvinists and Arminians, of course, claim to believe in both of these. Calvinists consider that Arminians, in effect, deny God's sovereignty in order to affirm man's freedom. Arminians consider that Calvinists, in effect, deny man's freedom in order to

---

[14]Arminius, III:196.
[15]Arminius, III:287.
[16]Paul K. Jewett, *Election and Predestination* (Grand Rapids: Eerdmans, 1985), 76.
[17]Ibid.
[18]Pinnock, "Responsible Freedom," 107.

affirm God's sovereignty. Both sides will often say that the two cannot be reconciled by men.

But Arminians believe that there is no threat to, or restriction of, God's sovereign freedom, who runs everything (nothing omitted) as He pleases, by having another personal and free (although limited) being in the universe.

And Arminians, assuming that God's plan or decree is that such a free and responsible being exist and make free choices, insist that therefore all those choices (which really are contingent) are incorporated into His plan (as He certainly foresees what those choices will be).

Arminians consider that this view magnifies God's omniscience. In the Arminian conception of the universe, God foreknows true contingencies. Man really can choose either of two ways, and God really knows which he will choose.

Likewise, Arminians consider that this view magnifies God's power, in at least two interrelated ways.

1. God was able to create a being who is not merely "determined," but an actor who also "determines" things, a being who is free and in His own image. He of the only truly sovereign will was able to endow man with a will that really has the power of decision and choice.

2. God is able to govern the truly free exercise of men's wills in such a way that all goes according to His plan. A God who created a complex universe inhabited by beings pre-programmed to act out His will for them would be great. But one who can make men with wills of their own and set them free to act in ways He has not determined for them, *and still govern the whole in perfect accord with His purpose* is far greater. "If the divine Wisdom knows how to effect that which it has decreed, by employing causes according to their nature and motion—whether their nature and motion be contingent or free, the praise due to such wisdom is far greater than if it employ a power which no creature can possibly resist."[19]

Like the Calvinist, the Arminian readily affirms that nothing is out of God's control. All goes according to His plan. His will cannot be thwarted. And, even so, men freely choose between true contingencies. As Arminius expressed this, "I place in subjection to Divine Providence both the *free-will* and even the *actions of a rational creature,* so that nothing can be done without the will of God, not even any of those things which are done in opposition to it."[20]

---

[19]Arminius, I:292.
[20]Arminius, I:251.

The Doctrine of the Divine Decrees in General

Arminians do not usually have a section under this heading in their theology books. They probably should have (although I would prefer to call such a section by a title like Hoeksema's "God's Eternal Counsel" or "The Eternal Purpose of God"). That they do not may be, in part, attributable to a truth that Wood calls attention to: namely, that though a doctrine of decrees is "integral to reformed doctrine," it is "deduced from rather than actually designated as such in Scripture."[21]

The Nature of the Decrees: Points of Agreement

I cannot say that I would reject any of the terms used by the Calvinist to describe the characteristics of the decrees (counsel, plan) of God in general. Surely the "ordaining decisions" of God are:

• *founded in the Divine wisdom.*

• *a simple unity* (that is, *one* plan).

• *all-embracing, including whatever comes to pass,* whether free or necessary, good or evil.

• *eternal.* "God does nothing in time, which He has not decreed to do from all eternity."[22]

• *immutable.*

• *unconditional,* in that nothing outside God can "condition" His decisions.

• *incapable of being overturned* (Calvinism: "efficacious"): that is, they are always successful. And this heading might well be subdivided into those that are positively efficacious and those that are permissively efficacious. Arminius simply distinguishes "efficacious action" from "permission," but notes that "Both are immutable."[23] He considers it "an impious supposition" that any decree of God be made in vain, for "the counsel of the LORD standeth forever"[24] (Ps. 33:11).

The Nature of the Decrees: Points of Disagreement

If this much of Calvinism's terminology is to be stipulated, what are the Arminian's points of departure? Three things stand out.

---

[21] A. Skevington Wood, "The Declaration of Sentiments: The Theological Testament of Arminius," (*Evangelical Quarterly* 65:2 [1993], 111-129), 121.

[22] Arminius, I:566.

[23] Arminius, III:285.

[24] Arminius, III:298.

• *Decrees unconditionally made are not necessarily achieved uncon-ditionally.* The unconditionality of God's sovereign "decisions" (plan, purpose) does not necessarily mean that all the ends God has pur-posed are achieved unconditionally or necessarily.

What seems clear is that God has unconditionally (sovereignly) decreed to administer salvation conditionally. And "conditionally" includes true contingency.

Calvinists at least *try* to include this concept: "The execution of the plan may require means or be dependent on certain conditions, but then these means or conditions have also been determined in the decree."[25] If this meant only that God determined *what* condition(s) must be met, then that would be no problem for the Arminian. Even if it meant that God foresaw the meeting of the condition as certain, the Arminian need not object. But "determined" and "condition" have a tendency to be mutually exclusive, at least in the sense that Calvinists use the word "determined."

Apparently Berkhof means that God, by His decree, made neces-sary not only the end but the means or condition required to achieve the end. In that case, the so-called "condition" has been decreed as unconditionally as the end. But if God has, by decree, "determined" that a certain action must take place, there is no real "condition" because there is no real contingency. Such an unconditionally deter-mined "condition" is no condition at all, but is identical with the effect or end decreed.

We may say, then, that God unconditionally decreed that salvation be conditional. When God decreed the plan of salvation, He did so with nothing outside Himself imposing any conditions on Him. Whatever He decreed, He did so in absolute sovereignty, being under no obligations to any consideration except those reflecting His own nature. The decree was made unconditionally; its content is condi-tional salvation.

• *God's ordaining of all things does not mean that all things are made necessary.* The "Points of Agreement," above, may seem too quickly made. Do Arminians agree that everything, from the begin-ning, was "ordained" by God to be the way it is? Yes, but this must be carefully explained; the word "ordained" is tricky.

What I am saying goes something like this: Before any creating act, God considered all possibilities and chose from them the very set He put in motion by His creating acts. Thus, from before the begin-

---

[25]Louis Berkhof, *Systematic Theology* (Grand Rapids: Eerdmans, 1949), 105.

ning, He saw all that would follow if He created Adam and Eve in the very set of circumstances He chose for them. Seeing all, He said "Let that be," and by that creating word set in motion the chain of events that certainly would encompass all that ever occurs. In that sense He "ordained" everything that is. But that ordination does not cause the free acts to be necessary ones, and it certainly does not cause evil.

Thus "ordain" is ambiguous. Arminius denied that it always means "to decree that something shall [necessarily] be done."[26] With contingent and free actions, "ordain" means not to make them *necessary* but to set in motion the chain of events that God sees will *certainly* lead to them *without* having to, and thus to permit them and govern them in accord with His will. If one does not make such a careful distinction, he will make God the author of sin.

Arminius considered the fall in this light: "God ordained the fall of Adam, not that it should occur, but that, occurring, it shall serve for an illustration of His justice and mercy."[27] Again, "The word [ordain] is used in a two-fold sense—that of decreeing and determining that something shall be done, and that of establishing an order in that which is done, and of disposing and determining to a suitable end, things which are done."[28] Only in the latter sense can it be said that God "ordains" free, contingent acts. Arminius cited Augustine, "God maketh and ordaineth the righteous, but he maketh not sinners, as such; He only ordaineth them."[29]

The Arminian will therefore readily acknowledge that God may bring about a set of circumstances (including internal "conviction") that He knows *will* produce a certain effect without being the responsible cause of that effect or making it a *necessary* effect. In such cases, the one affected really can choose otherwise in exactly the same set of circumstances.

To illustrate: a person may say he is going to work in his garden today, and God can make it rain knowing that the person will certainly decide otherwise. This can apply even in the matter of salvation. Arminius acknowledged that "Many acts of the divine Providence . . . are so administered by the Deity, that from them salvation certainly results."[30] Again, however, "certainly" is not "necessarily." But whenever God brings about a set of circumstances (externally or internal-

---

[26] Arminius, III:284.

[27] Arminius, III:389, 390.

[28] Arminius, III:407.

[29] Arminius, III:408, note.

[30] Arminius, III:276.

ly) that *must* produce a certain effect, God alone is responsible for the effect.

• *God's decree to create man morally free and responsible—a true person, an actor—logically precedes decrees respecting salvation.* This is obvious in that God could not consider salvation for an entity that did not yet exist, or need salvation, in His mind.[31] Furthermore, the decree to create man must be fundamental since the decree to create determines the nature and endowments of the being created.

The Arminian, therefore, is not in contradiction with the "doctrine of decrees" or with God's sovereignty when he regards man as truly free to choose for salvation or destruction. Either way, man fulfills the decree of God. As Arminius expressed it, "God . . . can not fail in His universal purpose. For, if any person should not consent to be converted and saved, God has still added, and purposes to Himself, another design according to His will as consequent, that He should be glorified in their just condemnation."[32]

The Relationship between God's Decrees and Man's Sin

Some of the Arminian's main emphases are these.

• *God is not the author of sin.* Man's fall and sin are, in no way, a means to effecting a decree of God. Sin is not "necessitated" by the nature or influence (active or passive) of God, or by the need to reveal His attributes.

• *Sin originates in the free exercise of the will* of the creature given that freedom by God. It is freely permitted by God, freely performed by man. The reasons God determined to permit sin are best left to Him, although some of these are reasonably clear.

• *Even sin, however, is incorporated into the overall plan of God* for His creation. He determined to create man all the while knowing man would sin. Knowing sinful acts as certain, God providentially governs man as sinner. Nothing—not even sin—can be performed apart from God's good pleasure to permit it, and to sustain man's ability to perform it! As creator, considering infinite possibilities before Him, God chose to put in motion that course of events He foresaw as certain

---

[31]One of Arminius' main concerns was to deny the unbiblical logic of those who made the decrees respecting salvation precede the decrees respecting the creation of man or, worse still, the fall. He hammered away at this throughout the lengthy "Examination of the Treatise of William Perkins," III:281-474.

[32]Arminius, III:337, 338.

and as including sin. But nothing in God's action made sin necessary. Each act of sin is *certain* (and contingent), but not *necessary.*

Predestination: The Plan of Salvation

Definition of Terms

The term "predestination" serves the Arminian, like the Calvinist, as a heading for the overall subject of the decrees or plan of God respecting salvation, with "election" and "reprobation" its two main subdivisions. (As we will see in the following chapter, this may not in fact correspond precisely with the way the New Testament itself uses the terms. But usage, once entrenched, is difficult to change, and this traditional usage works acceptably.)

• *Predestination:* Arminius defined in the simplest terms possible, as "the Election of men to salvation, and the Reprobation of them to destruction."[33] This leaves his theological emphasis for the definitions of election and reprobation, although sometimes his definition of predestination takes the positive slant otherwise reserved for election.[34]

• *Election:* He defined as "the decree of God, by which, of Himself, from eternity, He decreed to justify in (or through) Christ, believers, and to accept them unto eternal life, to the praise of His glorious grace."[35] His wording was not always the same, but the emphases were constant, especially that election is of believers and in Christ.[36]

• *Reprobation:* He defined as the "decree of the wrath, or of the severe will of God; by which he resolved from all eternity to condemn to eternal death unbelievers, who by their own fault and the just judgment of God, would not believe, for the declaration of his wrath and power."[37]

The Arminian Doctrine of Election

The following characteristics are the ones that need greatest emphasis and clarify the main differences between Arminian and Calvinist doctrine.

---

[33] Arminius, I:211.

[34] See for example Arminius, I:565, where the definition of Predestination is almost exactly the same as given elsewhere for Election.

[35] Arminius, III:311.

[36] Cf. Arminius, II:99, 100; III:266, 292.

[37] Arminius, I:568.

• *Election is Christocentric.* This was one of Arminius' main concerns; as Clarke puts it, his "final objection to Calvin was that his doctrine of predestination was just not sufficiently Christocentric."[38] He felt that the traditional Calvinistic approach did not adequately honor Christ. In the previous chapter I cited Berkhof's observation that Christ as mediator is *not* the impelling or moving or meritorious cause of election. The best Berkhof would say is that Christ is the "mediate" cause of the effecting of the decree, or that He is the "meritorious" cause of the salvation to which believers are elected.

But Arminius felt that such distinctions are unworthy, that election becomes the end and the salvation wrought in Christ only a means to the realization of that end: *"only a subordinate cause* of that salvation which had been already foreordained."[39] For him, Christ should be the foundation and focus of election, as of salvation or Christianity itself, the one "on whom that decree is founded."[40] Arminius insisted that "The love with which God loves men absolutely to salvation . . . has no existence except in Jesus Christ"[41]

In his "Declaration of Sentiments" Arminius expressed just how he felt: the predestination doctrine of his opponents was "not that decree of God by which Christ is appointed by God to be the Savior, the Head, and the Foundation of those who will be made heirs of salvation," and only such a doctrine can be the "foundation of Christianity."[42] Again he said, "Christ Jesus is here to be considered not only as the foundation on which is based the execution of the decree, but also as the foundation on which the decree itself is based."[43] Again, "Predestination is posteriori, in the prescience and preordination of God, to the death and resurrection of Christ."[44] Again, "Since God can love no sinner unto salvation, unless he be reconciled to Himself in Christ, hence it is, that there would be no place for Predestination, except in Christ."[45] And again, "Christ according to the Apostle is not only the means by which the salvation, already prepared by election, but, so to speak, the meritorious cause, in respect

---

[38]F. Stuart Clarke, "Arminius's Understanding of Calvin" (*Evangelical Quarterly* 54:1 [1982], 25-35), 35.

[39]Arminius, I:230.

[40]Arminius, II:100.

[41]Arminius, I:230.

[42]Arminius, I:216, 217.

[43]Arminius, III:266.

[44]Arminius, III:268.

[45]Arminius, III:295.

to which the election was made, and on whose account that grace was prepared."[46] A much longer list of passages could be cited.[47]

For this reason, Arminius' "order of decrees" relative to salvation begins with the appointment of Christ as Mediator or Savior. Then all the rest of the decrees relating to salvation flow logically from that foundation, as follows:

1. Appoint Christ as Mediator/Savior;
2. Determine to receive into favor those who repent and believe; thus,
   a. in and through Christ to effect salvation of believers, and
   b. to leave in sin and under wrath unbelievers, and to condemn them;
3. Determine to administer the means to repentance and faith in a manner appropriate with Divine wisdom and justice;
4. Determine to save (or damn) particular persons according to foreknowledge of who would (or would not) believe, and persevere in faith, through His grace.[48]

Clarke laments that, after Arminius' death, even Arminians neglected his emphasis on the Christocentricity of election and "reverted to seeing Christ as merely an agent who carried out a predetermined decree of the Father."[49] Perhaps this is the reason Cottrell, when discussing the "structure" of election, lists first "The Election of Jesus" which he calls "the central and primary act of election," affirming that "All other aspects of election are subordinate to it."[50] He cites Isaiah 42:1; Matthew 12:18; Luke 9:35; 1 Peter 2:4, 6, and even texts relating to Christ's death: Acts 2:23; 4:28; 1 Peter 1:20. He proceeds to emphasize that Ephesians 4:1 indicates that we are "chosen" (i.e., "loved") in Christ, and that this "preserves the Christocentric character of predestination."[51]

A word of caution is in order. Some Arminians have taken this point to mean something Arminius never meant. Shank, for example, insists that election is "primarily corporate and only secondarily particular: one becomes elect by coming to be in Christ."[52] If this idea is consistently pressed, it finally denies personal election and substi-

[46]Arminius, III:311.
[47]Cf. Arminius, I:217, 566; III:323.
[48]Arminius, I:247, 248; see also II:494, 495.
[49]Clarke, 35.
[50]Cottrell, 52.
[51]Cottrell, 61.
[52]Robert Shank, *Elect in the Son* (Springfield, Mo.: Westcott Publishers, 1970), 45.

tutes only a corporate election, the election of the body of Christ, the church. Arminius never suggested such a restriction.

Arminius' idea, then, may be expressed thus: *Christ* (not election *per se*) is the foundation of the church; salvation is by *Christ* (not by election, except as election is an expression of God's love in Christ); the gospel is about *Christ* (not about God's decree of election). When God saw man as lost, He said: "I will make my Son a mediator and love men in Him."

I may add, although space does not permit developing this, that Barth apparently recognized this weakness of traditional Calvinism and proceeded to restore the Christocentric nature of election. But he went about it wrongly, making Christ both the electing one and the truly elected one, as well as the truly reprobate one. Apparently this finally led Barth to embrace universalism. Jewett rightly rejects this and is more on track when he observes, "There is no reason for me to ask whether I am elect: the anxiety that might evoke such a question is dispelled when I look away from myself to him in whose election I see myself elect. Christ's election, in other words, assures me of my election."[53]

• *Election is personal and individual.* This is not to deny that there is such a thing, in the Bible, as national election or election to particular roles of service. But these are not election to salvation and so are not directly involved in the subject of this work.

Some Arminians, as already noted, err in making election entirely corporate, even when referring to election to salvation. Thus Wiley speaks of "class predestination,"[54] and Wynkoop observes that "the way of salvation is predestined."[55] As already noted, Shank gets much too close to this when he speaks of election as primarily corporate and only secondarily personal. As Jewett observes, "In the Bible the elect are generally spoken of as a class. . . . Yet the implication is plain . . . that each member . . . shares, as an individual, in the election of that people."[56]

Thus Arminius, as we have seen above, defined predestination as the election of men to salvation and the reprobation of them to destruction. And, in the order of the decrees, his fourth included the

---

[53] Jewett, 56. His critique of Barth's view on pp. 48-54 is helpful.

[54] H. Orton Wiley et. al, "The Debate Over Divine Election," *Christianity Today* (Oct. 12, 1959), 3.

[55] Mildred Bangs Wynkoop, *Foundations of Wesleyan-Arminian Theology* (Kansas City: Beacon Hill Press, 1967), 53.

[56] Jewett, 47.

salvation or damnation of "certain particular persons." Watson also indicates that election is "of individuals to be the children of God, and the heirs of eternal life."[57] Thus Wood is incorrect in saying that Arminius proposed "the election or reprobation of specific classes rather than of individuals as such."[58] What Arminius taught was election of individuals *as believers,* but individuals nevertheless.

Cottrell correctly expresses the classical Arminian position when he emphasizes that election is of persons, not merely the plan. He cites passages like Romans 8:29, 30; 16:13; 2 Thessalonians 2:13; Ephesians 1:4, 5, 11; and 1 Peter 1:1, 2, pointing out that in some cases specific persons are spoken of as among the elect. He also notes that the names of the elect are written in the book of life (Rev. 17:8; Lk. 10:20; etc.).[59]

• *Election is eternal.* God's will to save (which includes both determining what the condition is and knowing who will meet it and electing to save them) is as eternal as He is. Ephesians 1:4: "He hath chosen us in him before the foundation of the world." Arminius, citing both this verse and Acts 15:18, says, "We attribute Eternity to this decree; because God does nothing in time, which He has not decreed to do from all eternity. . . . If it were otherwise, God might be charged with mutability."[60]

Some Arminians have tried to avoid this by referring election to the saving event that takes place in time. I do not think that Watson meant to do this, but his discussion muddies the water rather than clearing it. Discussing personal election, he said that the elect are "they who have been made partakers of the grace and saving efficiency of the gospel." Election, he said, means that people were chosen out of the world and to obedience and the sprinkling of the blood of Jesus. This is an act done in time, subsequent to the administration of the means of salvation. All this seems to mean that, for Watson, election is identified with the saving event in time. But then Watson observes, more clearly, that "eternal election" can only mean the "eternal *purpose* of election," the purpose formed in eternity.[61] Precisely: and that eternal purpose of election is what "election" is.

True, some of the Bible's uses of "election" may very well refer to acts in time rather than in eternity (First Thessalonians 1:4 *may* be an

---

[57]Watson, 337.
[58]Wood, 115.
[59]Cottrell, 57, 58.
[60]Arminius, I:566.
[61]Watson, II:337, 338.

example). But, even if that is so, some of the Bible's statements clearly refer to election in eternity, to God's eternal counsel; and this is what the theologians are discussing when they speak of election.

Thus Arminius, as we have already seen, defined election as the decree of God by which He determined from all eternity to justify believers. And thus Cottrell correctly observes that "God determined even before the creation which individuals will be saved, and even wrote their names in the book of life."[62]

• *Election is conditional.* This is the Arminian's main point of departure from Calvinism, understanding the Bible to teach that specific persons are elected or reprobated (i.e., chosen or rejected) as believers or unbelievers.

Arminius' way of presenting this strikes me as the most appropriate and properly cautious. His definitions (cited above) indicate that he saw people elected as believers (or reprobated as unbelievers). Consequently faith is the "condition" for election. For Arminius, if salvation is by faith, then election is by faith. If salvation is conditional, election is.

This is not to say that God's decrees are conditionally made. To repeat what has been observed above, God's eternal decisions are made without any conditions imposed on Him. He has unconditionally decreed a conditional election, electing people as believers.

I am not attracted, therefore, to the idea that the condition is "being in Christ."[63] Compare Shank's view, cited earlier, that "one becomes elect by coming to be in Christ." This appears to say that Christ is the only elect one, and one must see to it that he gets "in Christ" in order to be among the elect. I have an idea that this is a poor way of trying to state a fine truth. True, we are "chosen in Him" (Eph. 1:4), but surely He places us in Him, and that union or identification is part of the work of salvation wrought by Him. That union, in fact, is conditioned on faith; and so it seems right to stay with faith as the condition of election. Arminius might have been answering such a view when he said, "Christ is a means of salvation to no one unless he is apprehended by faith"; and, "God regards no one in Christ unless they are engrafted in him by faith."[64]

---

[62]Cottrell, 58.
[63]Cottrell, 61.
[64]Arminius, III:311.

One of the most important points in linking salvation by faith with election of believers is that this does away with the necessity of assuming some difference between God's secret, unrevealed decree and the administration of salvation in time. As noted in the previous chapter, Calvinists often tend to emphasize this distinction, citing Deuteronomy 29:29, "The secret things belong unto the Lord our God: but those things which are revealed belong to us." For Arminius, however, as Charles Cameron has seen, "The unbeliever cannot find any excuse for his unbelief in any distinction between God's revealed will and his secret will. Both secretly and openly, God does want all men to be saved."[65] Otherwise, reality is irrational and truth would violate the so-called law of non-contradiction.

No doubt there are some facets of God's will that He has not revealed, but His love for people in Christ to save them is not one of the secret things. He has revealed His plan of salvation, and it is salvation by faith. We should therefore understand election in those terms. Arminius' observations on this point are powerful: "As believers alone are saved, so only believers are predestinated to salvation."[66] "It has been revealed to us, Without faith it is impossible for any man to please God, or to be saved. There is, therefore, in God no other will, by which he wills anyone to be absolutely saved without consideration of faith." He continues to urge that if the decree of election were unconditional, and faith subsequent to that as something God wills to bestow on the elect, God would be of "contradictory wills."[67]

Wesley also emphasized this, in commenting on the meaning of election: "I believe the eternal decree concerning both [the elect and the reprobate] is expressed in the words: 'He that believeth shall be saved; he that believeth not shall be damned.' And this decree, without doubt, God will not change, and man cannot resist."[68]

Without going on to this logical conclusion, Jewett acknowledges—citing the Westminster Catechism for support—that "There can be no other will of God apart from that proclaimed in Christ, no secret counsel [concerning our redemption] that has not been

---

[65]Charles M. Cameron, "Arminius—Hero or Heretic?" (*Evangelical Quarterly* 64:3 [1992], 213-227), 224.

[66]Arminius, I:380.

[67]Arminius, I:288.

[68]John Wesley, *The Works of John Wesley* (Grand Rapids: Zondervan reprint, n.d., 14 vols), X:210.

revealed in him."[69] Well, what has been revealed is, simply enough, that he who believes in Christ is saved (elected) and he who does not believe is condemned (reprobated). We had better not work too hard at finding some other, unrevealed truth behind it.

How can the individual's faith in time be the condition for God's election in eternity? The question is no more difficult than many others that involve the same dimensions. The answer is that God is not limited by time. In eternity, He sees them as believers (or unbelievers) and loves (elects) them as believers.

After all, the individual's faith (or unbelief), while truly contingent and free, is certain. Being certain, and clearly seen by God as certain, He freely elects those whom he foreknows as believers. Add to this, further, that their faith (or unbelief) is all part of the course of events He planned (without rendering their faith or unbelief as necessary; certain and contingent, but not necessary).

Does this mean, then (as commonly put): "predestination according to foreknowledge"? Apparently so; when we say God elected people, in eternity, as believers, their faith was foreknown faith. But this way of speaking is, after all, merely a convenience for us who have to wrestle with the confusing distinction between God's eternality and our temporality.

Arminius spoke in these terms. On the subject of predestination in general he notes that it "was made in view of sin, the occurrence of which in time, God foresaw in the infinity of His knowledge."[70] Elsewhere he cites Augustine as teaching that "God has chosen to salvation those who he sees will afterwards believe by the aid of his preventing or preceding grace, and who will persevere by the aid of his subsequent or following grace."[71]

Even so, Jewett makes a misleading choice of words when he says, "Arminians came to the final conclusion that God foresees the choice the sinner will make and bases his own choice thereon."[72] The last five words of this are not appropriate: saying that God "based" His choice on the choice of believers is not the same thing as saying that God chose believers. Did Jewett allow Arminians the same view of the tension between eternity and time that he chooses for himself,

---

[69]Jewett, 56.
[70]Arminius, III:267.
[71]Arminius, I:385.
[72]Jewett, 14, 15.

he would better understand Arminius' insistence that God "has in his decree considered [or looked upon] them as believers."[73]

Furthermore, "foreknowledge" in the Bible is, at least some of the time, something more than mere prescience. Arminius credited this, even in the discussion of predestination. He observed that some explain foreknowledge (in Rom. 8:29) as meaning "previously loved, and affectionately regarded as His own," while others define it as "prescience of faith in Christ." And then he proceeds to inquire whether one of these can be true without the other, concluding, "God can 'previously love and affectionately regard as His own' no sinner unless He has foreknown him in Christ, and looked upon him as a believer in Christ."[74]

My own view is that the wording "election according to foreseen faith" is not the best way to express conditional election, although it may be the best we can do while we continue to face the problem of eternity and time. I am content to refer to conditional election, to say that faith is the condition, and to insist that God elected people as believers.

One thing is very clear: Donald Lake has twisted the Arminian understanding of the nature of foreknowledge into something Arminius and the Remonstrants would never recognize, as follows:

> Jacobus Arminius and later Arminians interpreted this distinction to mean that God's decision to apply the atonement was based upon his knowledge and awareness of those who would, when rightly confronted with the claims of the gospel, believe. . . . God knows who would, under ideal circumstances, believe the gospel, and on the basis of his foreknowledge, applies that gospel even if the person never hears the gospel during his lifetime.
>
> The task of evangelism and missions is to bring the knowledge of salvation, not the salvation itself. That salvation has already been brought in the all-sufficient work of atonement through Jesus Christ.[75]

This is inaccurate interpretation of both Arminius and the Scriptures. Not Reformation Arminianism at all, it appears to be more like an Arminian form of Barthianism.

---

[73]Arminius, I:221.

[74]Arminius, III:313, 314.

[75]Donald M. Lake, "He Died for All: The Universal Dimensions of the Atonement," in *Grace Unlimited,* ed. Clark H. Pinnock (Minneapolis: Bethany Fellowship, 1975), 42, 43.

How does conditional election relate to the sovereignty of God? The answer seems obvious: if the sovereign God unconditionally established faith as the condition for salvation (and therefore for election), then His sovereignty is not violated when He requires the condition. Neither Calvinist nor Arminian, by "sovereignty," means that God acts in a way that men call "arbitrary."

Surely God's sovereignty means that He acts freely, under no conditions than that He be true to Himself. Neither *a priori* (from our logic) nor *a posteriori* (from Scriptural evidence) is there any reason to believe God could not sovereignly establish any condition He chose (or no condition at all, did He so choose) for salvation. As Arminius put this, "The freedom of the goodness of God is declared. . . when He communicates it only on the condition, which He has been pleased to impose."[76]

How does conditional election relate to the Scriptural presentation of salvation by grace? Most important here is the fact that faith is not a work and has no merit (as Ambrose apparently thought). Did faith present itself as a claim to merit, salvation could not be by faith and by grace at the same time.

This will be dealt with in greater detail in a subsequent section on the application of salvation. For now, it is sufficient to observe that it is the Bible itself that presents salvation by faith as salvation by grace, thus making clear that there is no contradiction. As Paul insists in Romans 4:16, salvation is by faith that it might be by grace. Faith, rightly understood, is the opposite of works.

Arminius certainly believed in salvation *sola gratia:* "This doctrine . . . establishes the grace of God, when it ascribes the whole praise of our vocation, justification, adoption, and glorification, to the mercy of God alone, and takes it entirely away from our own strength, works and merit."[77] Again: "As the gospel is purely gracious, this predestination is also gracious . . . [It] excludes every cause which can possibly be imagined to be capable of having proceeded from man, and by which God may be moved to make this decree."[78]

How does conditional election relate to the doctrine of "total depravity"? The Calvinist insists that, given fallen man's utter inability to exercise faith, God Himself must impart faith as a gift to the elect. Thus faith flows from election rather than conditions it.

---

[76]Arminius, III:274.
[77]Arminius, I:568.
[78]Arminius, II:100.

This matter will be dealt with in detail below, in the section on the application of salvation. For now, it is sufficient to indicate the Arminian answer briefly. Arminius saw the answer in what he called "prevenient grace." In other words, he readily acknowledged that fallen man, left alone and simply presented with the gospel, is incapable of faith. And so he indicated that the work of grace is necessary first: "That act of faith is not in the power of a natural, carnal, sensual, and sinful man," and "no one can perform this act except through the grace of God."[79]

This "enabling grace" (as we may call it) is performed before the sinner is able to believe: "We give the name of 'believers,' not to those who would be such by their own merits or strength, but to those who by the gratuitous and peculiar kindness of God would believe in Christ."[80] Arminius consistently insisted that this faith is a gift.

The difference between the Calvinist and the Arminian, at this point, is that the Arminian understands that God performs this work of enabling grace for those who will respond in faith (the elect) and for those who will not (the non-elect or reprobate).

Reprobation in the Arminian System

We have already noted Arminius' definition of reprobation above. Any further description of reprobation seems unnecessary, except for brief analysis of the definition given.

As election deals with people as believers, so reprobation deals with them as unbelievers.

Reprobation includes punishment not merely for the sin of rejecting Christ but for all the individual's sins. Arminius was quick to insist, correctly I believe, that the punishment to which unbelievers are reprobated is "not only on account of unbelief, but likewise on account of other sins from which they might have been delivered through faith in Christ."[81] Thus Lake is certainly something other than "Arminian" in the original sense of the word when he asserts:

> What condemns a man is not sins. Why? Because Christ's redemptive and atoning work is complete and satisfying. . . . The issue of every man's salvation turns not upon his sins, but rather upon his relationship to the Son! . . . There is only one sin God cannot forgive, and that is the rejection of the Lord Jesus Christ as one's Savior.[82]

---

[79] Arminius, II:102.
[80] Arminius, I:567.
[81] Arminius, II:101.
[82] Lake, 47.

This is precisely the reasoning that has led Neal Punt to put forth the view that only those are condemned who have consciously rejected the gospel offer.[83] I assume, without his saying so, that Lake would agree. As with similar matters, I have space and purpose here only to make clear that this is not the view of Arminius himself or of this work.

Sin is the sole, meritorious cause for God's wrath and condemnation, not some "secret" decree of reprobation.

In summary, reprobation is corollary to election. Unlike the Calvinistic system, the Arminian system makes election and reprobation essentially parallel (although as opposites). Election is gracious and eternal, founded in Christ, and conditional and personal in application. Reprobation is just and eternal, punitive (punishment for sin), and conditional and personal in application. The major non-parallelism is that election requires the included foreordination of the administration of the means to faith: namely, the Word and the Spirit; reprobation requires nothing more.

Excursus: Foreknowledge, Freedom, and the Future

I hesitate to go beyond what I have said on this subject earlier in this chapter; my purpose does not require it. But there is so much current discussion—some of it misguided, in my view—that I feel I must offer some observations, albeit briefly because of the limitations of space.[84] In truth, the view I have stated earlier in this chapter is often thought of as rather simplistic: namely, to accept as given that God can know the future certainly without thereby closing the door to human freedom and moral responsibility.

Admittedly, the issues are complex. In one form or another, the problem of an unchanging God and a changing world has been around for a long time. Zeno and Parmenides, centuries before Christ, were responding to the problem when they affirmed that all change is illusory. (One wonders, at times, if Calvinists are not affirming the same thing!)

There are different positions on these matters, as we relate them to the problem at hand.

1. Calvinists affirm that all events, including future ones, are certain and foreknown because God has predetermined all events. In that case, there is no problem with absolute foreknowledge, or with divine control; the question is whether there is any real freedom and moral responsibility for humans. To this Calvinists verbalize a positive

---

[83]See Neal Punt, *Unconditional Good News* (Grand Rapids: Eerdmans, 1980).

[84]For a more complete treatment, see my "Foreknowledge, Freedom, and the Future," *Journal of the Evangelical Theological Society* 43:2 (June 2000), 259-271.

answer, even though it seems to us who are Arminian that they are hedging.

Sometimes Calvinists make a distinction between the primary and secondary causes of an event, and represent human decisions as the latter. In this case, however, human agency is reduced to being God's instrumentality. This seems no different from a "hard determinism" that finally makes all freedom an illusion and traces all events to prior, necessitating causes.

Many Calvinists profess a "compatibilism" that attempts to combine determinism with human freedom by redefining "freedom" to mean the freedom to do as one desires, rather than the freedom to do something different from what one does. In other words, faced with a decision, a person chooses according to the sum total of influences, circumstances, and effects of previous choices that are operative at the time. Only one course of action is really possible, therefore, but the person involved "freely" chooses that course of action. Arminians unanimously deny that this "soft determinism" does justice to human freedom.

2. The classic Arminian view affirms that the future is perfectly foreknown by God and yet is, in principle and practice, "open" and "undetermined." That is, future free decisions are certain but not necessary. In other words, the person who makes a moral choice is free either to make that choice or to make a different choice.

Holding this kind of "indeterminism" (I prefer "self-determinism") is considered to be necessary to affirming the reality of both God's omniscience (infallible foreknowledge) and human freedom. These Arminians do not always attempt to explain how both of these can be true at the same time, nor do they necessarily think this is required. This is the view that I have attempted to outline earlier in this chapter.

3. Consequently some modern Arminians, who have permitted the supposed logical problems involved in this view to affect them, have redefined foreknowledge to mean that God knows all that is possible to know. Just as He cannot do what is not possible to do, He cannot know what is not possible to be known; and the future free acts of moral agents cannot be known. For lack of a better term, this may be called the "limited foreknowledge" view. As noted earlier, Clark Pinnock is perhaps the best known adherent of this view.[85] Richard Rice also takes this approach.[86]

---

[85]Clark H. Pinnock, "God Limits His Foreknowledge," *Predestination and Free Will*, ed. D. and R. Basinger (Downers Grove: InterVarsity, 1986), 156-158.

[86]Richard Rice, "Divine Foreknowledge and Free-Will Theism" in *The Grace of God, The Will of Man*, ed. Clark H. Pinnock (Grand Rapids: Zondervan, 1989), 121-139.

Indeed, as this movement has developed the result has been a revision of classic, Christian theism. Those who advance this view call themselves "open theists," by which they emphasize the openness of God both to the future and to give-and-take relationships with human beings. They use the name "presentism" for their view of God's knowledge, thus affirming that He knows the past and present exhaustively but does not know the future. They advance many arguments against foreknowledge, especially "logical" ones, and responding to these is beyond the scope of this work. Perhaps the best expression of this view is John Sanders' *The God Who Risks: A Theology of Providence.*[87]

This neo-Arminian movement has attracted some attention on the contemporary evangelical scene,[88] but it is not entirely new. Indeed, Richard Watson faced the very same approach in 1850: "From the difficulty which has been supposed to exist, in reconciling this [foreknowledge of future things] with the freedom of human actions, and man's accountability, some have however refused to allow prescience, at least of contingent actions, to be a property of the Divine nature."[89]

It will have to be sufficient, for now, to lodge objections from both sides. On the one hand, the view is falsified by the Bible itself. One would need to cite only a few of countless instances, in the Scriptures, where God demonstrates His perfect foreknowledge of future, free choices—both good and evil ones. For me, it is enough to observe that Christ's atonement for sin was foreordained before the foundation of the world (1 Pet. 1:18-20; Rev. 13:8). This alone destroys the view that sin is not foreknown by God.

On the other side, and equally important, this view is not logically needed; the reasons proposed do not require it. Rice, for example, reveals his reason for rejecting the classic Arminian approach:

> In spite of assertions that absolute foreknowledge does not eliminate freedom, intuition tells us otherwise. If God's foreknowledge is infallible, then what he sees cannot fail to happen. This means that the course of future events is fixed, however we explain what actually caus-

---

[87]Published at Downers Grove, Ill. by InterVarsity (1998). For my own detailed response to this work, see "An Arminian Response to John Sanders' *The God Who Risks: A Theology of Providence*" in *Journal of the Evangelical Theological Society* 43:2 (June 2000), 259-271.

[88]For a recent summary, with critical responses, see "Has God Been Held Hostage by Philosophy" in *Christianity Today,* Jan. 9, 1995, pp. 30-34.

[89]Watson, I:375.

es it. And if the future is inevitable, then the apparent experience of free choice is an illusion.[90]

But this is an all too shallow and careless set of affirmations, and it is certainly not the view of Arminius or the original Remonstrants. My intuition, for example, does not tell me what Rice's tells him. To say that "the course of future events is fixed" (as I have labored the point earlier in the chapter) may mean nothing more than that the course of future events is the course of future events. In other words, it is to speak of the factuality of the future, of its certainty as fact, without speaking of its necessity. The alternative to a certain course of future events is not an uncertain future but no future at all. If by "fixed" Rice means "inevitable" (in the sense of "necessary"), his claim is entirely unjustified.

The words "can" and "cannot" are ambiguous. Used in one way, the sentence "If God's foreknowledge is infallible, then what he sees cannot fail to happen" is true. In this sense, "cannot" is being used with respect to factuality. But if "cannot" is made to speak of necessity, the sentence is not true. For that reason, it is altogether best to avoid "can" or "cannot" and speak of certainty and necessity, of "will" and "must." (Watson was willing to stay with "can": "It is said, If the result of an absolute contingency be certainly foreknown, it can have no other result, it cannot happen otherwise. This is not the true inference. It will not happen otherwise; but I ask, why can it not happen otherwise? Can is an expression of potentiality."[91])

To repeat what has already been said: A future event can be both certain and contingent at the same time, without being necessary. That I will make a certain choice in the future does not mean that I am not free to make a different one. All that is required to grasp this is careful thinking and unambiguous use of words. The future, however certain, is not closed until it occurs.

4. Still another approach is currently being offered, its best-known spokesman being William L. Craig. He suggests, to use the title of one of his papers, that "middle knowledge" offers the possibility for rapprochement between Calvinists and Arminians.[92] What Craig means by "middle knowledge" is that God knows both everything that will

[90]Rice, 127.

[91]Watson, I:380.

[92]William L. Craig, "Middle Knowledge A Calvinist-Arminian Rapprochement?" in *The Grace of God, The Will of Man* ed. Clark H. Pinnock (Grand Rapids: Zondervan, 1989), 141-164.

come to pass and everything else that could or would come to pass in all other conceivable sets of circumstances.

What is the advantage of this? According to Craig, in a book he has written to present this theory:

> Since [God] knows what any free creature would do in any situation, he can, by creating the appropriate situations, bring it about that creatures will achieve his ends and purposes and that they will do so freely. ... In his infinite intelligence, God is able to plan a world in which his designs are achieved by creatures acting freely.[93]

No doubt there is some truth here, although its significance for the problem at hand is questionable. If it has any usefulness, that will be found in contributing to our understanding just how, at times, God is able to bring about the doing of His will freely by His creatures without in any sense acting on their wills causally. As I have said earlier in the chapter, if God keeps me from going to work in my garden by sending the rain, He has not thereby interfered with my freedom. But this will not do as a whole explanation of the problem. Nor does it seem to me that this "middle knowledge," as thus explained, is any advancement on traditionally conceived foreknowledge or omniscience. It is already clear that God knows not only all future facts but all other possibilities, and that helps nothing. In the final analysis, the difference between Calvinist and Arminian is not as much about foreknowledge and free will as it is about God's sovereign control and free will. And the proponent of this "middle knowledge" still cannot avoid having God decide which sets of circumstances—and therefore which human responses—to actualize, as David Basinger has pointed out.[94]

Once again, then, I must stress what seems to me the final set of facts to hold in tension. Either the future is certain or it is not. The Arminian, at last, must come to grips with the fact that the future is certain and is certainly foreknown by God. And this, in the end, is no problem once it is clear that certainty is not necessity, that it does not preclude freedom to act in more than one way.

---

[93]William L. Craig, *The Only Wise God* (Grand Rapids: Baker, 1987), 135.

[94]David Basinger, "Divine Control and Human Freedom: Is Middle Knowledge the Answer" (*Journal of the Evangelical Theological Society,* 36:1 [1993]), 55-64.

For Further Reading on the
Arminian Doctrine of Predestination

Arminius, James. *The Writings of Arminius,* tr. James Nichols and W. R. Bagnall. Grand Rapids: Baker, 1956 (vol. I, pp. 211-253, 289-299; vol. II, pp. 99-103).

Cottrell, Jack. "Conditional Election," *Grace Unlimited,* ed. Clark H. Pinnock. Minneapolis: Bethany Fellowship, 1975 (ch. 3).

Miley, John. *Systematic Theology.* New York: Methodist Book Concern, 1892, 94 (vol. I, pp. 180-187; vol. II, pp. 254-266). [Later Arminianism as represented in organized Methodism]

Pinnock, Clark. "God Limits His Knowledge," *Predestination and Free Will,* ed. David and Randall Basinger. Downers Grove: InterVarsity, 1986. [A neo-Arminian reading of the problem of foreknowledge in a book subtitled "Four Views of Divine Sovereignty and Human Freedom"]

Shank, Robert. *Elect in the Son.* Springfield, Mo.: Westcott Publishers, 1970. [More representative of later Arminianism than of Arminius]

Watson, Richard. *Theological Institutes.* New York: Nelson and Phillips, 1850 (vol. I, pp. 375-383; vol. II, pp. 306-312, 337-361). [An important, early Wesleyan theologian]

CHAPTER 4

Predestination in the New Testament

Very little space has been devoted, in the previous two parts of this section, to Scriptural discussion. Not because Scripture is unimportant in this discussion: indeed, it is too important to be treated in piecemeal, proof-text fashion. As Gordon Clark has said, "Although quoting verses is an indispensable prerequisite for formulating Christian doctrine, much more is required."[1] For this issue, as for any, we must try our best to grapple with the Scripture as carefully as we can. One's doctrine must never be determined by his "system," but by exegetical theology, by an honest effort to determine what God has said on the issues at stake.

Space does not allow us to treat, in detail, everything the Bible says about the matters of concern in this book. For each of the major topics, then, I will select those passages that are most crucial and treat them in the way that appears to offer the best hope of determining what they say about the topics at hand.

On the subject of predestination—that is, God's decisions about salvation made in eternity—I will deal most extensively with three key passages. These are Ephesians 1:3-14; Romans 8:28-30; and Romans 9–11. Following this, I will indicate a set of conclusions that seem justified in the light of this analysis, bringing into play (more briefly) some other Biblical statements.

First, I would note that there are some seven key Greek New Testament words (with their cognates) that are significantly involved, to one extent or another, in the discussion. Several of these words occur in each of the three passages. Since space does not allow for a detailed word study of each of these, I will have to be content to work some of the results of such a word study into the discussion at appropriate points.

The seven words I refer to are:

1. *proorizō*: predestinate, foreordain
2. *eklogē* (with *eklektos* and *eklegomai*): election, choice
3. *boulē* (with *boulēma* and *boulomai*): counsel, will
4. *prothesis* (with *protithemi*): plan, purpose
5. *thelō* (with *thelēma*): will, desire

---

[1]Gordon H. Clark, *Faith and Saving Faith* (Jefferson, Md.: The Trinity Foundation, 1983), 31.

6. *eudokia* (with *eudokeō*): good pleasure, will
7. *prognōsis* (with *proginōskō*): foreknowledge, prescience.

Ephesians 1:3-14

This important passage contains five of the seven key words just listed. It demands careful analysis.

Doctrinal discussion in Ephesians is more like a doxology to God than a systematic theology book. That is precisely true of this passage. It is one unbroken, complex sentence, difficult to "outline": "an almost ecstatic declaration of Paul's theology of salvation"[2] spoken as an occasion for praise. Careful study leads to the following analysis.

1. *Preamble: the God of all blessings* (v. 3)
   a. the God and Father of our Lord Jesus Christ
   b. the One who blessed (Greek aorist) us
      (1) with a complete and manifold blessing
      (2) in the realm of spiritual reality
      (3) in (union with) Christ
2. *God's eternal plan to bless us* (vv. 4-6)

"According as" (*kathōs*) connects the following, as explanation, to verse 3. Three times the pronoun "us" occurs as object of a verb that states God's action. These three, then, provide the basis for a reasonably precise syntactical outline.

   a. *God chose us* (v. 4). Like "blessed," this is aorist, a simple past action. "Chose" (*exelexato*), as the description in context makes clear, looks to the act of election in eternity—one of the key words listed above. Several characteristics of election are made clear by the modifiers.

      (1) He elected individuals, as the "us" makes clear.

      (2) He elected "in Christ." This is the thing Arminius wanted emphasized, the "Christocentricity" of election. Christ Himself, first and foremost, was God's darling, His chosen One. Individuals are chosen in saving union with Christ.

Hodge rightly objects to reading this as though God elected us *to be* in Christ, or *because* we are in Christ.[3] Both add to the text.

      (3) He elected "before the foundation of the world" was laid, thus making clear that *eternal* election is the subject here. The same phrase, *pro katabolēs kosmou*, occurs also in John 17:24; 1 Peter 1:20. In those passages, Christ is the one "loved" (essentially equal to

---

[2]C. Leslie Mitton, *New Century Bible: Ephesians* (Oliphant, 1960), 44, 45.
[3]Charles Hodge, *A Commentary on the Epistle to the Ephesians* (Grand Rapids: Eerdmans, 1954), 30, 31.

"elected") and foreknown (apparently, to provide His blood for our redemption) "before the world's foundation." Our election is thus closely associated with that which God foreordained concerning His Son—again calling attention to the Christocentric nature of election.

(4) He elected us to be holy and without blemish in His presence, in love: the objective of election. Comparing Colossians 1:22, I conclude that this is a futuristic look at the ultimate goal not only of election but also of Christ's redemptive work: "to present you holy and unblameable and unreproveable in his sight."

No "basis" or condition for election is stated here. If other New Testament passages do not indicate that election is conditional, it cannot be proved from this passage—unless one can show (and this is not far-fetched, after all) that election "in Christ" *implies* a condition, and that one comes to be "in Christ" by faith; see on verse 13 below. But the point to be kept in mind is that the passage also cannot be used to prove that election is *un*conditional. Conditions are simply not discussed. Paul neither affirms nor denies a condition for election.

b. *God foreordained us* (vv. 5,6a). This verb ("predestinated," *proorisas*) is another of the key words listed above. Here it is an aorist participle (simple past action, again) and there is no grammatical or contextual reason to place it *before* the electing (neither logically nor temporally). Indeed, the "foreordaining" is (at least grammatically) subordinate to the main verb: (literally) "He elected us, foreordaining us." In electing, He foreordained us. As Mitton puts it, this "reemphasizes the truth already affirmed in the word 'chose,' and indicates the purpose behind that choice."[4]

(1) He foreordained us to a position as His sons. "Adoption" (*huiothesia*) does not so much relate to bringing an outsider into one's family as to giving a child the status of an "of age" son and heir—as Galatians 4:1-7 makes clear. This emphasizes the rights and responsibilities of full-fledged *status* in the family, and in this sense "son" contrasts not only with "servant" but also with "child."

(2) He foreordained us by Jesus Christ. Again we have the Christocentric emphasis.

(3) He foreordained us "according to the good pleasure of His will." In summary, this phrase emphasizes that God's plan of salvation found no grounds or reason in man himself. The only basis is in God's own will and there our search for a "reason" must end.

---

[4]Mitton, 51.

"Good pleasure" (*eudokia*) and "will" (*thelēma*) are two more of the key words listed above. Here (and in other New Testament passages) they are not far from being synonyms. (Piling up synonyms is one of the stylistic tendencies of Ephesians.) If we regard *tou thelēmatos* as appositional genitive, we can even read this as "God's good pleasure which is identical with His will." And this may be defined as "the free good-pleasure which, grounded in God alone and influenced by none else, is His gracious resolution to save."[5]

We should note that, when God acts in a manner that is in accord with His sovereign good pleasure or will, *He may act unconditionally or on the basis of conditions He sovereignly establishes.* The words themselves do not tell us which applies in any given instance. Indeed, *all* God's acts are "according to the good pleasure of His will."

(4) He foreordained us to the praise of the glory of His grace. Already we have seen two phrases indicating God's purposes in election and foreordination: "for us to be holy and without blemish. . . " and "unto adoption." This is a third and *ultimate* purpose: for the glorification of God as a God of grace.

(5) He foreordained us as an act of grace. I single this out (already indicated indirectly) for special mention because all of verses 5, 6a imply this. God's plan of salvation is wholly gracious, owing nothing to man's work or merit. The "favor" we call salvation is entirely undeserved and unearned.

As will also be seen in the analysis of Romans 8:28-30, foreordination (predestination) therefore seems clearly to refer to *what* happens in salvation rather than to *who* is saved. "Election" sees the saved as people God has chosen; "predestination" refers to what He has chosen them for.

c. *He gave us grace* (v. 6b), a third action, even though it is grammatically subordinate to the noun "grace" in the preceding phrase; the "wherein" has "grace" for its antecedent. "Made us accepted" is the verb form cognate to the noun "grace"; what we have, then, is repetition for emphasis: His grace with which He "be-graced"[6] us; grace which He graciously bestowed on us.

"In the beloved" means in the Beloved One, Christ. (Cf. Col. 1:13, "the son of his love.") Again, then, we have the two-fold emphasis on Christocentricity and the role of union with Christ. We are objects of

---

[5]*Theological Dictionary of the New Testament,* ed. Gerhard Kittel (Grand Rapids: Eerdmans, 1964), II:747.

[6]F. F. Bruce, *The Epistle to the Ephesians* (Revell, 1961), 30.

God's grace only in Christ. Election and foreordination graciously flow to us in union with Christ—the only way God could elect us and maintain His holiness, given that apart from union with Christ we are sinful and cannot be objects of election. God's eternal decree to save, then, was not a sterile one that logically preceded the plan of redemption in Christ. Instead, it is grounded in the plan of redemption by Christ and grows out of it.

3. *The realization of these blessings in time* (vv. 7-14).

The orientation of the passage undergoes a subtle adjustment at this point. Everything in the previous verses looked to the eternal past. Now Paul looks at what "we have" (v. 7). True, some clauses in verses 7-14 will look back to God's eternal plan (vv. 9b, 11b) as background, but the passage as a whole looks at our experience in time that reflects (and reveals) God's eternal decisions.

a. *Redemption in Christ* (vv. 7, 8)

(1) The fact of redemption

(2) The means of redemption: "through his blood"

(3) The nature of redemption: "the forgiveness of sins"

(4) The basis of redemption: "God's rich grace which He made abound to us in a manner that manifests the highest order of wisdom and prudence"

b. *Revelation of the mystery of His will* (vv. 9,10)

(1) A making known in time. "Making known" (*gnōrisas,* another aorist participle) is subordinate to the previous clause and looks to one result of God's activity in effecting the plan of salvation in time. Calvinists are accustomed, rightly, to emphasizing that God's eternal decrees are not revealed—as such—to us, that we must learn their content by what He does in time. This is an emphasis the Arminian can support wholeheartedly: we learn the nature of God's eternal decrees about salvation from the way He applies them.

(2) A making known of "the mystery" of His will. In Paul, a "mystery" is something unknowable by man's natural powers, thus requiring that God reveal it. Here, the mystery is His will, specifically His will as it relates to salvation.

(3) The basis: "according to his good pleasure which he purposed in himself" (or, "in him": that is, in Christ). The phrase essentially repeats verse 5b, above, and so glances back at eternity again. The only difference is that "which he purposed" is substituted for "of his will." This shows that God's purpose (*prothesis,* another of the key words in the list above) is equal to His will.

(4) The ultimate objective. Here is another clause to indicate God's objectives: that Christ will be the unchallenged Head of all the universe.

c. *Inheritance* (vv. 11-14)

Verse 11 is structurally parallel to verse 7, as the "also" indicates. Growing out of God's eternal decisions about salvation, in time we have experienced redemption and the making known of His good pleasure for our salvation. We have also come to be, as His corporate people, His inheritance.

(1) We were made the Lord's inheritance (as the verse should probably be read, with a number of interpreters, especially if Deut. 32:8, 9 is reflected here).[7]

(2) This, too, is part of what was *foreordained* for the elect. Like verse 9b, then, verse 11b also glances back into eternity for the background of what is being experienced in time.

(3) The basis, again, is "according to the purpose of him who worketh all things after the counsel of his own will." This is the third time for this (essentially the same) phrase (see vv. 5, 9). Now, instead of "the good pleasure (*eudokia*) of his will," we have "the counsel (*boulē*) of his will," using still another of the key words in the list above. Apparently, then, "good pleasure" and "counsel" are essentially synonyms, and (as noted above) "will" and "purpose" are also essentially synonyms with them.

(4) The glory of God is, once more (cf. vv. 6, 14), the ultimate objective.

(5) Faith (which comes by hearing; cf. Rom. 10:17) is the condition for experiencing salvation. Paul indicates that salvation flows from faith (vv. 12, 13). Since the experience in time has already been seen as the way of understanding the decrees in eternity (v. 9, above), one feels confident in drawing the conclusion that the decree in eternity was one to administer salvation conditionally (by faith).

Thus Arminius could insist that to his view of election ". . . the passage in Eph. i, is not opposed. For believers are 'predestinated according to the purpose of Him who worketh all things after the counsel of His own will.' The purpose, according to which Predestination is declared to have been made, is that of adopting

---

[7]"The thought is essentially that which recurs often in the Old Testament when Israel is spoken of as God's portion (see Dt. iv.20, ix.29; Zc. ii.12)." Francis Foulkes, *The Epistle of Paul to the Ephesians* (InterVarsity and Eerdmans, 1983), 54.

believers in Christ to sonship and eternal life, as is apparent from many passages of Scripture."[8] Again: "The passage, in Eph. i, regards faith, as presupposed to predestination. For no one, but a believer, is predestinated to adoption through Christ—'as many as received him, to them gave he power to become the sons of God.'"[9]

(6) The indwelling of the promised Holy Spirit is the "seal" of salvation, the official "imprimatur" of God stamped in the lives of the elect.

(7) That Spirit is also the "earnest" of the inheritance promised to the elect.

Romans 9—11

Probably no passage is more important for our investigation than this. As lengthy as these three chapters are, space does not allow for the same kind of close analysis attempted above (of Eph. 1:3-14). Nor is that necessary. The first requirement is to get a grasp of the overall sweep of the section, as follows.

The key to the passage is 9:14: "Is there unrighteousness with God (in His treatment of Israel, which includes the present rejection of Israel)?" Paul's purpose for the three chapters is to answer this question with a resounding "No." The important thing, about any portion of the three chapters, is to understand that no one portion stands alone. Paul responds to the overall question with a series of "points" to make in establishing that the answer is negative. Each part of the answer must be understood in light of the other parts of the answer. The following broad "outline" will give the overall picture:

Main Point: God is not unrighteous in His present rejection of Israel.

Sub-points in developing this main point:
A. God elects and rejects whom He pleases (chs. 9, 10)
1. He never promised, unconditionally, to save all the fleshly descendants of Abraham, Isaac, or Israel (9:6-13).
2. He is Sovereign and has the right to save (or damn) whomever He pleases (9:15-24).
3. He always made clear (in prophecy) that not all of "Israel" would be saved (9:25-29).
4. He has rejected Israel because Israel has rejected salvation by faith in favor of salvation by works (9:30—10:21).

---

[8]James Arminius, *The Writings of James Arminius* (three vols.), tr. James Nichols and W. R. Bagnall (Grand Rapids: Baker, 1956), III:488.

[9]Arminius, III:490.

B. God has not rejected Israel after all (ch. 11)
  1. In fact, God has not rejected Israelites: any who will can be saved by grace through faith (11:1-10).
  2. The present rejection of Israel opens the doors of salvation for all nations (11:11-22).
  3. Indeed, the present rejection of Israel is not "final": Israel will yet be converted (11:23-32).

This "bare bones" analysis requires some fleshing out, and we begin with a clarification of the question at issue. One should realize that Paul, in this passage, is "arguing" (theoretically, at least) with any Jews who rejected his understanding of salvation by faith in Christ as leaving unbelieving Jews out of the Abrahamic covenant (as in Gal. 3:6-29; Rom. 4) and thus unsaved. Those Jews would contend that God had unconditionally promised to save all Israel and would therefore be unrighteous if He failed to keep that promise. Their concept—the corporate salvation of all Jews—is referred to by Hodge and connected with this passage: "Comp. Rom. 2:17; 9:6; and other passages, in which Paul argues to prove that being the natural descendants of Abraham is not enough to secure the favour of God. That such was the doctrine of the Jews is shown by numerous passages from their writings."[10]

The purpose of verses 6-13, then, is to start with something the Jews already would acknowledge and show that God never promised to save all of Abraham's seed just because they descended from him. The rejection of Ishmael and Esau (with the concomitant election of Isaac and Jacob/Israel) made this clear. (We will return to "the purpose of God according to election" below.)

And the purpose of verses 14-24 is to argue that the sovereign God is the one who determines who will be saved. Since this follows hard on the heels of the point of verses 6-13 (as just seen), the point now is that therefore the Jewish notion of universal corporate salvation for all Jews is unjustified. God still saves whom He wills and damns whom He wills, Jews or otherwise. Indeed, the use of Exodus 33:19 specifically supports the point that not all Israelites were destined to be saved; it was spoken to *Moses,* of all people. As I have written elsewhere:

---

[10]Charles Hodge, *Commentary on the Epistle to the Romans* (Grand Rapids: Eerdmans, 1972), 70.

Even in the wilderness, when we might think all the nation was automatically entitled to His favor, He said: "I will show mercy on whom I
will show mercy. . . ." Neither Moses nor Israel had any special claims
on Him that took away His sovereign right to act as He chose. Nor will
He show mercy to all of them just because they were Israelites in the
flesh.[11]

In other words, then, the Jew cannot raise his voice to heaven and
say, "I am a Jew; you have promised to save all Jews. You must save
me therefore. Paul's doctrine of salvation by faith in Jesus (which
would leave me out) is therefore wrong." To such a claim, Paul
responds: "God rejected Ishmael and chose Isaac; He rejected Esau
and chose Jacob. He saves whom He wills and rejects whom He wills.
You cannot speak thus to God. You cannot lay on Him the claim of
your Israelite lineage."

Finally, then, the purpose of 9:30 (and following) is to show that
the sovereign God, who saves whom He pleases and damns whom He
pleases, has pleased to save believers. In the way Israel has been
rejected, then, she has been rejected because she has rejected salvation by faith. Nothing could be much plainer than this: "Israel has not
attained . . . righteousness: Why? Because they did not seek it by
faith" (9:31, 32). "They . . . have not submitted to the righteousness of
God" (10:3). And this is reconfirmed in 11:20: "Because of unbelief
they were broken off."

In such a context, then, the "stage" of argument in 9:15-24 (the
most crucial part) is relatively obvious. As Forlines has expressed it,

When we read in Rom. 9:15 that God will have mercy and compassion
on whomever He wills, it behooves us to ask: On whom does God will
to show mercy and compassion?. . . When God chooses the one who
believes in Jesus Christ as his Lord and Savior to show His mercy in salvation, He is choosing whom He wills. . . . When salvation is offered on
the condition of faith in Christ, that in no way weakens the words, "I will
have mercy on whom I will have mercy. . . ." God's sovereignty is fully in
control in this view.[12]

To summarize: Paul is, in fact, arguing against the Jewish concept
of "unconditional" election (of all Jews by birth) and establishing, in

---

[11]Robert E. Picirilli, *The Book of Romans* (Nashville: Randall House Publications,
1974-75), 183.

[12]F. Leroy Forlines, *The Randall House Commentary: Romans* (Nashville: Randall
House Publications, 1987), 268.

its place, conditional election—election of believers. He does not "blame" the rejection of unbelieving Jews on the fact that God arbitrarily rejects whomever He pleases, but blames it on their own unbelief, which amounts to a rejection of His sovereign decision to ordain salvation by faith in Jesus.

One of the questions involved in the analysis of the section relates to 9:11. What does "that the purpose of God according to election might stand, not of works but of Him who calls," as related to the choice of Jacob and rejection of Esau, *before birth,* mean? Arminians tend to set this aside as election to office rather than salvation. Calvinists tend to take either of two approaches. Some (Shedd, Hodge) agree that this is election to patriarchal office but go on to regard Jacob and Esau, by analogy, as illustrative types of spiritual election and reprobation. Others (Murray, Piper) regard this, directly (not by analogy), as election to salvation.

In fact, the decision on these three possibilities *does not matter* for our purposes here. What Paul says is that the Jacob-Esau choice, even before their birth, disproves election *by works.* If the choice were based on the works of the individual, then it would not be by the (gracious) purpose of "Him who calls." But since Paul himself is the very one who has established that "by faith" is the very opposite of "by works" (as in Rom. 4), then "by faith" in no way contradicts what he says in 9:11. A subsequent section of this book will emphasize this point more; for now, it is crucially important to recognize that salvation by faith is, in fact, the very method by which God has chosen to establish salvation by grace and not by works (Rom. 4:16) and thus to base salvation on the work and decision of God rather than any human merit or deserving.

Such a view is what Paul is arguing for in this entire section of Romans (which obviously must not be separated from the preceding 8 chapters where the argument has been presented ever so forcefully): salvation is not by membership in the Israelite race but by faith, and this is precisely so that salvation will not be by men's doings but by God's, and this is precisely in accord with God's sovereign right to give salvation as an act of grace to whomever He wills. In order to establish salvation by His own "sovereign grace," He made faith, rather than works, the condition. Accordingly, all man can do is hold out the *empty* hands of faith and turn away from himself to receive God's free and entirely unearned gift.

A related question is whether the "anticipated" objection in 9:14 comes in response to the selection of Jacob and rejection of Esau (in

v. 13). The answer must surely be, No, in spite of the fact that Haldane, Shedd, and others take it this way. As Forlines observes,

> Let it be said that the Jews had no difficulty with the rejection of Ishmael and Esau. . . . The concern that the unbelieving Jew would have had about God's righteousness was that for God not to follow through with the unconditional election of all Jews meant that God had not kept His word.[13]

The argument of the *entire* passage makes this clear: Paul's "opponents" (imaginary or otherwise) had no objection to the rejection of Ishmael or Esau, but to the idea that some Israelites were not going to be saved.

In this light, then, the entire section (chs. 9-11) has consistency and presents no problem at all for the one who believes in conditional election. References in 11:5ff to "the election of grace" accord exactly with the idea of election of believers. Paul contrasts gracious election with election of "workers," not election of believers. In context, the point is that some Israelites have not obtained the promises; they are those insistent on salvation by Israelite nationality or by the works of the law given to Israel. But other Israelites, in accord with the election of grace, have obtained the promises; they are those who have submitted to the righteousness of God that is gained on condition of faith in Jesus Christ. To repeat: 11:6 contrasts grace with works, not with faith; Paul is the very one, and in this same epistle, who emphasizes that salvation is by faith that it might be by grace (4:16).

What, then, about the "hardening"? In the first place, one must note that "hardening" is made the opposite of "showing mercy" (9:18). And this fits well with what is said in 11:7ff; there, those who have put faith in Christ, in accord with the election of grace, have obtained the promises; the rest have been "hardened." One may say, then, that the withholding of saving mercy is all that is needed to accomplish this hardening. Nothing more active is necessary. Even Piper, a consistent Calvinist, observes that "The hardening in 9:18 has reference, just as the hardening in 11:7, to the action of God whereby a person is left in a condition outside salvation and thus prepared for destruction."[14] John Brown concurs, suggesting that the word is "equivalent to 'treat with severity' in withholding favor and inflicting deserved punish-

---

[13]Forlines, 265.

[14]John Piper, *The Justification of God, An Exegetical and Theological Study of Romans 9:1-23* (Grand Rapids: Baker, 1985), 159.

ment."[15] The Arminian has no problem with such an understanding. Just as God shows mercy to (saves) whom He wills, and wills to save believers; so He withholds saving mercy from (damns) whom He wills, and wills to damn unbelievers. Once the positive has been established as conditional, the negative follows logically and Biblically.

Romans 8:28-30

This important passage refers to three of the key ideas in the list given at the beginning of this chapter: foreknowledge (*proginōskō*), predestination/foreordination (*proorizō*), and purpose (*prothesis*). All three refer to works of God.

The relation of ideas in the passage appears to be as follows (which is probably better than a traditional "outline" in conveying the meaning):

1. The overall subject is the fact that the circumstances of a believer's life work together (perhaps, directly, God works them together) for good.

2. That "good" equals God's "purpose"; that, in turn, is that believers are "being conformed to the image of His Son so as for Him to be firstborn among many brothers."

3. This purpose is being worked out for "those called for that purpose"; these are identical to "those loving God."

4. The order of working in their lives, toward this end, is:

> *in eternity:*
> foreknew
> foreordained/predestinated
> *in time:*
> called
> justified
> glorified

Logically, then, foreknowledge precedes predestination. Verses 29, 30 appear to set a deliberate order:

> *foreknew* → *foreordained* → *called* → *justified* → *glorified*

(It also logically precedes election in 1 Peter 1:2, which will be commented on below.)

Various meanings for foreknowledge seem possible.

---

[15]John Brown,*Analytical Exposition of the Epistle of Paul the Apostle to the Romans* (Grand Rapids: Baker, 1981), 338.

a. A meaning close to election would fit: lovingly acknowledged as His. Certainly foreknowledge, in this verse, is directly personal: *whom He foreknew.*

b. A meaning similar to foreordination (pre-planning) seems less likely. That meaning would seem more appropriate for things than people (although this is not a killing objection). Further, if that were the meaning, the following "foreordained" would be tautological, essentially repeating. Some answer this objection by saying that the repetition serves to add purpose to the preplanning: those whom He foreknew (as pre-planning) He foreordained (same meaning) in order to. . . . " But against this is the grammatical structure, including the parallelism of the phrase with the distinct repetition of the "and/also" (*kai*).

c. The meaning of (mere) prescience is possible. Even though prescience does not seem as appropriate for persons as for things about persons, it would be possible to translate this as "those whom He knew [about] in advance" (one probably needs to add an "about" to the idea of foreknowing in Acts 26:5).

Even so, this last meaning strikes me as unlikely here, given the distinctly personal emphasis (unless one wishes to regard "those whom He foreknew" as something of a condensation representing "those whose faith [?] He foreknew"). I therefore regard the first of the three meanings as more likely here. (And in that case, the typical systematic theology terminology, placing "election" as one of two subdivisions of "predestination," is not precisely in accord with the use of the terms here.)

What then is the meaning of the "foreordination/predestination"? (1) It assumes the personal foreknowledge. Thus, their *identity* as those foreknown by God is already settled before the "predestination." (2) Then predestination/foreordination speaks of God's purpose *for those already foreknown as His:* namely that—by calling, justification, and glorification—they be brought into full conformity to the image of His Son. This is therefore not predestination to be among the elect (to be a Christian) but a foreordained purpose of God *for the elect,* one for which He works out the circumstances of their lives. This agrees precisely with the understanding of "predestinated" suggested in the treatment of Ephesians 1 above.

This leaves one crucial question: On what basis is the foreknowing, *loving identification of these as His* (= election) performed? We are not told; on this point the passage says absolutely nothing. It tells us that, from eternity, God has "foreknown" His own. It does not tell us whether there is any basis for this or not, or, if so, what that basis is.

We will have to learn that from other sources. But especially important is the fact that, therefore, the passage neither affirms nor denies
that the eternal selection is conditional or unconditional.

Even here, however, Arminius offered a pregnant suggestion that
"foreknew" means *both* "whom He previously loved and affectionately regarded as His own" *and* "prescience of faith in Christ," since "the
former cannot be true without the latter": "God can 'previously love
and affectionately regard as His own' no sinner unless He has foreknown Him in Christ, and looked upon him as a believer in Christ."[16]
He may well have been right, but the latter is at best implicit, not
explicit, in what Paul says.

One further observation. I find interesting the way Jewett—a
Calvinist, if not always typically so—concludes his observations
about the passage: "[God] saves us not according to our works but
according to his purpose and grace, which were given us in Christ
Jesus 'ages ago.'"[17]

One can only agree, all the while observing that he has caught the
right emphasis of Paul in contrasting salvation by God's eternal
design and initiative to man's *works*—a point that has nothing to say
about whether man must meet the condition of *faith,* which always in
the Bible stands likewise in sharp contrast to works.

Brief Comments on Other Texts

1 Peter 1:1, 2

"Peter [writes his letter] to elect sojourners of the disper-
sion . . . according to the foreknowledge of God the Father, in the
sanctification of the Spirit, unto obedience and sprinkling of the blood
of Jesus Christ."

In spite of difficulties of interpretation, one seems reasonably safe
in concluding that election, here, is subordinate to foreknowledge.
The order is, "elect . . . according to foreknowledge."

Nothing answers the question, Foreknowledge of what? Any
answer we may arrive at will reflect our understanding of the meaning of "foreknowledge" here. That word (*prognōsis* or *proginōskō*) is
used 7 times in the New Testament (all by Peter or Paul, in epistles or
speeches). Only twice does the word refer directly to the plan of salvation (here and Rom. 8:29; see above). It can be foreknowledge of

---

[16]Arminius, III:313, 314.
[17]Paul K. Jewett, *Election and Predestination* (Grand Rapids: Eerdmans, 1985), 26.

persons (Rom. 8:29; 11:2; 1 Pet. 1:20; Acts 26:5—although things are incorporated in this last reference) or of *things* (Acts 2:23; 2 Pet. 3:17). The word obviously has a variety of meanings.

1. Once (Acts 26:5), perhaps twice (Rom. 11:2), it means *knowledge of the past* ("knowing previously").

2. Sometimes it means (mere) *prescience* or precognition (Acts 2:23; 2 Pet. 3:17), although this idea may incorporate the added notion of "foresight" in the sense of wise foresight.

3. *Pre-planning* (thus close to foreordination) is a possible meaning in 1 Peter 1:20 (the KJV prepared us for this with its translation of "foreknown" as "foreordained").

4. And *forelove* may be the meaning in Romans 8:29, as discussed above—in which case it is close to the idea of election, a loving acknowledgement by God of those who are His own.

Of the four shades of meaning just indicated, only two seem possible here in 1 Peter 1:1, 2, the second and third. (The fourth is ruled out on the grounds that making it equal to election would be tautology; then Peter would be saying, "Elect according to the election of God.") To give it the meaning of "foreplanning" would fit well enough: election according to the foreplanning of God. So would the meaning of prescience, with or without the added notion of foresight. Without any dogmatism, the meaning that strikes me as most likely is prescience, with a hint of wise foreplanning.

Acts 2:23; 4:28

These two verses do not relate directly to election of individuals to salvation, but are important for understanding the way the New Testament presents the idea of God's foreordination and eternal counsel. In both verses, the crucifixion of Christ is presented on two sides: (1) as by the plan of God, and (2) as at the hands of wicked men.

God's side is indicated, in 2:23, as "delivered up by the having-been-determined counsel and foreknowledge of God"; and, in 4:28, as "things your hand and your counsel foreordained to come to pass." Without taking space for detail, I think it is clear that God's eternal counsel (plan), foreknowledge, and foreordination are being closely linked. Christ's death is in accord with that eternal plan.

Man's side is indicated, in 2:23, as "you, by the hand of lawless men, slew [Him], nailing [Him] to a cross"; and, in 4:27, by "Against Jesus were gathered together both Herod and Pilate, together with the Gentiles and the people of Israel."

There is fine interplay here between Divine and human responsibility. On the one side, Jesus' crucifixion was according to God's eternal plan. On the other hand, blame and responsibility—worthy of condemnation—are emphatically placed on the men involved. Peter was not conscious of any contradiction between judging men liable for moral agency in the crucifixion and regarding it as carefully provided for in the eternal plan of God at the same time. As Calvinists are accustomed to observe, since both facts are affirmed without sense of contradiction, there must not be a contradiction.

Only we hasten to add that, if there really is no contradiction, then God's "foreordination" of the events *must* be in such a manner that those events are *not necessary* but *contingent* (see the discussion in ch. 3). If, in fact, those who crucified Jesus *had* to do so, if God's foreordination by its own efficacy made their actions unavoidable, then they were not free to do otherwise—*could* not do otherwise—and were therefore not responsible.

In fact, however, the acts were contingent and the actors were free to crucify Him or not. Insofar as their moral responsibility was concerned, they really could have chosen not to do so. And none of these observations contradicts in the slightest the fact that all their actions were known to God from eternity as *certain,* and that He in fact foreordained the events by choosing in His perfect knowledge and wisdom to set in motion the course of events and circumstances that He knew certainly (but not necessarily) would lead to what happened, thus incorporating all the events into His perfect plan.

Calvinists themselves (although they may reject the way I have just expressed this) are quick to avow something very similar, insisting that God's foreordaining of wicked acts was done in such a way that He did not "cause" those wicked acts and thus become author of sin. Well: if, in fact, He can foreordain wrongdoing without causing that wrongdoing (and I certainly agree), then that admission will serve us well as we proceed throughout this work to comment on the relationship between the Divine and the human in *any* actions where moral agency is involved. And if His foreordaining of the crucifying acts did not cause those acts, it likewise does not make those acts *necessary,* although they are *certain.*

1 Corinthians 1:21

[Since the world knew not God] "God took pleasure (*eudokēsen*) through the 'foolishness' of the proclamation [of the gospel] to save the ones believing."

The verb "took pleasure" is cognate to the noun *eudokia,* referring to God's "good pleasure" which is for all practical purposes identical to His will or decree; see the discussion above on Ephesians 1:3-14, where "the good pleasure of His will" (v. 5) is essentially equal to "the counsel of His will" (v. 11). (See also Mt. 12:18, where "took pleasure" is consciously parallel to "chose.")

Here Paul lays the "credit" for salvation directly on the "good pleasure" of God, a point to be affirmed by Calvinist and Arminian alike. I have little doubt that the action in "took pleasure" is consciously intended, here, to express the sovereign decision of God in eternity—in other words, His eternal *decree.*

We should note, then, that the decree to save is qualified, here, in two ways. (1) The decree logically followed God's foreknowledge of man's fall: "after/since the world knew not God, God planned in His good pleasure to save." This is distinctly an infralapsarian or sublapsarian (see chs. 2, 3) view. (2) Even more important, the salvation decreed is salvation *of believers.* This is conditional salvation, election of believers—the Arminian viewpoint precisely.

Luke 7:30

"The Pharisees and the lawyers rejected the counsel of God for themselves, not being baptized by him [i.e., by John]."

The counsel of God is clearly in view. It is also clear that this counsel (or will) can be rejected by men.

2 Peter 3:9

"The Lord is not delaying the [fulfillment of the] promise, as some reckon delay, but is exercising longsuffering toward us, not being willing [for] any to perish, but for all to have (or, make) room for repentance."

Arminians tend to stress this verse, with good reason. If *boulomai* is to be distinguished from *thelō* (see the next verse), the distinction usually made is that *boulomai* tends to be the stronger word, more likely to refer to God's eternal will and plan. But here is this word (like *thelō* in 1 Tim. 2:4; see below) used to express God's *will* that none be lost (in other words, that all be saved).

The Scriptures are clear, of course, that not all are saved, that many do perish. How can that be, if God's will or counsel is otherwise? Obviously, it can. As with Luke 7:30 (above), then, God's will can be resisted.

If this requires that some kind of distinction within God's "will" be made, then neither Calvinist nor Arminian will necessarily object to this. Witness, for example, the distinction (noted earlier) made by Shedd between the "legislative" will of God ("will of complacency") and the "decretive" will of God ("will of good pleasure"). But once such a distinction is allowed, thus permitting some kind of ambiguity in the meaning of God's *boulē* (or *thelēma,* for that matter), the Calvinist will not have so strong a ground to stand on if in any given passage he wishes to insist that it has the decretive force. (Many Calvinists avoid this dilemma by interpreting the "universality" of this—and any other similar—passage in another way. See part three of this book for discussion of that issue, and of this verse.)

God's will can be expressed, and fulfilled, from different perspectives. Clearly He does not delight in the death of the sinner; he desires/wills that all be saved. But, even more basic than that, He wills/decrees that men be free to decide their own destinies. And He obviously does not override the latter in favor of the former.

1 Timothy 2:4

[God] "who wills for all men to be saved and come to [the] knowledge of the truth."

The meaning of the "all" is crucial to the interpretation of the verse, and it cannot be separated from the entire context (vv. 1-7), which refers to "all men" three times. This passage will be treated in the section to follow, on the provision of salvation: was the atonement universal, and in what sense?

For now, then, it is enough to observe that this passage apparently makes the same point as 2 Peter 3:9, which has been examined above in the treatment of God's counsel (*boulē*). What was said there will apply here, even though one word for God's will is used there and the other (*thelō*) here. Even so, God's general will, from the perspective of eternity, and as respects salvation, is certainly in view.

John 5:21; 6:39, 40

"For just as the Father raises the dead and [thus?] makes alive, thus also the Son makes alive those whom He wills/desires."

"Now this is the will (*thelēma*) of the one who sent me, that—everything that He has given to me—I not lose [any] of it but raise it in the last day. For this is the will (*thelēma*) of my Father, that everyone who is beholding the Son and believing in Him be having eternal life, and [that] I raise him in the last day."

The first of these expresses the "will" (*thelō*) of the Second Person of the Trinity rather than of God the Father. But that should make no difference, given the identity between them. And this is confirmed by the second of these.

Standing alone, the claim of Jesus (5:21) might be taken to say that His decisions about whom to restore to life are made without attention to anything about them that distinguishes them from anyone else. But, in fact, the words do not stand alone. Verse 24 tells precisely whom He chooses to give life to: "the one hearing my word and believing in the one who sent me has eternal life." The Son chooses to make alive believers. The will of God, in giving eternal life, is to give it to believers.

The second verse goes well with the first one, indicating the same basic truth. God's will is that those who exercise faith in Jesus Christ have eternal life. His will respecting salvation is a will for believers. The will of God in eternity, as expressed by the Son in time (and, as we have seen, this is the only way we can learn the content of God's decrees), is to save believers. (And on the relationship between God's decree or purpose in eternity and revelation of that purpose, in Christ, in time, see 2 Timothy 1:9 and the comment below.)

One should note that any number of passages from the Gospel of John can be used to establish the fact that salvation is by faith. This fact will be treated in greater detail in part four of this work under the heading "The Application of Salvation."

Some Conclusions About Election and Foreordination

My purpose, here, is to draw from the Scriptural analysis of this chapter some observations relative to the matter of God's eternal plan of salvation. I trust that they rest firmly on the Biblical analysis that precedes.

1. God, in eternity, elected some to be saved. Ephesians 1:4 uses the word "elected." Romans 8:29 uses "foreknew" in a sense very close to meaning "elected": "in love acknowledged them as His."

2. This election is "in Christ" (Eph. 1:4). Ephesians 3:11 speaks of "the purpose (*prothesis*) of the ages [i.e., the eternal purpose] which He made *in Christ Jesus our Lord.*" Compare 2 Timothy 1:9, where God's purpose to exercise [saving] grace "was granted to us *in Christ Jesus* before the times of the ages [i.e, in eternity] and now was revealed through the appearing of our savior Jesus Christ."

3. This election is election *of believers* (1 Cor. 1:21). John 6:39, 40 (along with 5:21, 24) indicates that the will of God in eternity, as

revealed by His Son in time, is that *believers* be saved. Romans 9-11 indicates that God shows saving mercy to whom He pleases and that He pleases to show this saving mercy to those who put faith in Jesus Christ. Thus election is conditional and faith is the condition.

4. This election is "according to foreknowledge" (1 Pet. 1:2), where "foreknowledge" may mean either prescience, foresight, or foreplanning—or a blending of all three.

5. For the elect God has "foreordained" (KJV, "predestinated") certain salvation blessings (Rom. 8:29, 30, Eph. 1:3-14).

6. In election and foreordination, everything is grounded on, and in accord with, the sovereign will (= good pleasure, purpose, counsel) of God (Eph. 1:3-14).

For Further Reading on the New Testament Treatment of Predestination

Forlines, F. Leroy. *The Randall House Bible Commentary: Romans.* Nashville: Randall House Publications, 1987 (pp. 232-241, 248-319). [An Arminian colleague of this writer]

Jewett, Paul K. "The Biblical Data Summarized," *Election and Predestination.* Grand Rapids: Eerdmans, 1985 (pp. 24-29). [A brief summary of the Biblical passages involved, from a—not entirely traditional—Calvinistic perspective]

Marshall, I. Howard. "Predestination in the New Testament," *Grace Unlimited.* Minneapolis: Bethany Fellowship, 1975 (pp. 127-143). [A "Biblical theology" treatment of the language of predestination in the New Testament]

MacDonald, William G. "The Biblical Doctrine of Election" in *The Grace of God, the Will of Man,* ed. Clark H. Pinnock. Grand Rapids: Zondervan, 1989 (ch. 11). [Offers some helpful exegesis of key passages]

Picirilli, Robert E. "Ephesians" in *The Randall House Bible Commentary: Galatians through Colossians.* Nashville: Randall House Publications, 1988 (pp. 132-144).

The Provision of Salvation

When dealing with the basic assumptions of Calvinism and Arminianism, there is probably no more crucial issue than the extent of the atonement. All agree that salvation is provided for by virtue of Christ's redemptive work. The question, then, is: For whom did Christ die—for the elect only, or for all?

The question is not quite that simple, but that is the issue. As in the previous section, we will examine first the systematic argument of the Calvinists for a "limited" atonement, then the corresponding arguments of the Arminians for a "general" or unlimited atonement—again using a more or less brief, outline approach. In each of these two chapters, I will indicate the response of the antagonists to the arguments of the other side. Then will follow a more careful analysis of some key passages of Scripture, striving for conclusions based on a more Biblical theology.

PART THREE

CHAPTER FIVE

Calvinistic Arguments
for a Limited Atonement

A systematic discussion of the atonement is usually structured around two subjects: the *nature* of the atonement and its *extent*. Calvinists and Arminians do not *necessarily* disagree about the first of these. When they have done so, that disagreement has typically placed Calvinists on the side of the "satisfaction" view and Arminians on the side of the "governmental" view.

In fact, however, the original Arminians did not depart from the satisfaction view. Neither did Arminius himself. Nor should Arminians today. At this point, then, I will stipulate the satisfaction view of the atonement and reserve any further discussion of that matter for passing comments to follow.

The most important thing, therefore, is to examine the arguments involved in discussing the extent of the atonement. In this chapter, my purpose is to outline the logical and Biblical arguments used by Calvinists to uphold the view that Christ died to provide salvation only for the elect. That view has usually been called "limited atonement," but some prefer "definite atonement" or "particular atonement."

Before proceeding to the arguments, two other matters require brief attention. First, I should make reference to the fact that there is some debate whether Calvin himself taught limited atonement. Even among his followers there are differences of opinion on this subject. In his *Institutes* Calvin devoted no special section to the extent of the atonement. Consequently, his view must be determined from more or less passing comments here and there in the *Institutes* and in his commentaries. This leaves one less than dogmatic.

R. T. Kendall has argued, very insistently, that Calvin believed in a universal atonement.[1] Among those who have responded to Kendall, some affirm that Calvin did not commit himself on the question.[2] Others have been equally sure that Calvin taught that Jesus died for the elect only.[3] Charles Bell concludes his assessment of the arguments thus:

---

[1]R. T. Kendall, *Calvin and English Calvinism to 1649* (New York and Oxford, 1979).

[2]For example, R. W. A. Letham, "Saving Faith and Assurance in Reformed Theology: Zwingli to the Synod of Dort," Ph.D. thesis (Aberdeen, 1979).

[3]For example, Paul Helm, *Calvin and the Calvinists* (Edinburgh: Banner of Truth, 1982).

> The emphasis in Calvin's teaching is certainly on the unity of the death
> and intercession of Christ, and upon the idea that Christ's intercession
> flows from his sacrificial death, which, according to Calvin, was offered
> for all. More than that is difficult to state with certainty. For, since Calvin
> did not fully or consistently develop his teaching on this subject, we
> should hold our evaluations of it to be somewhat tentative, especially
> when they differ from his own emphasis.[4]

Enough said. For my purposes here, there is no need to pursue
the matter. After all, in this work I am not comparing Calvin with
Arminius but developed Calvinism with the Reformation Arminianism
of Arminius himself. No one will dispute the fact that developed
Calvinism teaches limited atonement. (For exceptions, see below.)

Second, we should gives some attention to what is *not* at issue in
the debate. Calvinists do not deny the *sufficiency* of the atonement for
all. In other words, they are quick to agree that Christ's redemptive
work would have been the very same as it was had God intended it to
provide for all human beings who ever live. As Roger Nicole expresses this, "It is freely granted by all parties to the controversy, and
specifically by the Reformed, that the death of our Lord, by virtue of
His divine nature, is of infinite worth and therefore amply sufficient to
redeem all mankind . . . if He had so intended."[5] He continues to
express the Calvinistic view succinctly: namely, that the purpose of
the atonement, for God, was that it was "intended to secure the salvation of all those and those only who will in fact be redeemed."[6]

This may likewise be stipulated, as the view of consistent
Calvinists, without further discussion. I proceed then to the main
arguments used to support that teaching.

Calvinistic Argument 1: Limited atonement is implied in the doctrine of unconditional election, as dealt with in the preceding section
on "The Plan of Salvation." If salvation by grace means that it is sovereignly and unconditionally the work of God, applied to elected individuals in such a way that they make no choice prior to regeneration
(and withheld from the non-elect in such a way that they never really

---

[4]Charles Bell, "Calvin and the Extent of the Atonement" (*Evangelical Quarterly* 55:2 [1983], 115-123), 123.

[5]Roger Nicole, "The Case for Definite Atonement" (*Bulletin of the Evangelical Theological Society* 10:4 [1967], 199-207), 199.

[6]Nicole, 200.

can be saved), then it makes sense to say that atonement was made only for the elect.

In other words, the doctrine of limited atonement is implied in, and logically necessary to, the Reformed teaching about unconditional salvation. As outlined in the previous section, all men are both lost and so depraved that they cannot respond positively to the offer of salvation until they have been regenerated. God, seeing in eternity that this is the case and justly condemning all mankind, determined to save some from that predicament; we cannot define why he chose the ones he did and left the others to be lost. Having determined those whom he would save, unconditionally, he sent Christ to die for them and effect their salvation. As Shedd has expressed this,

> It is most rational to suppose that in the covenant between the Father and Son [in eternity], the making of an atonement was inseparably connected with the purpose to apply it: the purpose, namely, to accompany the atoning work of the Son with the regenerating work of the Holy Spirit. The Divine Father, in giving the Divine Son as a sacrifice for sin, simultaneously determined that this sacrifice should be appropriated through faith by a definite number of the human family.[7]

One can hardly deny the force of this logic. Once unconditional salvation is granted, limited atonement logically follows.

Even so, a minority of otherwise Calvinistic theologians have violated this "logic" and argued for a universal atonement.[8] As noted earlier, some believe that Calvin himself would not have agreed with this "logic." Donald Lake, not a Calvinist, confidently affirms that the idea of limited atonement "does not appear in Calvin." While it is difficult to be that certain, as I have indicated earlier, Lake is certainly on the right track when he observes that for Calvin the question whether God wills to save all "is a question of election, not of the atonement."[9] At any rate, the scope of this work does not allow for an evaluation of consistency when some Calvinists affirm unlimited atonement.

---

[7]W. G. T. Shedd, *Dogmatic Theology* (Grand Rapids: Zondervan reprint, n.d.), II:475, 476.

[8]See, for example, Robert P. Lightner, *The Death Christ Died* (Schaumburg, Ill.: Regular Baptist Press, 1967).

[9]Donald M. Lake, "He Died for All: The Universal Dimensions of the Atonement," in *Grace Unlimited,* ed. Clark Pinnock (Minneapolis: Bethany Fellowship, 1975), 33.

Arminian Response: One must agree that limited atonement follows logically from the doctrine of unconditional election, which equates to unconditional salvation. The response, therefore, is two-fold.

1. Since this argument rests the doctrine on the system, the system itself must be challenged. Indeed, the Arminian denies that salvation is unconditional. The Bible teaches salvation by faith rather than salvation by unconditional election. Furthermore, the Bible condemns the damned not merely for their sins but for rejecting Christ's redemptive work—a point to be returned to in the next chapter.

Without developing this response in more detail now, I merely observe that it is the aim of this entire book—as of all Arminian objections to Calvinism—to deny the system that makes limited atonement logical.

2. Teaching about the extent of the atonement should be determined by Biblical exegesis rather than by the logic of one's system. If the Bible does, in fact, teach that Christ died to provide salvation for all, then Calvinists should probably reexamine the basic assumptions of their entire system. It may be that those Calvinists referred to above, who have affirmed universal atonement, have done so for such reasons. At any rate, it will be the purpose of chapter 7 to show that the Bible does, in fact, teach universal atonement (but not universal salvation).

Calvinistic Argument 2:   Limited atonement is taught in the Bible: specifically in those passages that declare that Christ died, particularly, for the elect rather than for everyone indiscriminately. Berkhof summarizes this argument: "Scripture repeatedly qualifies those for whom Christ laid down His life in such a way as to point to a very definite limitation. Those for whom He suffered and died are variously called "His sheep,". . . "His Church,". . . "His people,". . . and "the elect."[10]

Various Calvinistic writers list a number of Scriptures in this vein. The most significant among these passages are as follows.

Matthew 1:21—He shall save *his people* from their sins.
John 15:13—He lays down his life for his *friends*.
John 10:15—He lays down his life for *the sheep*.
Ephesians 5:23-26—He loved and gave himself for *the church*.
Acts 20:28—He has purchased with his own blood *the church*.
Matthew 20:28 (Mk. 10:45)—He gives his life a ransom for *many*.

---

[10]Louis Berkhof, *Systematic Theology* (Grand Rapids: Eerdmans, 1949), 395.

Matthew 26:28—His blood is shed for the remission of sins for *many*.

Titus 2:14—He gave himself for *us* that he might redeem *us*.

Romans 8:32—God delivered up His Son for *us all* (and "us all" seems parallel with "God's elect" in v. 33).

Arminian Response:

1. To such passages *as a group:* statements that Christ died for some particular group or person fall far short of saying that He died *only* for them. In logic, a restricted statement does not invalidate a universal one. Any universal truth can include a restricted statement about some portion of the universal. In other words, if all S is P, than some S is P.

To illustrate: That I might say, at times, "I love my family" in no way speaks to the question whether (or denies that) I love others also.

In Galatians 2:20, Paul says that Christ "gave himself for me." This certainly does not mean that Jesus died only for Paul and not for others (but might according to Calvinist logic). Then neither do the passages above mean He died only for the saved and not for others. As William Sailer observes, "If Christ died for all, it is quite proper to state, under special circumstances, that he died for some."[11]

2. Beyond this sufficient answer, these passages can be answered *individually* and thus shown to fall short of teaching limited atonement.

Matthew 1:21—"Save" is more than "atone for." It is true that Christ will save (note the future) only those whom He will actually save.

John 15:13—In fact, the one referred to here is not Jesus specifically, but any person. The truth stated is a general one.

John 10:15—The words are determined by the illustration on which the statement is based: namely (v.11), that a good shepherd willingly dies for his sheep. This means the verse has nothing to say about limited or universal atonement.

Ephesians 5:23-26—Again, the words are determined by the illustration of a good husband (v. 25). Certainly, there is special love, on Christ's part, for the church as His bride: so much that He gave Himself for her in anticipation of presenting her to Himself.

---

[11]William S. Sailer, "The Nature and Extent of the Atonement—A Wesleyan View" (*Bulletin of the Evangelical Theological Society* 10:4 [1967], 189-198), 190.

Acts 20:28—the church is singled out as precious, purchased by Christ's blood, because the elders are to feed and protect it.

Matthew 20:28; 26:28—in such passages where "many" is used (cf. Romans 5:15ff) there is good reason to believe that "many" is a Hebraistic way of using an unrestricted plural meant to stand in contrast with one or some rather than with all. If so, the passages may turn out to argue more strongly for universal than for limited atonement.[12]

Titus 2:14; Romans 8:32—precisely the same kind of statements as in Galatians 2:20 (see above) except for the use of the plural "us" rather than the singular "me." As Arminius observed, that Christ died for the elect signifies only "that the death of Christ secures for the elect only, the blessing which is bestowed through an application of Christ and his benefits."[13]

Calvinistic Argument 3:   Limited atonement is shown by the fact that the Scripture speaks of the death of Christ as *actually* accomplishing salvation rather than merely making it possible.

To suggest, as Arminians do, that the atonement provided opportunity for salvation rather than salvation is to make it incomplete. This would mean that Christ did not effect redemption by his work. It would also mean that men must complete the work of redemption by their actions.

Some of the key words used to explain what actually happened on Calvary speak of accomplishment rather than mere provision. There is *redemption* or *ransom*, for example, as in Matthew 20:28. Jesus gave His life as a ransom. There is *propitiation*, as in 1 John 4:10. God sent His Son to be the propitiation for our sins. And there is *reconciliation,* as in 2 Corinthians 5:19. God was in Christ reconciling the world to Himself.

The point of all this is that Jesus actually redeemed, ransomed, made propitiation for, reconciled persons; he did not merely *provide* for the possibility of such things to transpire. He did not just make salvation possible, He saved. Nicole speaks forcefully:

---

[12]This may well be true, at least, for Rom. 5:18, 19 where "all" and "many" are parallel; this is one of the passages where Calvin's comments seem to uphold universal atonement. See Bell, 117; Lake, 33.

[13]James Arminius, *The Writings of James Arminius* (three vols.), tr. James Nichols and W. R. Bagnall (Grand Rapids: Baker, 1956), III:454.

What kind of redemption would this be where the redeemed are still under the power of the enemy? What kind of propitiation, where God still deals in wrath? What kind of reconciliation where estrangement continues to exist and is even sealed for eternity? These three terms, severally and jointly, bear witness to the fact that the Scripture views the work of Christ as bringing about the effectuation of salvation.[14]

The logic requires another step. Since all men are clearly *not* saved, as indicated both in the Bible and in experience, then His death clearly did not save them. He did not redeem, reconcile, make propitiation for them, else they would be saved. Berkhof makes this point well:

The doctrine that Christ died for the purpose of saving all men, logically leads to absolute universalism, that is, to the doctrine that all men are actually saved. It is impossible that they for whom Christ paid the price, whose guilt He removed, should be lost on account of that guilt. The Arminians cannot stop at their half-way station, but must go all the way.[15]

Arminian Response: This may well be the Calvinists' most significant argument.

1. It is typical of language usage to speak of an action as *actually* accomplishing what it was *intended* to accomplish, even if that action only made possible the accomplishment. In this way, the *potential* of an action is spoken of as contained in the action itself, even if some further condition or application is required. I may properly say that a doctor's diagnosis, on a given date, saved my life; but I still had to take the medicine he prescribed for the effect to be mine. (The illustration is not meant to be analagous with salvation; it merely shows the nature of language use.) Any action may linguistically be spoken of as containing its results.

It may be best to let Calvinists answer Calvinists on this point. Shedd observes, "Atonement in and by itself, separate from faith, saves no soul . . . this sacrifice in itself, and apart from its vital appropriation, is useless. . . . It is only when the death of Christ has been actually confided in as an atonement, that it is completely 'set forth' as God's propitiation for sin."[16] Again, "Vicarious atonement without

---

[14]Nicole, 201.
[15]Berkhof, 395.
[16]Shedd, II:477.

faith in it is powerless to save. It is not the *making* of this atonement, but the *trusting* in it, that saves the sinner. 'By *faith* are ye saved.' "[17]

The point is that if propitiation, say, or reconciliation were actually *finished* on the cross, then all those whose sins were actually propitiated were on the day Christ died removed from the wrath of God and reconciled to Him. Indeed, those elect not yet born would therefore never be under the wrath of God or estranged from Him in their real lifetimes. But in fact the Bible speaks of Christians as having lived under the wrath of God and in a state of estrangement from Him before their conversion; see Ephesians 2:3, 13, for example.

I may observe that the Calvinist's presentation of this point is certainly a forceful presentation of the atonement as *full satisfaction* of the wrath of God for sins. But one must note that the Calvinist, with the double insistence that the satisfaction is complete before application, and that it is this only for the elect, effectively denies his earlier insistence (see above) that the atonement is sufficient for all. If the atonement satisfies the just demands of a holy God merely by its making, and if it does this only for the elect, then God *can not* forgive the reprobate and so the atonement *is not sufficient* for any but the elect. As Shedd appears to have realized, the Calvinist will do well to drop the argument that the atonement actually accomplishes redemption in and of itself and therefore can be only for the elect.[18]

In Biblical terms, then, as Shedd understands, redemption is not individually finished until it is *applied*. The provision was fully finished, no further work being required except for the work of the Spirit in applying the perfect provision. If that work of application is conditional, as the Arminian believes (see part 3 of this work, "The Application of Salvation"), then the redemption itself is conditional. In his extended epistle to William Perkins, Arminius observed on this point, "You confound the result with the action and passion, from which it exists . . . the obtainment of redemption with its application . . . . reconciliation made with God by the death and sacrifice of Christ, with the application of the same, which are plainly different things."[19]

2. It is especially appropriate for one who has experienced the intended result of an action to speak of that action as having accom-

---

[17]Shedd, II:440.

[18]See the treatment of Arminius, III:352-353, on this same issue. He shows clearly that he understood the atonement as full satisfaction of God's just demands.

[19]Arminius, III:456.

plished that result. Thus (to continue the illustration introduced above) I may with perfect justification and accuracy say, "That doctor's diagnosis saved my life!"

In this light, it is significant that most of the passages cited by Calvinists for this particular argument affirm the experience of those actually saved. Thus Nicole cites Ephesians 1:7: *We* have redemption through his blood. Most certainly, but without any implication that it was applied to us against our wills. This same point can be made of other verses that Nicole cites: 1 Peter 1:18,19; 1 John 2:2; 4:10; Colossians 1:21; Romans 5:10; 2 Corinthians 5:18, and others.

3. It is also significant that some of these very verses make clear that faith is the condition required for application of Christ's atoning work. Nicole uses, for example, Romans 3:24, 25. This very passage is one of the reasons for the observation of Shedd, above, that only when Christ's death "has been confided in" is it made effective as propitiation: "Whom God hath set forth to be a propitiation through faith in his blood."

4. Furthermore, some of the passages that speak of the atonement as the accomplishment of salvation, cited by Nicole, speak not only of believers but of the *world*. First John 2:2, for example, says that not only is Christ the propitiation for our sins but also for the whole world. Second Corinthians 5:18, 19 says both that He reconciled us and that He was reconciling the world. Only tortured exegesis of these passages will give "world" a meaning that is as narrow as the elect. I leave this as a claim at this point and will return to it in chapter 7. But if this claim is correct, as I am confident, it means that we must interpret the verses in the way I have indicated above: namely, that the Bible speaks of the actions themselves as accomplishing results that require subsequent application.

5. Finally, this entire argument of the Calvinist can ultimately be reduced to the claim that Christ, on the cross, effectively saved only those whom He effectively saved. In that form, no Arminian will deny it. In that sense, He did not effectively redeem any but the elect—which in no way denies that He died for all.

Calvinistic Argument 4:   Limited atonement is necessary because an unlimited atonement, unless it actually saves all, leaves it to humans to determine who is saved and who is not, thus "a human ingredient is to be superadded to the work of Christ," one "which determines the difference between the saved and the lost," in which case, "the work of Christ by itself actually saves no one."[20]

Arminian Response:

1. If this argument is expressed in Scriptural terms, it winds up being the same as the previous argument. The last sentence, above, shows that this is actually the case, and that Nicole is still concerned with the idea that the atonement actually accomplished redemption. The answers already given still apply.

2. If, on the other hand, the argument is left as a mere matter of logic, one may respond, first, that it is true, that atonement *by itself* does not save: as already shown, the atonement does not save apart from the application of its effects, in time, by the work of the Holy Spirit. And if that application is conditional, then salvation itself is conditional and only those who meet the condition are saved.

3. One may also respond, however, that this logical affirmation is false—unless the condition required is a further work required to provide salvation. But Reformation Arminianism insists that the condition people must meet is faith, not works. This in no sense "works" or helps provide salvation. Salvation is not synergistic, as noted in the previous section. Faith is an absolute denial of one's own works and a total abandonment of anything one can do for his own salvation, a holding out of *empty* hands to God.

This matter need not be pursued here. It will be a major concern later; see chapter 7, "The Application of Salvation."

Calvinistic Argument 5:   Limited atonement is required by the fact that saving faith is a gift of God given only to the elect. A universal atonement, in light of that, would be illogical, not to mention ineffective for anyone else. Berkhof further clarifies the point: "The Bible clearly teaches that Christ by His death purchased faith, repentance, and all the other effects of the work of the Holy Spirit, for His people. Consequently these [faith, repentance, etc.] are not conditions of which the fulfilment is simply dependent on the will of man. The atonement also secures the fulfilment of the conditions that must be met, in order to obtain salvation, Romans 2:4; Galatians 3:,13, 14; Ephesians 1:3, 4; 2:8; Philippians 1:29; II Timothy 3:5, 6."[21]

---

[20]Nicole, 201, 202.
[21]Berkhof, 395.

Arminian Response: This argument assumes a further doctrine that is not in evidence: namely, that saving faith is in fact a gift *as part of* the application of salvation rather than a condition for the application of salvation. To say it this way—which is precisely what Calvinists claim—is to expose it as unbiblical. This matter will be treated at length in chapter 7.

I would add that once again the Calvinist undercuts his own prior insistence that the atonement is sufficient for all. If the atonement actually secures saving faith for those covered, and did not secure saving faith for the non-elect, it is not sufficient for the non-elect.

Calvinistic Argument 6:   Limited atonement is required when one believes that the atonement was full, penal, vicarious, sacrificial satisfaction for the sins of those included within its scope. Therefore, if such an atonement were universal, then all must be saved. Otherwise, anyone finally condemned to Hell would be making a second payment for what had already been paid for once by Christ. Only those actually saved were actually substituted for. Nicole expresses this well:

> Particular redemption is an inevitable implicate of a recognition of the penal substitutionary nature of the atonement. . . . If we do hold that Christ died substitutionally for all mankind bearing the divine penalty for the sins of all man, it would appear that at the day of judgment there will remain nothing to be punished, and consequently all men should be saved.[22]

Arminian Response:

1. This argument in fact resolves into the same as the third argument, already treated above. As there, it depends on seeing Christ's redemptive work as actually accomplishing its intended results, for those it was designed for, without faith on their part. Once we understand how the New Testament language of atonement is being used, proleptically incorporating all potential results of the action into the action itself, then to speak of the atonement as full, penal satisfaction of the just demands of a holy God for our sins presents no problem at all for universal atonement. To quote Shedd again, it is "not the *making* of this atonement, but the *trusting* in it, that saves the sinner"; by that faith, the Divine satisfaction is applied to the case of the individual sinner.

---

[22]Nicole, 202.

2. We should not overlook the fact that this argument introduces another doctrine about the *nature* of the atonement and links it to one about its *extent*. *Some* Arminians in fact retreat from the doctrine of penal substitution—and perhaps do so because they have been swayed by this argument. By no means however will I argue along those lines; as already observed, neither Arminius nor his first followers abandoned the Reformed doctrine of full, penal satisfaction. And as I have indicated above, there is no good reason to do so.

3. We grant, then, that Calvinists correctly understand the nature of the atonement to be penal, vicarious satisfaction; there is no problem there. But to *use this argument against universal atonement* (or to let it turn one away from the satisfaction view) implies (if unintentionally) a mathematical, quantitative view of the value of atonement. In other words, such an argument assumes that God, knowing exactly how many elect ones had committed exactly how much sin, exacted just that very amount in penalty from his Son. Then only their sins were "paid for," and not those of the non-elect.

Such a rationalistic concept of redemption is manifestly misguided. The suffering of Christ was suffering for sin, of infinite worth. For Him to substitute for 10 or ten million would require the same penalty. The number of those for whom He died does not affect the nature of His atoning work.

At their best, Calvinists realize this, and that the satisfaction view of the atonement does not settle the question of extent. Charles Hodge, for example, acknowledged that "Admitting the work of Christ to have been a true satisfaction for sin, its design [i.e., for whom intended] may still be an open question"[23]

4. Even more indicative and important, as we have noted, most Calvinists are very accustomed to insisting that Christ's atonement was *sufficient* for all. This insistence alone negates using the nature of atonement as argument against universality. If, in fact, His atonement was sufficient for all, then what was paid was adequate to make atonement for the sins of all, to be full, penal satisfaction for all. Conversely, if in His death He was not a substitute for some, then His death was not sufficient for them. One wonders if Shedd were on the verge of realizing this when he observed, "Although Christ's atonement, in the discussion of its value and sufficiency, can be separated from the intention to apply it, yet in the Divine mind and decree the two things

---

[23]Charles Hodge, *Systematic Theology* (Grand Rapids: Eerdmans, n.d.) II:544.

are inseparable."[24] I would agree that the sufficiency of Christ's atonement can be affirmed only for those to whom it may potentially be applied.

Calvinistic Argument 7:   Limited atonement is implied by the fact that Christ interceded, in His high-priestly prayer in John 17, for the elect only and not for the world. It would be illogical to think His atonement would be broader than His intercession. "The sacrificial work of Christ and His intercessory work are simply two different aspects of His atoning work, and therefore the scope of the one can be no wider than that of the other. Now Christ very definitely limits His intercessory work, when He says: 'I pray not for the world, but for those whom thou has given me.'"[25]

Arminian Response: This is pure assumption and human logic. In fact, there is no a priori reason to assume that Christ could not desire the salvation of all, and plan to die for all, and yet offer intercessory prayers for those truly His. The context of John 17 is such that the prayer of intercession offered there would be suitable only for the saved.

Calvinistic Argument 8:   Limited atonement is implied by the fact that when Christ died many were already in Hell. Furthermore, He already knew who would be lost and go to Hell after His death. Surely, then, He would not have "wasted" His death on those. "At the time of our Lord's death on the cross, the eternal destiny of many reprobates had already been sealed. . . . Can we suppose that our Lord died with the intent of bearing the sins of those who were then and there in Hell?"[26]

Arminian Response: This, too, is mere human logic, and poor logic at that. One may as quickly respond that when He died there were many already in Heaven: did He die for them? We may not be able to reconcile, in our finite thinking, the relationship between human history and God's eternity, but it is clear that an event in history had clear reference to things before and after it because of God's eternal knowledge and decrees. It is enough to remind anyone who has a

---

[24]Shedd, II:475.
[25]Berkhof, 395.
[26]Nicole, 203.

problem with this that Christ was the lamb slain before the foundation of the world.

As with the sixth argument, above, this one also tends to reflect a quantitative, numerical view of the value and design of Christ's redemptive work: there as a matter of amount, here as a matter of time.

Calvinistic Argument 9:   Limited atonement is necessary from the fact that God's purposes cannot be thwarted. Arminians believe that Christ's death was intended to save all. In that case, all must be saved since humans cannot thwart the purpose of God. As Berkhof says, "The designs of God are always surely efficacious and cannot be frustrated by the actions of man. . . . If it had been His intention to save all men, this purpose could not have been frustrated by the unbelief of man."[27] Nicole observes, "To attempt to combine universal redemption with particular salvation is to introduce an intolerable disjunction in the divine purpose."[28]

Arminian Response: I have saved this argument for last because it helps pave the way to the next chapter, which will present the Arminian arguments. And the very first thing that must be done is to clarify what the Arminian really claims.

My point is that this argument of the Calvinist misstates the Arminian position—and is wrong for that reason. It assumes the Arminian teaches that the redemptive work of Christ was intended by God to save all. In fact, the evangelical Arminian does not believe this. The Arminian view is that Christ died to provide salvation for all, a provision that is effective only when applied to those who believe, as was also part of the Divine intention.

Certainly, any purpose of God cannot be thwarted. He purposed to provide salvation for all in Christ, a salvation to be applied only to believers. That is exactly what transpired. His purpose was not thwarted. Only in this way, in fact, could the purpose of God relative to man be accomplished: namely, that each person have the freedom of will to accept or reject Christ. As I will insist in the next chapter, a person cannot reject a Christ who did not die for him.

I would add, once again, that this argument is also a subtle restatement of the third argument above and likewise confuses potential result with actual accomplishment (efficaciously saving).

---

[27]Berkhof, 394.
[28]Nicole, 204.

For Further Reading on the Extent
of the Atonement (Calvinism)

Berkhof, Louis. *Systematic Theology.* Grand Rapids: Eerdmans, 1949 (pp. 393-399).

Boettner, Loraine. *The Reformed Doctrine of Predestination.* Grand Rapids: Eerdmans, 1954 (pp. 150-161).

Boettner, Loraine. *Studies in Theology.* Grand Rapids: Eerdmans, 1947 (pp. 315-327).

Custance, Arthur. *The Sovereignty of Grace.* Grand Rapids: Baker, 1979 (pp. 149-174).

Hodge, A. A. *The Atonement.* Grand Rapids: Eerdmans, 1950 (pp. 347-429).

Hodge, Charles. *Systematic Theology.* Grand Rapids: Eerdmans, n.d., vol. II (pp. 544-562).

Kuiper, R. B. *For Whom Did Christ Die?* Grand Rapids: Eerdmans, 1959.

Nicole, Roger. "The Case for a Definite Atonement." *Bulletin of the Evangelical Theological Society* 10:4 [1967], 199-207.

Packer, James I. *What Did The Cross Achieve?* Theological Students Fellowship, n.d., booklet reprinted from *Tyndale Bulletin* 25 (1974).

Shedd, William G. T. *Dogmatic Theology.* Grand Rapids: Zondervan, n.d. (vol. II, pp. 464-489). [Some Calvinists regard Shedd as too speculative in some matters.]

CHAPTER SIX

Arminian Arguments for a Universal Atonement

Introduction: The Point at Issue

Clarifying the issue may be the single most important factor in the debate between Arminians and Calvinists about the extent of the atonement. Berkhof, for example, undertakes to do this, indicating both what is at issue and what is not. He takes pains to say that the disagreement is not:

(1) the *sufficiency* of Jesus' atonement for all, since Calvinists believe this as much as Arminians do;

(2) the *application* of the saving benefits of the atonement to all, since Arminians no more believe this than Calvinists;

(3) whether a *universal offer* of salvation is made, since Calvinists believe that the gift of salvation by the redemptive work of Christ is genuinely offered to all;

(4) whether there are *some* benefits of the atonement that are universal, since the Calvinists allow that there are some ways, short of the experience of saving grace, that all people benefit from the atonement.

And then he hastens to clarify, positively, that the issue is one of *design*. The question, he says, is: Did God design or purpose, by the atonement, to save only the elect or all?[1]

Herein lies a good lesson: on the one side, do not let your opponent state the issue without carefully evaluating his expression; on the other, do not let your statement of the issue rest until your opponent agrees you have stated it well. The fact is that Berkhof's statement of the issue is not correct. Arminians do *not* believe that God intended by the atonement to save all people. Had God designed the atonement with that intention, all would be saved. What God intends to do, He does. His final purposes are never thwarted. Had God sent His Son with the purpose that by His death all men would be saved, without actually saving all, He would have been both thwarted and in error as to the facts. Calvinists and Arminians agree on that much.

We need, therefore, to add Berkhof's statement of the issue to his four others: neither is the issue whether God designed the atonement

---

[1]Louis Berkhof, *Systematic Theology* (Grand Rapids: Eerdmans, 1949), 393, 394.

with the intention or purpose of saving all people from their sins. Instead, the issue is about *provision*, and that explains the name I have given to this section of the work. Roger Nicole, in similarly clarifying the issue, is more accurate: "The point at issue here is simply this, whether the Father in sending the Son . . . did intend to provide salvation for all men and every man."[2] "Provide" is the significant word here.

Simply put—and I think Calvinists can agree—the issue is whether by the redemptive work of Christ God provided salvation for all. The Arminian position is that He did, that Christ died to provide equally for the elect and those who will certainly be eternally damned. That by His redemptive work salvation was made accesible to all. That "The price of the death of Christ was given for all and for every man."[3]

Perhaps some further word about "sufficiency" is in order. Calvinists typically say what Berkhof has said, that the issue is not sufficiency, that the atonment of Christ "is not intended to be applied to non-elect men though it is sufficient for them."[4] Let us grant them their sincerity, although as I have shown in the brief responses in the previous chapter that they proceed to use arguments against universal atonement that undercut sufficiency. As Arminius said, "They say the price was sufficient for the sins of all, but if the necessity of divine justice demands that some sinners should be damned, then the price was not sufficient for all."[5] Again, "If [the atonement] is not a ransom offered and paid for all, it is, indeed, not a ransom sufficient for all."[6]

I have no desire to pursue this matter further and will stipulate that the Calvinist sincerely but inconsistently affirms the sufficiency of Christ's atonement for all. I think it is important, however, to add yet one more item to Berkhof's list, although he would object. Neither is the issue necessarily the nature of the atonement as full, penal satisfaction for the Divine justice.

To be sure, that is the issue for some Arminians, for those who hold to the governmental view of the atonement. That view is appar-

---

[2]Roger Nicole, "The Case for Definite Atonement" (*Bulletin of the Evangelical Theological Society* 10:4 [1967], 199-207), 200.

[3]James Arminius, *The Writings of James Arminius* (three vols.), tr. James Nichols and W. R. Bagnall (Grand Rapids: Baker, 1956), I:316.

[4]W. G. T. Shedd, *Dogmatic Theology* (Grand Rapids: Zondervan reprint, n.d.), II:478.

[5]Arminius, III:77.

[6]Arminius, III:346.

ently owed to one of Arminius' later followers, Hugo Grotius—not incidentally a legal scholar. I can only surmise that some of the Calvinists' arguments about the effectiveness of the atonement led to this variation of Reformation theology. But for Arminius himself, and the first Remonstrants, that was not the issue. Nor should it be. As I have tried to show in the previous chapter, once one understands that the atonement itself can be described in terms of its eventual effects, viewing it as full satisfaction does not contradict the fact that many for whom it was made will be eternally condemned.

That Arminius set forth the penal satisfaction view is clear from such statements as these: "He prepared merited punishment even for the sins of the elect . . . by laying them upon Christ, that he might expiate them."[7] "The most complete satisfaction was made to the justice of God by the sacrifice of Christ."[8] Again, by the atonement "it is effected that God may now be able, as Justice, to which satisfaction has been made, . . . to remit sins and to bestow the spirit of grace upon sinful men."[9] (It is clear that the early General Baptist theologian, Thomas Grantham, also affirmed the satisfaction view,[10] as did Wesley.)

For a thorough, Arminian presentation of the satisfaction view over against the governmental view of atonement, and the consequent implications for the doctrine of justification, I highly recommend the chapter "Atonement and Justification" by Leroy Forlines.[11]

I proceed, therefore, to the Arminian arguments for universal atonement, both logical and Scriptural. (One may note that some prefer to speak of "general" atonement. The two terms are being used in the same sense.)

Arminian Argument 1:   Universal atonement is implied in the doctrine of conditional salvation or election, as dealt with in the earlier section on "The Plan of Salvation." This argument corresponds precisely to the first argument for limited atonement as listed in the previous chapter. Just as limited atonement makes sense for uncondi-

---

[7]Arminius, III:191.

[8]Arminius, III:348.

[9]Arminius, III:352,353.

[10]See Matthew Pinson, "The Diversity of Arminian Soteriology," (unpublished paper), 7-9, for evidence of this.

[11]Leroy Forlines, *Biblical Systematics* (Nashville: Randall House Publications, 1975), 149-173. See also Forlines, *The Randall House Bible Commentary: Romans* (Nashville: Randall House Publications, 1987), 90-96.

tional salvation, so does universal atonement for the Arminian system. If, in fact, there is a condition that man must meet and may meet it or not as he chooses, then it follows that there must be a general work of redemption that provides each one this "live" option.

Calvinist Response: Indeed, in the Arminian system, universal atonement is logical. But that is precisely the problem: the system itself is misguided and unscriptural. The way to disprove the claims of universal atonement is to disprove the entire system. Both Calvinists and Arminians agree that the basic parts of the system must stand or fall together.

In addition, the Calvinist must agree with the Arminian's earlier response: the question of the extent of the atonement should be determined by Biblical teaching on the subject rather than simply by relying on the logic of a system. If the Bible really teaches, as has been maintained in the preceding chapter, that the saving benefits of the atonement were by design provided for the elect and for them only, then the whole Arminian system will crumble.

(One should note that this is the classical Calvinist approach. Those who have deserted the logic of the system to hold universal atonement would by no means agree that such a position will destroy the basic Calvinist system. It is not the purpose of this work to judge the force of that claim, although I am satisfied it is not consistent.)

Arminian Rejoinder: No rejoinder is needed. Most proponents of both ways will agree that their views are coherent within the system. For each person the question should therefore be, What does the Scripture teach? The final issue, therefore, is which does the better work of interpreting the Scripture accurately.

Arminian Argument 2: Universal atonement matches the plain Biblical assertion that God wills the salvation of all. An atonement that did not provide for all would be inconsistent with this and self-defeating. Two Scriptural affirmations are especially important at this point:

Second Peter 3:9—"The Lord is . . . not willing that any should perish, but that all should come to repentance."

First Timothy 2:4—"[God] will have all men to be saved, and to come unto the knowledge of the truth."

As David Scaer observes, "The a priori exclusion of even a few persons from the atonement and its results is contrary to 2 Peter 3:9."[12] In Peter's words, "is . . . willing" is the Greek *boulomai*, the verb form of *boulē*, a word frequently used in the New Testament of God's will, translated variously counsel, purpose, plan, decision, resolution, etc. God's counsel, says Peter, is that none perish and that all have opportunity (or, make room) for repentance. (See my commentary on Peter's epistles for more detailed exegesis.[13])

In Paul's words, the verb "will" is the Greek *thelō*, a verb that is variously rendered desire, wish, will, be willing. (In an article on the Greek *epignōsis*, used here for "knowledge," I have shown that both in Peter's letters and in the Pastorals, there is a tendency to use this compound as the equivalent of saving knowledge of Christ: conversion, in other words. The two parts of God's desire here, therefore, are essentially equal in meaning.)[14]

There is considerable disagreement, even among thoroughly Calvinistic interpreters, as to the relationship between *boulomai* and *thelō*, and between these two words and the doctrine of God's eternal counsel. Some regard one as the stronger, some the other. The interesting thing is that both are used in stating this universal desire and will of God relative to salvation.

Calvinist Response:

1. *As a group*, these passages show the *general* benevolence of God, who delights in the salvation of people and certainly does not delight when any are lost. But they do not imply that He "wills" the salvation of each person individually. In chapter two we have noted Shedd's distinction between God's *legislative* will (or "will of complacency") and His *decretive* will (or "will of good pleasure").[15] It is the first of these that is referred to in these two crucial passages: God's natural, spontaneous, "constitutional," sincere, abiding, compassionate desire that is manifested toward all alike. Neither Peter nor Paul was referring to God's decretive will.

---

[12]David Scaer, "The Nature and Extent of the Atonement in Lutheran Theology" (*Bulletin of the Evangelical Theological Society* 10:4 [1967], 179-187), 183.

[13]Robert E. Picirilli, "Commentary on the Books of 1 and 2 Peter" in *The Randall House Bible Commentary: James, 1, 2 Peter and Jude* (Nashville: Randall House Publications, 1992), 304-307.

[14]Robert E. Picirilli, "The Meaning of 'Epignosis'" (*Evangelical Quarterly* 47:2 [1975], 85-93).

[15]See Shedd, I:451-457.

2. Beyond this sufficient answer, these two passages can be satis-factorily treated *individually* in such a way as to show that they do not necessarily teach that God actively wills the salvation of all.

In 2 Peter 3:9, the phrase "longsuffering to *us*" may suggest that the "any" and "all" are intended to mean "any of *us*" and "all of *us*"— rather than any and all persons indiscriminately: "the reference is specific to those who, as Peter, are among the redeemed."[16]

In 1 Timothy 2:4, the "all" may mean "all kinds" of men (as it often does): in other words, persons in all categories to include even the unlikely rulers mentioned in verse 2.[17] This would not necessarily mean, therefore, every individual human being. For comparison, see 1 Timothy 6:10 where "all evil" surely means "all kinds of evil" rather than every specific instance of evil.

3. A third response will be indicated as the third response to the next argument, below.

Arminian Rejoinder:

1. That God's "will" does not always mean exactly the same thing may be admitted. But the use of both *boulomai* and *thelō* in these two verses tends to weaken the claim that His "will" is used in both of them only in the weaker sense of a desire that God has by nature but does not carry out in His decrees. Indeed, while we must make some distinctions, I find it difficult to sustain Shedd's distinction as the way to do this. Whatever God is by nature He manifests in His decrees.[18]

Furthermore, regardless what kinds of "spin" we can put on the words for God's will (whether in Greek or in English), the words by themselves do not tell us which way they are being used. If we are to distinguish between different ways the word "will" can be used, the probability is that our theology will govern how we distinguish them in specific verses rather than vice-versa. And that is not good: the point is that, finally, the theology of these verses depends on their exegesis in context rather than on some artificial (or genuine) dis-tinction we can find in the way the words are used on occasion. To say this another way, our view of the extent of the atonement and the con-ditional or unconditional nature of salvation will affect the way we view the word "will" in these verses.

---

[16]Nicole, 204.

[17]Nicole, 204.

[18]For some refreshingly transparent discussion of the problem of making distinc-tions in the will of God, see Paul Jewett, *Election and Predestination* (Grand Rapids: Eerdmans, 1985), 97-101.

A far better way to make distinction between aspects of God's will, I believe, is to understand that some things God wills are willed in subordination to other things He has willed. Perhaps a better way to say this, in view of the fact that God's will is *one* (see section two of this work), is to affirm that some expressions of God's will in Scripture must be understood in the light of other (more basic or broader) expressions of His will. Their truth, then, is part of the whole truth indicated elsewhere.

I have already acknowledged that whatever God decides to accomplish He will most certainly accomplish without fail. No person thwarts such an unconditioned intention on His part. If that is so, and I don't see how it can be argued against Biblically, then how is it that I have been able to see in Peter and Paul's words an intention on God's part that all be saved—when, in fact, all are manifestly not going to be saved?

The answer is that the expression of God's desire for all men to be saved must be understood in the light of His (more basic) desire that all men have, as created in His image, the freedom of choice to decide for or against Him. This understanding will make sense both of passages like 2 Peter 3:9 and 1 Timothy 2:4 (as well as those that more directly teach universal atonement) and of those that require us to believe that not all are saved. As I have written elsewhere, God's will that all have the freedom to choose, "because it relates to His fundamental will concerning the *nature* of man as man, must logically 'condition' His purpose that all be saved."[19]

2. The Calvinist's exegesis of the two passages illustrated above appears to be tortured. In neither case will careful exegesis or context sustain the view that the "all" means merely "all of us who are saved" (2 Pet. 3:9) or "elect among all categories of people" (1 Tim. 2:4). In this case, the more obvious meaning is the correct meaning.

One should notice Berkhof's inconsistency in citing these very passages. At one place he names both of them as referring to the revealed will of God that both Jews and Gentiles be saved[20]—thus all kinds of people, not all people individually, in spite of the fact that there is no Jew-Gentile contrast or comparison in the context of either passage! But later he cites 2 Peter 3:9 as referring to *all* sinners' opportunity for repentance[21]; and 1 Timothy 2:4 as evidence of God's

---

[19]Picirilli,"Commentary," 306.
[20]Berkhof, 396.
[21]Berkhof, 442.

"favorable disposition" and "untold blessings" on all men, including the non-elect.[22]

Arminian Argument 3:   The New Testament plainly asserts that Jesus died redemptively for all, and this includes passages where the "all" is distinguished from the saved. Some of the most important of these are:

First John 2:2—He is propitiation for our sins, and not for ours only but also for *the whole world.*

First Timothy 2:6—[Christ] gave himself a ransom *for all.* (This should be linked, especially, with verse 4 as used above.)

Hebrews 2:9—Jesus tasted death *for every man.*

John 3:16-18—God so loved *the world* that He gave His Son . . . that *the world* through him might be saved.

Second Corinthians 5:14,19—One died *for all.* God was in Christ reconciling *the world* to Himself. (Compare especially v.18.)

Romans 5:18—The free gift came upon *all men* unto justification of life.

Titus 2:11—The grace of God that brings salvation *to all men* has appeared. (This is apparently the correct order of the words.)

Calvinist Response:

1. In general, we must realize that words like "all" and "world" have varying meanings in the New Testament, depending on the context. The Greek *pas* does not always mean, exhaustively, *all*, nor does *kosmos* always means everyone in the world. In these passages, the words are not universal but must be defined by the context.

2. Specifically, then, each of the verses must be examined more closely, and such an examination will show that they do not finally teach universal atonement.

First John 2:2—There are ways of understanding the contrast in this verse that do not uphold the Arminian position. One possibility is that, in this epistle, "ours" refers to a small group (of elect persons) including John and his fellow Jewish-Christian readers, rather than the whole body of Christians. Then the "whole world" is a short way of referring, by contrast, to other elect persons in the whole world, Gentiles included.

An alternative possibility is that "but also for the whole world" means His is the only propitiation available to anyone in the world.[23]

---

[22]Berkhof, 445,446.

[23]For a fuller presentation of these two options, along with others, see John Murray, *Redemption Accomplished and Applied* (Grand Rapids: Eerdmans, 1955), 82-84.

Or it may be that "the word 'world' is sometimes used to indicate that the Old Testament particularism belongs to the past, and made way for New Testament universalism."[24] "World" means "all mankind [in general], in distinction from the Jews,"[25] not all men individually.

First Timothy 2:6—The explanation is the same as for 1 Timothy 2:4, indicated above: "all" means all kinds or classes or levels of people, including (in context) "even rulers who seem to be such unlikely objects of divine grace,"[26] as well as common people.

Hebrews 2:9—In context, "every one" means, specifically, every son He brings to glory (verse 10), in other words His "sanctified brethren" (verse 11).

John 3:16-18—This merely indicates the general worldwide love of God, especially as contrasted with narrow Judaistic concepts that would restrict His love.

Second Corinthians 5:14, 19—The last clause of verse 14 shows that "all" means all who died in Him: "the body of believers, because it is described as 'the living'" (verse 15).[27] In verse 19 the "world" is only those whose trespasses are not imputed to them.

Romans 5:18—In the whole passage, verses 12-21, the "all" is but the "many" for whom Christ is the federal Head (that is, His elect), in contrast to the "all" for whom Adam was federal head (that is, the whole human race).

Titus 2:11—Regardless what "to all men" modifies, the following verses (12-14) show that "all men" "really means all classes of men."[28]

3. These references, and those cited above under the Arminians' second argument, would prove *too* much if the "all" and "world" are taken to be individually universal. The reason for saying this is: if God really willed to save all (argument 2, above), then all really would be saved; if verses like 1 John 2:2 and 1 Timothy 2:6 (argument 3) really mean all persons in the whole world, then they would likewise prove that the cross actually accomplished propitiation and redemption for all.

Arminian Rejoinder:

While one may readily acknowlege that "all" does not always mean every human being exhaustively, in none of these specific pas-

---

[24]Berkhof, 396.
[25]Shedd, II:480.
[26]Nicole, 204.
[27]Shedd, II:480.
[28]Berkhof, 396.

sages does the Calvinist's explanation of "all" or "world" seem correct. Each case by itself appears to be a deliberate attempt to read the
"all" or "world" in a way *not* justified by the context. As Vernon
Grounds has expressed the matter of interpreting these verses, "It
takes an exegetical ingenuity which is something other than learned
virtuosity to evacuate these verses of their obvious meaning."[29]

Instead of attempting to demonstrate this, verse by verse, I have
chosen instead to treat the most important of these verses in the
more thorough Scriptural argument in the following chapter. There is
simply not space in this volume to deal with all of these passages in
an exegetical, Biblical theology manner. And to deal with them briefly
would run the risk of relying on prooftexts.

With reference to the third response above, we may observe that
this is nothing more than a restatement of the Calvinist's third argument on his own side, outlined and answered in the previous chapter.

As this applies to 1 Timothy 2:4 and 2 Peter 3:9, I have dealt with
this above. Again, we readily acknowledge that His "will" that all be
saved does not mean that all are saved. We are not told why not:
apparently because His will that all people make their own free choice
"takes precedence" over His will that all be saved. We might call this
a distinction between His *absolute* and His *conditional* will. Calvinists
make similar distinctions, as I have pointed out for Shedd, above.[30]

Whether this is helpful or not, Scripture *does* indicate that God's
will for man's salvation can be thwarted—in *some* sense without
being absolute—by man's rejection. Matthew 23:37 contains an excel-
lent illustration of this: Jesus laments over Jerusalem that He "willed"
(*thelō*) to gather her children, but they "willed" (*thelō*) not. Luke 7:30
carries essentially the same idea, in that the Pharisees and lawyers
rejected the "counsel" (*boulē*) of God for themselves.

As this applies to verses like 1 John 2:2 and 1 Timothy 2:6, which
speak of propitiation and redemption in the atonement for "all," I have
already answered the Calvinists' argument that these would prove the
actual salvation of all if all persons exhaustively are meant. See the
preceding chapter and the Calvinists' third argument.

---

[29]Vernon Grounds, "God's Universal Salvific Grace" in *Grace Unlimited,* ed. Clark
Pinnock (Minneapolis: Bethany Fellowship, 1975), 27.

[30]Berkhof, 77.

Arminian Argument 4: Universal atonement is implied in Scriptural references to the perishing of some for whom Christ died. If redemption was provided for some non-elect in the atonement, then there is no reason to limit it at all.

Two such passages are 1 Corinthians 8:11 and its parallel in Romans 14:15. In both of these the subject is the limitation of Christian liberty for the sake of "weak" fellow believers. In the first Paul warns against abusing liberty lest the weak one, "for whom Christ died," *perish.* The parallel gives similar warning not to *destroy* the one "for whom Christ died." In both of these we are dealing with one whom Paul regards as saved, to whom the redemptive benefits of the atonement have been applied. And in both he raises the distinct possibility that this one may perish if his spiritual welfare is deliberately disregarded by those proud of their liberty in Christ. (Hebrews 10:29 might also be cited here, but I will save it for argument 5, below.)

Another such passage probably deals with some never regenerated. In 2 Peter 2:1 the apostle speaks of false teachers as "denying the Lord that bought them," and that they will "bring on themselves swift destruction."

Calvinist Response:

The first two of these refer to hypothetical situations: "a supposition, for the sake of argument, of something that does not and cannot happen."[31] The point of the passages is that the so-called "strong" Christians were so indifferent to the spiritual welfare of others that their actions would "offend the weaker brethren, to cause them to stumble, to override their conscience, and thus to enter upon the downward path, the natural result of which, if continued, would be destruction."[32] But Romans 14:4 shows that the Lord would not allow that course to be continued to their actual destruction.

An alternative explanation, held by some Calvinists, is that "perish" and "destroy," in these verses, do not mean eternal destruction.

If, in fact, these two verses indicate that some genuinely regenerated could actually perish eternally, then that would mean that a saved person can be lost. And that is a manifestly false doctrine based on salvation by works. Since the Bible teaches that a truly regenerate person cannot apostatize and perish in hell, we can be sure Paul did not mean to raise this possibility.

---

[31]Shedd, II:481.
[32]Berkhof, 397.

Second Peter 2:1 is to be explained as follows: Peter for the moment views the false teachers as if they really were the Christians they claimed to be. In other words, he means this ironically: they are denying the very Lord who—by their claim (though not actually)—bought them![33]

Arminian Rejoinder:

To regard these as "hypothetical" is to rob the warning of its force. This is a somewhat typical Calvinist explanation of similar warnings to Christians. In fact, the passages explained this way are patently straightforward. None of the hidden assumptions required to take them as hypothetical are ever indicated in the passages themselves. As Pieper observes, "The objection that these passages refer to cases that cannot actually occur would destroy the whole argument of the apostle."[34]

A careful study of the New Testament occurrences of "perish" and "destroy" will show that the alternative explanation is likewise lame. As Paul uses them in these verses, the words can not fail to mean eternal destruction.

The Calvinist is correct, of course, in observing that the Arminian's use of this argument, as it applies to the first two verses cited, implies the real possibility of apostasy. The rejoinder to this observation is simply to prove the possibility of apostasy. The force of this particular argument for universal atonement, admittedly, depends on the larger argument between Calvinists and Arminians relative to perseverance. That will be the task of the fifth section of this book, and further argument will be saved for that section. No doubt a Calvinist will be ready to acknowledge universal atonement if he is converted to belief in the possibility of apostasy!

The Calvinist explanation of 2 Peter 2:1 is another example of reading into the sentence something manifestly not implied. These words, too, are straightforward: The Lord Jesus, by His death, bought them. They deny Him. Nothing else is justified by the text. As Sailer observes, "The Bible as a rule designates men to be what they really are—not what they pretend to be"; he goes on to point out that in the same verse the ones involved are called " 'false teachers,' although they hardly professed to be such."[35] It seems strange that in the same

[33]Nicole, 205.

[34]Francis Pieper, *Christian Dogmatics* (St. Louis: Concordia, 1951), II:21, note.

[35]William S. Sailer, "The Nature and Extent of the Atonement—A Wesleyan View" (*Bulletin of the Evangelical Theological Society* 10:4 [1967], 189-198), 193.

verse one statement would represent them according to their profession and the other according to God's true understanding. (For a more complete treatment, see my commentary on Peter's epistles.)[36]

Arminian Argument 5: Expanding on the previous argument, universal atonement is clearly implied in the fact that the truly saved may apostatize and eternally perish.

At issue here, of course, is the possibility of apostasy by one to whom the redemptive benefits of the atonement have been savingly applied. Scriptures that teach this will include: (1) the two verses mentioned first for argument 4 above; (2) any passage that teaches the real possibility of apostasy from saving faith, like Hebrews 6:4-6 and 2 Peter 2:18-22; (3) especially Hebrews 10:29, which not only teaches the possibility of apostasy but specifically indicates the prior application of the saving benefits of the atonement to the apostate.

Calvinist Response:

That the truly regenerate may finally fall away and perish eternally is not Biblical. Proving that will invalidate this argument.

Hebrews 10:29 may be explained in a way like that used for 2 Peter 2:1 above. Where the words read "wherewith he was sanctified" we may understand the writer's unspoken addition "so he claims." Or, as Hoeksema puts it, "Although for a time they appeared as if they belonged to the true church, they did not."[37] The person spoken of was never really regenerate, thus apostasy is from profession, not possession.

Arminian Rejoinder: If proving the impossibility of apostasy will invalidate this argument for universal atonement (and it apparently will), then, conversely, proving its possibility will sustain it. As already indicated, section five of this work will be devoted to that issue.

Arminian Argument 6: Universal atonement is the view that best accords with the bona fide gospel offer of salvation to all, and correlatively with the command to preach that gospel to all.

---

[36]Picirilli, "Commentary," 261-264.

[37]Herman Hoeksema, *Reformed Dogmatics* (Grand Rapids: Reformed Free Publishing Association, 1966), 556.

It is true that Calvinists affirm that salvation is sincerely offered to all by the gospel, but their affirmation has to fly in the face of the apparently otherwise implications of their doctrine of atonement. The Arminian view that salvation was provided for all in the atonement gives weight to the gospel offer and impetus to its proclamation.

It is also true that one cannot fault the Calvinist system itself for those extremists who use it as a basis to deny evangelistic endeavor, and Calvinism is by no means invalidated by that perversion. Even so, those extremists have found something in their own doctrine that they—regardless how mistakenly—saw as implying such a denial. The Arminian view would never lead to that error (even though it might well lead to others).

Calvinist Response:
This is a logical, rather than a Scriptural argument. The fact is that Calvinists affirm both the genuineness of the universal offer of salvation and the correlative responsibility of the church to proclaim the gospel to all: "We believe that God . . . sincerely . . . calls all those who are living under the gospel to believe, and offers them salvation."[38] If this *seems* to Arminians to be contradictory, Calvinists may deny that it is contradictory on the simple grounds that the Bible teaches both the limited atonement and the universal offer. Whether the consistency between these can be explained satisfactorily or not, they must be consistent.

Furthermore, the two teachings are not really contradictory after all.

One "reconciliation" of them lies in the fact that the preacher, to whom God has not revealed the identity of the elect in advance, *must* preach to all indiscriminately in order that the gospel message can reach those (secretly) known to God as elect and be the means of their conversion. The means is foreordained as well as the end.

Another point is that the offer of the gospel to the non-elect, which is certainly followed by their refusal, serves to demonstrate both their wicked condition and the justness of their damnation. Indeed, by the gospel

> . . . the judgment of the ungodly is aggravated. . . . For by virtue of the remnants of natural light that are in him, he certainly understands this calling of the gospel. . . . He does not come to the light, for he loves the

---

[38]Berkhof, 397.

darkness rather than the light. And . . . the preaching of the gospel becomes to him a savor of death unto death. He is fully revealed as a sinner that stands in rebellion against the loving God.[39]

Still further: the gospel sincerely offers salvation to any who will meet the conditions of repentance and faith. The fact that only the elect, who are *given* repentance and faith, will (or can) meet the conditions does not detract from the truthfulness and sincerity of the offer. That the non-elect neither can nor will respond serves to magnify the grace of God who enables the elect to do so and to demonstrate that none would be saved if He did not save some against their will.

Finally, the offer does *not* consist in declaring to all that Christ died for all, but in declaring to all that any who will truly repent and believe will obtain the blessings of the salvation procured by His death for them specifically.

Arminian Rejoinder:

This complex explanation serves to divert attention from the main issue by introducing other issues. In fact, regardless of the Calvinist's claim, he faces difficulty in making the universal offer of the gospel a genuine offer. Indeed, Calvinists often appear to be speaking tongue-in-cheek when they speak of the universal offer of the gospel. Hoeksema, for example, finally observes that the preacher of the gospel is not at liberty "to change the Word of God into a well-meaning offer of salvation to all men on the part of God."[40] In other words, he realizes that salvation is not being offered in the gospel to the non-elect; only just condemnation is being offered.

Always the Calvinist is saying more than that sinners *will* not accept the offer; he is saying that they *can* not. And an offer that *can* not be accepted is not really an offer at all.

Furthermore, in the Calvinistic system, the gospel is not really offering salvation to *any*, since neither the elect nor the non-elect can accept the offer or meet its conditions. In fact, the "conditions" are not really conditions in the Calvinist system. They are part of the "package" of salvation-benefits given to the elect by virtue of the death of Christ for them.

---

[39]Hoeksema, 471.
[40]Hoeksema, 478.

Without realizing it, the Calvinist is finally saying that repentance and faith (as the gift of God in the salvation "package") are being offered to all who will repent and believe, when in fact none can do so. This reduces to pure tautology and is no offer at all.

I will return to this subject in the next section of this work, entitled "The Application of Salvation." The question really is, Is faith a condition of salvation or a saving benefit?

If not all who hear *can* respond to the gospel, as the Calvinist insists, then only those *given* repentance and faith can do so. In consequence, *no* person who hears the gospel can do so with any confidence that he can respond. Conversely, all who hear and are not given the gift may conclude that the offer is not intended for them and therefore not rejected by them. What a person *cannot* receive, he can not really reject. Nor can he be rightly blamed for rejection (although he might well be blamed for being in the condition that brought on his inability). This leads to the next argument for universal atonement.

Arminian Argument 7: Unlimited atonement is the view that best accounts for the blame attached to men for rejection of Christ. The point is that Scripture condemns people not just for their sins but also for not putting faith in Christ and thereby being delivered from their sins. Any sinner—having heard the gospel or not—can be justly condemned for his sins; but if the death of Christ made no provision for the salvation of the non-elect, he cannot be justly charged with unbelieving rejection of Christ.

In other words, the Bible is *not* saying, "You have sinned and will remain in your sins without hope *or atonement* and receive your just reprobation in hell"—which would certainly be just. But the Bible says again and again, in effect: "You have sinned and on that account deserve hell. Worse still, you have rejected the atonement made for your sins by the death of Christ, the atonement that could in fact be your deliverance. Your reprobation in hell is therefore all the more tragic and deserved."

In pursuing this argument, Sailer comments specifically on 1 John 5:10, 11, which explains the condemnation of the unbeliever as because he has not believed the witness that God has borne concerning His Son: namely, the witness that God gave eternal life in His Son. He then asks: "If Christ died only for the elect and for no one else, why should these non-elect souls believe this witness concerning

Christ? If, on the other hand, Christ has indeed died for them and yet they refuse to believe on Him—then their refusal is a heinous thing."[41]

John 3:18 is another example of many passages, especially in John's gospel, that affirm a specific condemnation for not putting faith in the redemptive work of Christ.[42] This is hard to understand if Christ did not die for them. And this difficulty is increased by the Calvinists' own insistence that the atonement, per se, was effectual in redeeming the sinner. In that case, the atonement did not redeem the non-elect and if they should believe that it did they would believe falsehood!

Calvinist Response:

Like the previous argument, this is logical rather than Biblical. It may be answered in exactly the same way as the first response to that argument: whether appearing to be "logical" or not, the Bible teaches both limited atonement and condemnation of the non-elect for rejection of Christ. Consequently, there must not be any real contradiction between those.

The gospel offer of salvation sincerely made to the non-elect is rejected by them not because Christ did not die for them (even though He did not), but because of their own wicked rebellion against God. They are therefore rightly condemned for such rejection.

Arminian Rejoinder:

This is to beg the question. The real issue is, simply, whether God made an atoning provision in Christ that actually *can* avail for the non-elect. If He did, they can be blamed for rejecting what is the offer of a real possibility. If He did not, they have rejected nothing possible for them to accept. An Arminian can hardly avoid observing that the Calvinistic concept of the offer to the non-elect is *prima facie,* but not genuine in the sense that it is a real possibility.

To reflect a point made in the previous section of this work, we will readily acknowledge that the non-elect certainly *will* not accept the offer. But in that certainty there is no necessity. The most coherent position is that the gospel offer is universal because the provision is universal and all who hear may, in fact, receive the salvation offered.

---

[41]Sailer, 195.
[42]Sailer, 194, also cites Jn. 8:24; 2 Cor. 6:14 [?]; 2 Thess. 2:11,12; 1 Jn. 5:10, 11; Rev. 21:8.

Arminian Argument 8: Universal atonement is strongly supported by the Scriptural indication that the provision is as broad as the sin. This argument has not received the attention, even among Arminians, that it deserves. Romans 3:22-25 is the best example of this indication, with its tightly knit logic, as follows:

(a) there is no difference,

(b) because *all* have sinned,

(c) being justified by His grace

—through the redemption that is in Christ,

—whom God set forth as propitiation

—through faith, in His blood.

Clearly, the propitiation and redemption purchased by the atoning death (blood) of Christ undergirds justification. This, in turn, modifies the "all" who have sinned, of whom Paul specifically says "There is no difference." The specific reason there is no difference is that all have sinned; that alone speaks strongly for atonement for all. And this, in verse 22, is cited as the reason justification is freely provided through Christ's atonement by faith. One may compare Romans 10:11, 12 where again the fact that salvation is by faith is connected to the fact that "There is no difference"; Acts 15:9 should also be noted.

In other words, God grounds the fact that there is no difference in the need, in the desperate state of fallen man. And that, in turn, is grounds for the provision for justification.

Calvinist Response: Since I have never heard this argument put to a Calvinist, I am unable to say how he would respond. I assume two things. First, the Calvinist will probably approach the passage with a different exegesis: specifically, he may reinterpret the "all" as we have seen him do in verses above.

Second, I think the Calvinist will return to the third response given to argument 3 above—and this is the same as the Calvinist's third positive argument for his position dealt with in the previous chapter. In other words, he will probably point out that this argument proves too much: namely, that if this "all" really is universal, referring to all human beings exhaustively, then they *must* by this verse be justified.

Arminian Rejoinder: The exegesis outlined above should stand the test of any careful analysis: the fact that the "all" means all in the broadest sense is indicated by the fact that "all" in that sense have sinned.

The second point has already been answered in the previous chapter; see the Arminian response to the Calvinist's third argument.

Arminian Argument 9:   Universal atonement accords best with the fact that "God is no respecter of persons" (Acts 10:34; Rom. 2:11; Deut. 10:17).

Calvinist Response: Such passages mean that God has not awarded grace to any persons *because of who they are* (cf. James 2:1ff). In other words, He does not regard people by whether they are noble or lowly, Jew or Gentile, rich or poor. Salvation by a particular election that was based on *nothing in man* does not violate this truth.

Arminian Rejoinder: The Calvinist's understanding of the main point of this Biblical affirmation, that God is no respecter of persons, is essentially correct. Even so, there may be some grounds to say that particular election does play "favorites"—even if there was nothing in the elect that deserved that favoritism.

Perhaps a better way of saying this is that an unconditional salvation of some versus others does mean that God treats some differently from others. And the passages that state this basic principle appear to be implying thereby that God deals with men on the basis of no predisposition on His part but solely on the basis of how they respond to Him who has dealt equitably with all.

Summary

In a "systematic theology" mode, the Arminian's contention is that universal atonement is the more coherent view, according best with the other aspects of Biblical soteriology, with Scriptural assertions that are universalistic in tone and that indicate His will that all be saved, with the possibility of apostasy, with the universal offer of the gospel, and with the blame attached to the unsaved for rejecting Christ.

Coherence is one thing, precise Scriptural teaching is even more important. For that reason, the following chapter undertakes to treat the most significant Biblical affirmations of universal atonement.

For Further Reading on the
Extent of the Atonement (Arminianism)

Bell, M. Charles. "Calvin and the Extent of the Atonement." *The Evangelical Quarterly* LV:2 [1983], 115-123. [A discussion by a non-Arminian of Calvin's views on the subject]

Lake, Donald. "He Died for All: The Universal Dimensions of the Atonement," *Grace Unlimited*, ed. Clark H. Pinnock. Minneapolis: Bethany Fellowship, 1975 (ch. 2). [In many ways Lake represents neither Reformation Arminianism nor historic Arminianism.]

Lightner, Robert P. *The Death Christ Died*. Schaumburg, Ill.: Regular Baptist Press, 1967. [A "Calvinist" defense of universal atonement]

Miethe, Terry L. "The Universal Power of the Atonement" in *The Grace of God, the Will of Man*, ed. Clark H. Pinnock. Grand Rapids: Zondervan, 1989 (ch. 4).

Sailer, William. "The Nature and Extent of the Atonement—A Wesleyan View." *Bulletin of the Evangelical Theological Society* 10:4 [1967], 189-198.

Scaer, David. "The Nature and Extent of the Atonement in Lutheran Theology." *Bulletin of the Evangelical Theological Society* 10:4 [1967], 179-187. [In many respects, the traditional Lutheran view of the extent of the atonement is parallel to that of Reformation Arminianism.]

Shank, Robert. *Elect in the Son*. Springfield, Mo.: Westcott Publishers, 1970 (pp. 59-87).

Torrance, James B. "The Incarnation and 'Limited Atonement'." *The Evangelical Quarterly* LV:2 [1983], 83-94. [Not an Arminian source]

Watson, Richard. *Theological Institutes*. New York: Nelson and Phillips, 1850 (vol. II, pp. 281-306). [An important, early Wesleyan theologian]

Wiley, H. Orton. *Christian Theology*. Kansas City: Beacon Hill Press, 1952 (vol. II, pp. 295-300). [A representative of later Arminianism]

CHAPTER SEVEN

New Testament Evidence for Universal Atonement

There is not space in this work to analyze every passage that bears directly on the scope of the atonement. I will treat in detail but a few. Meanwhile, one could hardly present a better survey than that of the Calvinist Jewett, who observes as follows in order to face honestly the difficulty of the New Testament evidence against "particular" atonement:

> Even more perplexing, if possible, is the content of the kerygma itself. The apostles preached a message that not only imposed the obligation on all to repent and believe the gospel, but assured all who came within earshot that God in Christ was "reconciling the world to himself, not counting their trespasses against them" (2 Cor. 5:19). This reconciliation was effected by him "whose act of righteousness leads to acquittal and life for all," for "by [his] obedience many will be made righteous" (Rom. 5:18-19). This act of righteous obedience culminated in his death on a Roman cross. As Christ crucified, "he is the propitiation for our sins; and not for ours only, but also for the sins of the whole world" (1 John 2:2, ASV). To this "Lamb of God, who takes away the sin of the world" (John 1:29), to this "man Christ Jesus, who gave himself as a ransom for all" (1 Tim. 2:5-6) the apostles bore eloquent witness in due time. And so through their witness the grace of God appeared for the salvation of all (Titus 2:11), even the grace of the God who will have all men and women to be saved (1 Tim. 2:4)—the God who "so loved the world that he gave his only Son" (John 3:16), because he is "not wishing that any should perish, but that all should reach repentance" (2 Pet. 3:9).[1]

1 John 2:2

"And he is propitiation concerning our sins, and not concerning ours only but also concerning the whole world."

As indicated in the previous chapter, Arminians claim this verse as one of those teaching universal atonement. "Few biblical texts are stronger in their stress upon the universal potentiality of Christ's

---

[1]Paul K. Jewett, *Election and Predestination* (Grand Rapids: Eerdmans, 1985), 28, 29 [italics his].

atonement than 1 John 2:1-2!"[2] Calvinists protest this exegesis. Berkhof, for example, observes:

> "World" is sometimes used to indicate that the Old Testament particularism belongs to the past, and made way for New Testament universalism. The blessings of the gospel were extended to all nations. . . . This is probably the key to the interpretation of the word "world" in such passages as . . . 1 John 2:2.[3]

Roger Nicole apparently agrees—after saving this verse until last, as the one needing the most attention: "It may be possible to hold that the apostle John had in view not only a small group, perhaps of Jewish Christians, to whom he was addressing his letter, but the universality of the redeemed elected out of every nation and category."[4] He adds two other possible explanations, "helpfully presented" in Murray's *Redemption Accomplished and Applied*: (1) that the contrast between "our" and "the world" is between John's and later generations; (2) that John simply meant to emphasize that Christ's is the *only* propitiation available to anyone in the whole world.[5]

Such exegesis shows that a meaning other than the apparently obvious one *can* be adopted: one notes these writers' own use of "probably" and "may," not to mention their uncertainty which explanation is better. Even so, an apparently obvious meaning is not always the correct one, and none of us is always perfectly free of *eis*egesis. What we must do, then, is consider as carefully as possible the precise meaning of the words John used. And in that study we will seek to do good exegesis and discover whether 1 John 2:2 does, in fact, teach universal atonement.

Use of "world" in 1 John
The most basic point of difference between Calvinist and Arminian understandings of the verse is about how "world" is being used. The exegete's first task, then, is to investigate the meaning of the word in the entire letter.

---

[2]Donald M. Lake, "He Died for All: The Universal Dimensions of the Atonement" in *Grace Unlimited*, ed. Clark Pinnock (Minneapolis: Bethany Fellowship, 1975), 39.

[3]Louis Berkhof, Systematic Theology (Grand Rapids: Eerdmans, 1949), 396.

[4]Roger Nicole, "The Case for Definite Atonement" (*Bulletin of the Evangelical Theological Society* 10:4 [1967], 199-207), 206.

[5]Nicole, 206.

Kosmos occurs 23 times in 1 John, thus frequently enough to give us confidence that we can discern how he uses it. It tends to occur in clusters, as the following will show.

2:2 (our text)	Its first appearance
2:15-17 (6 times)	The Christian is not to be loving the world or the things in the world. The world, and its lust, is passing away.
3:1	The world does not know us, because it did not know Him.
3:13	Do not be annoyed if the world is hating you.
3:17	Whoever has the means of life of the world and does not share with one in need is not demonstrating the love of God.
4:1-5 (6 times)	Greater is the one in you than the one in the world. They, being of the world, speak of the world and the world hears them.
4:9	God sent His Son into the world in order than we might live through Him.
4:14	The Father sent the Son to be Savior of the world.
4:17	As He is, so are we in the world.
5:4, 5 (3 times)	The believer overcomes the world.
5:19	We are of God, and the whole world lies in the evil one.

1. Some of these use "the world" personally (3:1, 13 for examples) and some impersonally (perhaps 2:15)—more the former than the latter. Calvinists and Arminians will agree that the word is personal in 2:2.

2. Whether personal or impersonal, "the world" is being used very consistently by John in a sense antipathetic to the church or Christians. The only four instances where this negative sense is not necessary are 3:17 and 4:17 (where "the world" is neutral as the context in which we live and have our livelihood); 4:9 (which may be viewed either as local-neutral or in the same sense as in 4:14); and 4:14 (where it has whatever meaning it has in 2:2).

Otherwise, "the world" must not be loved by Christians (2:15-17), did not recognize Jesus and does not recognize Christians (3:1), hates Christians (3:13), has the spirit of antichrist in it (4:3, 4), is overcome by Christians (5:4, 5), and is in the grip of the wicked one (5:18, 19).

It already seems clear that, given this consistent use, one would hardly be prepared to find "the whole world" in 2:2 (or 4:14) to stand as some kind of shorthand for "the elect of all nations (or generations)."

To this we may add one especially telling comparison. Except for 2:2, the only other place in the letter where *holos* ("whole") modifies "world" is in 5:19. The two verses should be compared side by side:

2:2	5:19
not for ours only, but also for *the sins of the whole world.*	We are of God, and *the whole world* lieth in the wickedness.

This serves to strengthen the impression that John's use of "world" elsewhere in this letter provides absolutely no reason to think it might represent the worldwide elect in 2:2. Indeed, it provides every reason to believe otherwise.

(I would add that, although there is not space in this work, an examination of John's use of "world" in the rest of his New Testament writings will assuredly lead to a similar conclusion.)

Use of the first plural in 1 John

It is also part of the Calvinist's view that 1 John 2:2 uses "we/us" in a limited way to mean John and his circle only (usually conceived as Jewish Christians) in contrast to a broader group of believers (Gentiles, or later believers), rather than as an unrestricted reference to Christians in general. We should therefore also examine closely his use of the first plural elsewhere in this letter.

Too much space would be required to list all instances of the first plural in 1 John. But a careful reading tends to lead to the following observations.

1. An effort to read the other first plurals as meaning "we in our particular group of elect ones"—a relatively small circle of homogeneous believers—in contrast to the elect worldwide is sure to fail.

2. The only part of 1 John where the first plural may have some kind of limitation of its breadth is in the prologue. There "we" may be taken, specifically, as apostolic in reference. But once 1:5 has been passed, no other first plural can sensibly be read as "we apostles."

3. A few examples of typical usage will underscore the conclusions above:

GRACE, FAITH, FREE WILL

1:7   we walk in the light and experience fellowship and cleansing;

1:9   if we confess our sins He forgives and cleanses us;

2:3   we know that we know Him if we keep His commandments;

3:1   God has bestowed such love on us that we are called His children;

3:2   when He appears we will be like Him;

3:14   we have passed from death to life, we love the brethren;

4:6   we are of God;

5:11   God gave us eternal life;

5:14   if we ask in His name, He hears us.

Add to these 3:16; 4:9, 11, 17, 19; 5:2—and indeed any other first plural in the letter. There is nothing here that cannot most sensibly be read, "We Christians, all of us." Conversely, there is nothing that would sensibly be read, "We, in our particular sub-group of Christians." Indeed, all these uses tend to argue that John pregnantly uses "we/us" as shorthand for "we Christians" in general, at least everywhere except in the prologue.

One should also look again at the comparison above between 2:2 and 5:9. This tends to confirm that "we/ours" stands in deliberate contrast to the "whole world" that lies in the grip of Satan.

4. For the sake of thoroughness, we may also check the other places in the letter where "our" modifies "sins," as here in 2:2:

1:9	If we confess our sins, He is faithful to forgive;
3:5 ("our" not in all mss.)	He was manifested to take away our sins;
4:10	God loved us, sent His Son as propitiation concerning our sins.

This does not really add to the weight of the conclusion already reached. Still, one may observe that there is not the slightest suggestion in any of these that the "our" is limited to *some* elect ones, as the Calvinist suggests for the "our" in 2:2. Indeed, 4:10 so specifically corresponds to 2:2 that it sounds like a standard Christian confession. If this is the case, and it seems likely, that is all the more reason to believe John is speaking of Christians in general in 2:2 (and 4:10).

Use of contrast between "the world" and "we/us" in 1 John

Since the Calvinist has suggested that the contrast in 2:2 is between "us" elect and the other elect in the "world," we should examine the rest of the places in the letter where a similar contrast occurs. There are at least four of these.

3:1   we are called children of God, because of which *the world* does not know *us*.

4:5, 6 they are of *the world* and *the world* hears them; we are of God and the one who knows God hears us. (The entire passage, 4:1-6, is instructive.)

5:4, 5 this is the victory that overcomes *the world*, even *our* faith.

5:19   we are of God, and the whole *world* lies in the evil one.

One hardly needs to observe that these cannot refer to a contrast between "us" elect ones and other elect ones of the world. Nor is there any greater reason to regard the "world" in 2:2 as referring to anyone other than the unsaved referred to in these passages.

So far, the results of exegesis seem absolutely clear: in 1 John 2:2, the "ours" stands in deliberate contrast with the unbelieving "world."

Doctrine of atonement in 1 John

The final thing to be investigated in our pursuit of the meaning of 2:2 is the teaching of this letter about the meaning of the death of Christ. In one way or another this is found in the following references.

• *1 John 1:7:* "The blood of Jesus, his Son, cleanseth us from all sin." The context provides this logic:

1. God is light (verse 5).

2. Walking in darkness gives the lie to a claim to be in fellowship with him (verse 6).

3. Conversely, if we walk in the light we have fellowship with each other and *Jesus' blood cleanseth us* (verse 7).

4. Still, a claim to be without sin is false (verse 8).

5. But confession of our sins brings forgiveness and cleansing (verse 9).

Atonement ("the blood of Jesus"), therefore, yields forgiveness and cleansing from sin. This, in turn, is linked with fellowship—with both God and other Christians. To be noted is the way John links the *effectiveness* of the atonement with its *application* in the experience of the believer, not to be separated from "walking in the light" (probably more relational than behavioral here) and confession of sin.

• *1 John 2:2*—"He is propitiation for our sins, and not for ours alone but also for the whole world." This observation grows out of the context just discussed (in 1:5-8), and so the logic continues:

6. Even though it is false to claim sinlessness (1:8, 10), we should strive to avoid sin (verse 1).

7. But if anyone sins, we have Jesus Christ as a righteous Paraclete with the Father (verse 1).

8. And he is propitiation for our sins, as well as for the sins of all the world (verse 2).

Atonement, therefore, is propitiation for sins. Space does not permit pursuit of the debate whether *hilasmos* means "expiation" (forgiveness, removal) or "propitiation" (appeasement, satisfaction of wrath). I am satisfied that the latter is the correct understanding of the word. Regardless, this work of propitiation is the grounds for confidence in Christ's advocacy when we sin. Once again, then, the historic atonement—even as propitiation—is linked with its *application* in the experience of the believer: in this case, intercession and forgiveness for post-conversion sins (which, in the context, has already been conditioned on confession).

(Comment about "but also for the whole world" will be saved for the end of this section.)

• *1 John 3:5, 8*—"That One was manifested in order that he might take away [our] sins. . . . For this purpose the Son of God was manifested, that he might destroy the works of the devil." In light of John 1:29, where "taking away the sin of the world" is linked to Jesus as the [sacrificial] Lamb of God, "was manifested" probably implicitly refers to the atonement. The context here calls for Christians to avoid sin:

1. True Christians keep themselves pure (verse 3).

2. Jesus was manifested to take away sin (verse 5).

3. In him is no sin (verse 5).

4. Whoever abides in him does not live in sin (verse 6).

5. The one who practices righteousness is righteous, and the one practicing sin is of the devil (verses 7, 8).

6. Jesus was manifested to destroy the works of the devil (verse 8).

The fact that the atonement "takes away" sin and "destroys the works of the devil" is apparently being used as a basis for ethical injunction to avoid sin. In other words, there would be a basic contradiction between claiming to experience the fruits of the atonement and going on in our former sinful ways. Whatever else the destruction of the works of the devil might mean, in this context it certainly includes freeing us from bondage to sin. As before, then, the efficacy of atonement is closely linked with application in experience.

• *1 John 3:16*—"By this we have come to know love, because That One laid down his life in our behalf (or, stead)." This context, like the previous one, is ethical; the admonition is now to be loving one another. In His death, Jesus exemplified what true love demands and we ought to emulate him.

The atonement, therefore, is a demonstration of God's love, although what we have already seen (not to mention the rest of the New Testament) keeps us from the error of thinking this is *all* it means. Given the fact that *huper* can mean either "in behalf of" or "instead of," there is no need to emphasize the vicarious nature of the atonement here; it is well enough emphasized in many other passages. I would observe, however, that there are many things one cannot do in *behalf* of another without doing them in his *place*. For that reason, there is absolutely no doubt that *huper* often implicitly indicates substitution, and that would appear to be the case here.

• *1 John 4:9, 10*—"By this God's love was manifested in (or, among) us, that God has sent his one-of-a-kind Son into the world in order that we might become alive through him. In this is love, not that we have loved God, but that he loved us and sent his son (as, to be) propitiation for our sins." As in the preceding we see again that the atonement was a manifestation of God's love for us, and in this context too that truth is basis for ethical obligation. As in 2:2, we see again that atonement is propitiation—appeasement of God's just wrath for our sins.

Added to what we have already seen is the fact that atonement produces *life*. This "ingressive" aorist *zēsōmen* is most certainly the new birth. And that regeneration is viewed as a purpose of the atonement. Once again, then, efficacy is linked with application.

• *1 John 4:14*—"The Father has sent the Son (as, to be) Savior of the world." In light of 4:10 above, surely this "sent" has the same atonement implications. Thus being "Savior of the world" is clearly meant to parallel His propitiating death. The verse performs the same universalizing function as the last clause in 2:2:

2:2	4:10, 14
He is propitiation for our sins, and not ours only but for all the world.	He sent his Son as propitiation for our sins; he sent his Son as Savior of the world.

Atonement, therefore, is provision of a savior, of salvation, and that for all the world. (Again, comment on "the world" will be made below.)

• *1 John 5:6-8*—"This is the one who came by water and blood, Jesus Christ: not in the water only but in the water and in the blood; and the Spirit is the one bearing witness, because the Spirit is the truth. Because the ones bearing witness are three, the Spirit and the water and the blood, and the three are as the one." For our present purpose, we need spend little time on this more or less cryptic passage. The "blood" certainly appears to be a reference to the shedding of Christ's blood on the cross (as in 1:7). John is apparently linking together the testimony of Jesus' baptism (which included "Behold the Lamb of God") and the testimony of the cross (the "blood," indicating His atoning death) with the testimony of the Holy Spirit (as the "unction" indwelling the believer, 2:20; 4:13) as a three-fold, identical, and undeniable testimony to Jesus' deity, His mission, and the cleansing from sin experienced through him.

With everything else, then, the atonement is also a witness to the deliverance it provides for those to whom it is applied.

By way of summary, these (direct or implicit) references in 1 John to the atonement lead to the following observations.

1. As to the *nature* of the atonement, John emphasizes propitiation as basic. He also makes clear that the atonement is for forgiveness, cleansing, removal of sins, for life, and for the destruction of the works of the devil.

2. John views the *effects* of the historical atonement as inseparably linked with the *application* of benefits in individual experience. In other words he does not regard the atonement as automatically achieving its results until applied by the Spirit.

(I would have to stretch the epistle to see in it any *emphasis* that these benefits are applied only on condition. That does not seem to be a major concern of John's. Still, in light of the context in 1:7 and 4:14, at least, there is clear room for the understanding that the application is conditional, should we find that to be the case in the rest of the New Testament. See the next section of this work.)

3. John does, however, have an ethical interest when he speaks of the atonement. This does not lead him to speak of condition, however, so much as of result. In other words, if atonement is what we say it is—taking away sin, destroying the devil's works, manifesting God's love—then we must not claim to be experiencing its fruit and at the

same time live in sin, do the works of the devil, or fail to practice love. Especially do the contexts of 3:5, 8, 16; 4:9, 10 teach us this.

4. As to the *extent* of the atonement, one concludes finally that the "world" in 2:2 and 4:14 can have no meaning other than all of unsaved mankind. John's purpose is to say that believers, even when discussing the benefits of Christ's atoning death for themselves, must remember that He also died for the whole world, including the lost. Both "world" and "us" in these two texts are used in the very same way they are used consistently throughout the rest of the epistle.

In conclusion, I feel I must refer once more to Nicole's observation, about 2:2 (and similar texts), that if "the whole world" is taken to mean all of mankind then universal salvation must result: "If the texts prove anything at all, they prove too much."[6] What he means is the same as has been argued earlier (argument three in chapter 5): namely, since 2:2 says Christ's historic atonement actually made propitiation for all, propitiation was then and there made effective.

My answer there is my answer here, except to add that John himself, in 1:7, 2:2, for example, presents the *effects* of atonement as depending on *application*. As I observed there, normal language usage is involved: we often speak of an action as incorporating all its potential effects. Earlier, I quoted the Calvinist Shedd on this point. I do so again:

> Vicarious atonement without faith in it is powerless to save. It is not the making of this atonement, but the trusting in it, that saves the sinner. . . . If it were made, but never imputed and appropriated, it would result in no salvation. . . . In this state of things, the atonement of Christ is powerless to save. It remains in the possession of Christ who made it, and has not been transferred to the individual. In the Scripture phrase, it has not been imputed. . . . After the vicarious atonement has been permitted and provided, there is still another condition in the case: namely, that the sinner shall confess and repent of the sin for which atonement was made, and trust in the atonement itself.[7]

Shedd is a good (if somewhat speculative at times) Calvinist. He thinks that this appropriating faith is itself given unconditionally to all those (the elect) for whom the atonement was intended. Even so, he has shown us how to explain that the atonement made propitiation

---

⁶Nicole, 206.

⁷W. G. T. Shedd, *Dogmatic Theology* (Grand Rapids: Zondervan reprint, n.d.), II:440-442.

for all without actually saving them. It is not applied until appropriated by faith. A conditional and universal atonement can be made without securing universal salvation.

I may add that Shedd, and we ourselves, have good reason for insisting that the atonement, apart from faith, does not save. If it did, then the elect would never in their lifetimes, *not even before their regeneration*, be unsaved! And if that were the case, Scriptures like Ephesians 2:1-10 would be completely off the mark.

Herein lies the solution to the problem some Arminians have had, leading them to the so-called "governmental" view of the atonement. Arguments like that given by Nicole have convinced them that if they regard the atonement as full, penal satisfaction for sin, as a vicarious bearing of men's guilt and punishment, and that if they regard it as being substitionary in this sense for all men, then no one could possibly be lost (else the "payment" for some would be demanded twice). They have therefore resorted to a lesser view of the value of the atonement.

As I have noted earlier, Arminius did not resort to such a view, nor did his immediate followers among the Remonstrants. The jurist Grotius invented that alternative to the Reformed view. Generations later Wesley saw that this was entirely unnecessary and faithfully proclaimed a full satisfaction of the Divine wrath and holy demand. Once we understand that the atonement only accomplishes propitiation as it is applied to the believer in saving union with Christ by the work of the Spirit of God, once we understand that the New Testament statements affirming that Christ accomplished redemption and made propitiation for our sins and those of all the world are speaking anticipatively and depend on application, we have no need to avoid the satisfaction view of the atonement in order to hold that it was universal and provided for the salvation of all.

1 Timothy 2:1-6

"I appeal therefore, first of all, for petitions to be being made, prayers, intercessions, thanksgivings, in behalf of all men, in behalf of kings and all those who are in authority, in order that we may lead a quiet and tranquil life in all piety and respectability. This is good and acceptable before our Savior, God, who desires for all men to be saved and to come to knowledge of the truth. For one is God, one also is mediator of God and men, a man, Christ Jesus, the one who gave himself a ransom in behalf of all."

The obvious question, here, is whether "all men" in verse 4 and "all" in verse 6 are truly universal and encompass the entire human race. The Calvinist view is that they do not. Some Calvinists interpret the "all" to mean people of all kinds or classes, and thus to "refer to the revealed will of God that both Jews and Gentiles should be saved"; such passages "imply nothing as to the universal intent of the atonement."[8] Others, having distinguished between the *sufficiency* and the *intent* of the atonement, suggest that this passage refers to its sufficiency for all: "Owen remarks that [1 Tim. 2:6] must be understood to mean that Christ's blood was sufficient *to be made* a ransom for all, *to be made* a price for all."[9]

Shedd, with Owen, is at least due credit for recognizing that "all" means "all" in the passage. No wonder he proceeds, therefore, to say that "Atonement must be distinguished from redemption," and that "Atonement is unlimited, and redemption is limited"[10]—a statement an Arminian might well agree with, especially in light of Shedd's insistence that *redemption* "includes the *application* of the atonement."[11]

Arminians insist, however, that this passage indicates a provision for universal redemption. As Sailer notes, "The context . . . is universalistic throughout." To summarize his treatment *in loco*,

(1) the passage opens with appeal to believers to pray for all men, which must be broader than believers since it includes kings and all in authority;

(2) this is based on God's desire that all men be saved;

(3) this in turn reflects that there is one God and one mediator between God and men, again a universal emphasis;

(4) and this in turn rests on the fact that the one mediator gave himself a ransom for all. He concludes by observing that "The context demands a universal application."[12] His exegesis is convincing.

To simplify: in the passage at hand we find:

(1) prayers for all
(2) desire for all
(3) ransom for all.

Those who would interpret the "all" to mean "all classes" point to the reference to kings and authorities in verse 2 as supporting this

---

[8]Berkhof, 396, 397.
[9]Shedd, II:468; [italics his].
[10]Shedd, II:469, 470.
[11]Shedd, II:469.
[12]William Sailer, "The Nature and Extent of the Atonement—A Wesleyan View" (*Bulletin of the Evangelical Theological Society* 10:4 [1967]), 192, 193.

view. In other words, we should pray for people at all levels, whether kings or commoners, princes or peasants.

Well, then, if we are to sustain that interpretation, given the unity of the passage, "all men" must have that meaning throughout. In verse 6 we find that the "all" referred to are those ransomed. They must therefore be the elect. Consequently we must read the passage thus:

Verses 1, 2—the prayers exhorted must be made for all the elect among all people of whatever classes, including believing kings and authorities.

Verses 3, 4—the basis of this exhortation is that this will be well-pleasing to the God who desires that the elect of all classes of men, high and low, be saved.

Verses 5, 6—in turn, the basis of this is that there is one God and one mediator, Jesus Christ, between God and elect men, who gave himself a ransom for all elect men of all classes.

I submit that this is a consistent reading, using the Calvinist's understanding of the "all men," but that it is not coherent. The obvious lack of continuity between verses 1, 2 and verses 5, 6 is almost enough, by itself, to disqualify this exegesis. It is reasonably clear that Paul is not asking for prayers for Christian authorities only.

To those who insist that the mention of kings and authorities supports the understanding "all classes" of men, I would respond by saying that the passage as a whole makes better sense if God's universal desire for the salvation of all and Christ's ransom for all provide the universal basis that will include kings and authorities. It is the universal (all) that incorporates the particular (kings), not the particular that determines the meaning of the universal. On the grounds that prayers should be offered for all, Paul can readily include a request for kings and authorities in view of the fact that their good graces are needed for believers to live in piety and respectability and pursue the mission of the God who wills that all be saved.

Are there specific exegetical tasks that may help establish or undermine this view? One that occurs immediately is, Does Paul use "all men" elsewhere in this letter, and if so with what meaning? In this passage it occurs three times (verses 1, 4, 6), twice modifying "men" expressed and once with "men" left to be supplied.

The answer to the question is that it occurs three more times in 1 Timothy: namely in 4:10, with "men" expressed, and in 4:15 and 5:20, with "men" left to be supplied. Analysis of these is instructive.

4:10   ... the living God, who is Savior of all men, most of all of
       believers.
4:15   ... that your progress may be evident to all.
5:20   Rebuke those sinning in the presence of all. ...

When I say that these are instructive I mean that they help us
determine how to read the word "all." In the latter two, Paul is speaking to Timothy in the direct light of his relationship to the believing
community. It is obvious, as one reads the verses, that "all" means all
those in that community (and not all men universally).

But the very sound of 4:10 is different, not to mention the specific verbal content. Even without the addition "most of all of believers"
we would automatically understand "all men" to be all men universally. No doubt some interpreter would attempt to change our minds
on that point; for that reason we are glad we have the added "most of
all of believers." That leaves us in no doubt, then, that "all men"
means everyone. That He is Savior of all men speaks of provision; that
He is Savior especially of believers speaks of application.

(I can hear some Calvinist arguing, as before, that if God is Savior
of all then all will be saved. And I repeat, as before, that this reading
is unwarranted. See above in this chapter and my answer to the
Calvinist's third argument in chapter 5. Indeed, this particular passage is helpful in answering that argument since it explains both how
He can be Savior of all and especially of believers, to whom alone His
Spirit applies Christ's atoning work.)

This use of "all men" argues strongly for the same interpretation
in 2:1-6. Indeed there, just as here in 4:10, Paul is speaking without the
kind of self-evident limitation that "all" has in 4:15 and 5:20.

We are probably justified in extending our search for Paul's use of
"all men" to the letter to Titus, given that the two letters were apparently written at about the same time and with similar concerns and
circumstances. In that letter "all men" occurs twice, both times with
"men" expressed:

2:11   The grace of God bringing salvation to all men has
       appeared (or, has appeared to all men).
3:2   ... showing all humility to all men.

Again, one needs no agonizing analysis to recognize that both of
these are unlimited. In neither one is Titus being addressed regarding
community life specifically. In both verses the subject is the Christian

life in the midst of the world. In 2:11 Paul exhorts believing slaves to adorn the doctrine of salvation with right behavior because God's saving grace toward all men has made its appearance and teaches godly living. They will undermine that grace with lives that are not commensurate with it. I will not argue the connection of the phrase "to all men" beyond saying that it seems more likely to be linked to the unique adjectival use of *sotērios*, bringing salvation: "For the grace of God *for the salvation* of all men has appeared"[13] (I tend to think that the somewhat parallel ideas in 3:4 support this, but one cannot be dogmatic.) Regardless, the impact of the verse is the same and is universal: God's saving grace, which made its appearance in history in the redemptive work of Jesus Christ, is provided for all men.

In 3:2, as in 1 Timothy 2:1-6, the subject of rulers and authorities is again involved, and they are obviously not all (not even usually) believers. But in the face of unbelieving rulers, as also of all men, the Christian recalls his own formerly wicked life and manifests subjection to rulers and meekness to all.

The argument about 1 Timothy 2:1-6 does not depend on this usage in Titus, of course, but the usage, if it means anything, adds a measure of support for the universalistic understanding of "all men" in the passage before us.

I would conclude this chapter with what I believe is an important observation, although I offer it without hubris. All of us who handle God's Word do well to remember that we do not honor Him with our interpretive ingenuity but with submission to what He says. To say, even to show, that a given statement *can* be interpreted in a certain way does us no credit at all. The question is always not what the words *can* mean but what they *do* mean, here. In 1 John 2:2 and in 1 Timothy 2:1-6, the most obvious meaning of "world" and "all men" is universalistic. In these cases, careful exegesis supports the obvious meaning.

---

[13]K. H. Schelkle (on *sotērios*), *Exegetical Dictionary of the New Testament,* ed. Balz and Schneider (Grand Rapids: Eerdmans, 1993), III:329.

For Further Reading on the New Testament
Evidence for Universal Atonement

Marshall, I. Howard. "Universal Grace and Atonement in the Pastoral Epistles," in *The Grace of God, the Will of Man*, ed. Clark H. Pinnock. Grand Rapids: Zondervan, 1989 (ch. 3).

Osborne, Grant R. "Exegetical Notes on Calvinist Tests" in *Grace Unlimited*, ed. Clark H. Pinnock. Minneapolis: Bethany Fellowship, 1975 (ch. 9).

Outlaw, Stanley. "Commentary on 1 Timothy" in *The Randall House Bible Commentary: 1 Thessalonians through Philemon*. Nashville: Randall House Publications, 1990 (pp. 199-206).

PART FOUR

The Application of Salvation

When it comes the turn of the individual to be delivered from the kingdom of darkness into that of the Son of God's love, how does such a thing come to pass? How does salvation become his personal experience?

I suggest that there is more of significance here, for the purpose of this work, than is usually thought to be. Indeed, in a way, the entire argument between Calvinism and Arminianism comes down to this. For it hardly needs saying that if salvation is unconditional, that means it is applied unconditionally. Likewise, if salvation is conditional, it is applied conditionally.

This is the reason *application* is a perfectly good term for us to use, even though the Arminian Pope rejects both *application* and *appropriation* as appropriate, the former on the grounds that it suggests "the predestinarian error which assumes that the finished work of Christ is applied to the individual according to the fixed purpose of an election of grace"; the latter because it "tends to the other and Pelagian extreme, too obviously making the atoning provision of Christ a matter of individual free acceptance or rejection."[1] But by themselves the terms do no such thing: there is application and there is appropriation—and either term means whatever it is used to mean. Pope goes on to prefer the *administration* of

---

[1] W. B. Pope, *Compendium of Christian Theology* (London: Wesleyan-Methodist Book-Room, 1880), II:319.

redemption, which is certainly acceptable but does not improve on *application*.

This part of Soteriology, in the systematic theology books, will typically treat such doctrines as union with Christ, calling, regeneration, justification, sanctification, and so on. The subject is far too big for all its implications to be discussed in detail here. Consequently, while some of these must be touched on, we must get more to the roots of the matter. Instead of the whole range of soteriological questions, then, I want to focus on two more fundamental issues. These are *depravity* and *conditionality*.

Integrally related to the matter of depravity are such questions as: What are the effects of the fall? Is man *totally* depraved? If so, is there such a thing as "free will"? How does one's view of depravity affect the way he understands that salvation becomes a person's experience?

Related to the matter of conditionality are equally serious questions: Is salvation by faith? How is the *ordo salutis* (order of salvation) involved? Is faith the gift of God? How does salvation by grace relate to salvation by faith—or, for that matter, to salvation by works?

As in the previous two sections, I will offer first a chapter that explains the Calvinistic viewpoint on these issues, then a chapter from the Arminian perspective. (I venture in passing that I think this is the area where the Calvinist least understands the Arminian, at least the Reformation Arminian.) Following this will be a chapter devoted to some of the Biblical theology involved.

CHAPTER EIGHT

Calvinism and the Administration of Salvation

One can hardly help admiring the tight logic of the Calvinist's system, typically—although with some oversimplification—presented by the acrostic TULIP:

T otal Depravity

U nconditional Election

L imited Atonement

I rresistible Grace

P reservation of the Saints

In this section we look more closely at the implications of the first and fourth of these points. In summary, the Calvinist's view is that fallen man's depravity is such that his constitutional freedom is effectively negated. His will is bound, not free. Regardless how generous God's offer of salvation in Christ, no human being either will or can accept it in his natural state. That is the reason salvation must be applied by a gracious work that is "against" man's will, that supernaturally overcomes his natural resistance. And that is the reason salvation begins, logically, with regeneration: a person must be regenerated before he is capable of faith.

To the key elements of this view we now turn our attention.

Man After the Fall

Adam and Eve, as created, were both good and free. But the first sin brought them, and all born into their race, into bondage to a corrupt nature. This is depravity and it is total, befouling every aspect of man's being.

1. This does not mean (a) that every person is as bad as he can be, or (b) that every person commits every sin. Indeed, unregenerate persons have a conscience that distinguishes between right and wrong, and they often choose not to violate that conscience. Sinners often have some measure of appreciation for what is noble and virtuous. They may even, at times, be deliberately altruistic in action or motivation. But total depravity is the condition in which all human beings are naturally born.

2. Closely associated with this depravity are two other results of the fall: (a) the guilt of "original sin" and (b) consequent condemnation by God. The purpose of this work does not require us to treat these matters, or to pursue the difficult issue that divides even those who are fully loyal to Calvin: How is it that the guilt and condemnation for Adam's sin are imputed to the whole race? Some prefer the Augustinian view, claiming "natural headship" as the basis. Others prefer "federal headship."[2]

3. But there is no such difference of opinion about the nature of depravity. As depraved, fallen man is naturally inclined to evil, preferring that to any good. He is in a convinced state of rebellion against God, suppressing and blind to the truth. He cannot genuinely desire the good so as to turn from wrongdoing and embrace it; all such desires are too contaminated by self will to prevail. His will is therefore bound, he is no longer free to choose God. Indeed, there is no true good, in relation to God, in him at all—only perversion.

a. That this is *total depravity* means that it pervades man's whole being: "all the faculties and powers of both soul and body"[3]

b. It may also be called *total inability*, which means, in spite of what has been allowed above: (1) that the unregenerate person can not do anything that is fundamentally good or meets God's approval, and (2) that he cannot change from his radically selfish love for sin to a genuine desire for what is holy or meets the demands of God's law.[4]

4. This view has significant consequence for our understanding of the gospel offer of salvation. The moment we consider the gracious offer God has made to all, to give salvation in Christ to any who will believe, that very moment we realize that no unregenerate human being can in fact respond to that offer. Total depravity has rendered fallen man helpless and incapable of believing the gospel. He cannot exercise faith in Christ.

The Crucial Role of Regeneration

The "solution" to this problem of depravity is regeneration, which may be defined as that supernatural work of the Holy Spirit, based on the merits of Christ's redemptive work, which is exercised directly on

---

[2]For a helpful presentation of these, see Leroy Forlines, *Biblical Systematics* (Nashville: Randall House Publications, 1975), 123-128. See also W. G. T. Shedd, *Dogmatic Theology* (Gand Rapids: Zondervan reprint, n.d.), II:13-94.

[3]Louis Berkhof, *Systematic Theology* (Grand Rapids: Eerdmans, 1949), 247.

[4]Berkhof, 247.

the spirit of man to bring him from death to life, from separation from God to a living relationship with Him.

The Nature of Regeneration

Some of its important attributes are as follows.

1. Regeneration implies a "mystical" union between Christ and the elect which logically—not chronologically—precedes it and provides a basis for it.

2. Regeneration is an immediate and internal work within man. "The influence of the Spirit is distinguishable from that of the truth; from that of man upon man; and from that of any instrument or means whatever. His energy acts *directly* upon the human soul itself."[5] This means that the Spirit of God operates without using even the Word of God. Regeneration does not require faith on the part of the individual; as Shedd observes, "A dead man cannot assist in his own resurrection."[6]

3. Regeneration is, in itself, entirely subconscious. The one regenerated has no awareness of the work and is altogether passive. Any awareness of regeneration that may develop in one's experience is based on a perception of its effects.[7]

4. Regeneration is logically the first work involved in applying salvation. All other aspects of the experience of redemption grow logically from this and require it as prerequisite.

5. Regeneration is not necessarily linked to conversion, although the two typically occur simultaneously. Where regeneration is unconscious, conversion is conscious and may coincide with regeneration or follow it after some separation in time. While regeneration does not require the Word, conversion does.

The Effectual Calling

Calvinists emphasize, in the application of salvation, the role of the Holy Spirit in "effectively" calling the person to conversion.

1. The distinction between the *external* and the *internal* call.

a. The external call is presented in the indiscriminate proclamation of the gospel. It is thus general or universal, offering salvation in Christ, inviting sinners to repent and believe, and promising salvation to any and all who will do so. Although none but the elect will

---

[5]Shedd, II:500.
[6]Shedd, II:503.
[7]Berkhof, 469; Shedd, 502-509.

respond, this is a *bona fide* offer. This call, however, is not efficacious in itself.

 b. The internal call is the external call made effective internally by the direct operation of the Holy Spirit on the heart of the elect. It may thus be termed *effective, effectual,* or *efficacious.*

 2. The characteristics of the effectual calling.

  a. It requires the Word and is conscious.

  b. It is a powerful and supernatural work of the Holy Spirit and therefore cannot successfully be resisted.

  c. It is effective because regeneration has provided the person with what Berkhof calls a "spiritual ear"[8] so that he can now hear responsively: "There is now a spiritual vitality that can respond to the truth."[9]

  d. It necessarily issues in conversion.

Some earlier Calvinists essentially equated regeneration and effectual calling, but that is not typical of Reformed theology in its more carefully developed forms. Some do suggest that "regeneration proper," in its strictest sense, is the implanting of divine life discussed above, while this effective calling is the completion of the work of regeneration in the broader sense and is thus equal to the "new birth" as the first, and conscious, manifestation of the life implanted in regeneration proper. This distinction enables the Calvinist to acknowledge that the "new birth" requires the Word, while regeneration proper does not.

Regeneration in the Ordo Salutis

This Latin phrase translates into the "order of salvation." Calvinists conscientiously delineate the several aspects of the salvation experience and relate them to each other in a *logical* order. (One must emphasize that this is not meant to be a *chronological* order.)

There is no need to enter here into a detailed treatment of the *ordo salutis.* For the present purpose it is sufficient to relate regeneration to other major elements.

As already indicated, regeneration is the first work of application. The Calvinistic order, therefore, is:

---

[8]Berkhof, 471.
[9]Shedd, 508.

regeneration
effectual calling
conversion, including two elements:
    a. repentance
    b. faith
justification
sanctification.

The logic of this arrangement is significant. Regeneration makes all the rest possible, because it enables the otherwise depraved individual to hear the gospel with understanding and to respond to the effectual calling in repentance and faith, themselves gifts of God. Thus, while that person would have had no consciousness of regeneration as such, the conversion made up of personal repentance and faith is indeed a conscious experience. And while the proclamation of the gospel is not necessary for regeneration, it is essential to effectual calling and conversion.

Then, based on the faith thus received, the converted person is justified. And sanctification, as the on-going work of the Holy Spirit, proceeds from there.

Some lesser points are not absolutely required for the discussion here. Among these are possible implications of that period of time that may, but does not typically, separate conversion and the rest of the order from regeneration. One of these is that a person may well be regenerated as an infant, with conversion to follow after enough maturity for personal understanding has been realized. This is more likely to occur among the children of elect parents than otherwise: "The new life is often implanted in the hearts of children long before they are able to hear the call of the gospel."[10] (There is also the possibility that a person may be regenerated and never—for want of hearing the gospel—truly be converted in this life. Shedd discusses this at some length, hastening to observe that such a case is an "extraordinary" work of the Spirit and is not to guide the church in its evangelistic endeavor.[11] Some Calvinists insist that Shedd is being too speculative in allowing this possibility.)

---

[10]Berkhof, 471; cf. Shedd, 508, note.
[11]Shedd, 706-711.

The Role of Faith

Given the order just outlined, it follows that faith is, in fact, a part of the work of salvation wrought for the elect rather than a condition the individual must meet in order to be saved. Berkhof defines saving faith as "a certain conviction, wrought in the heart by the Holy Spirit, as to the truth of the gospel, and a hearty reliance (trust) on the promises of God in Christ."[12]

1. As we have seen, saving faith is not possible for the unregenerate person; his depravity prevents it. This faith is not within the capacity of the bound will of natural man and he is therefore unable to exercise faith in order to be saved from his unregenerate condition.

If faith were within natural man's capacity to exercise or withhold at will, then man's unpredictable will would be the direct cause of salvation. Salvation would then be by the whim of man rather than by the decree of God. Indeed, such "faith" would in fact be a *work* of man's, an activity that makes man at least co-responsible for his salvation. Such a view is "synergistic," and such a salvation is not a pure work of God's grace.

2. Faith (along with repentance) is therefore primarily a gracious gift of God and only secondarily an activity of man that issues from the work of God. If Ephesians 2:8, 9 does not say this explicitly, it does so at least implicitly. This way, man gets no more credit for faith than for Jesus' atoning work: "The seed of faith is implanted in man in regeneration"[13] "A man is not regenerated because he has first believed in Christ, but he believes in Christ because he has been regenerated."[14] Again, "Faith is an effect of which regeneration is the cause."[15]

3. It is more technically correct, then, to speak of "justification by faith" than to speak indiscriminately of "salvation by faith." The latter phrase can correctly be used, but if so the broader word "salvation" is being used by synecdoche for "justification" as one of its key elements. And it would certainly be incorrect to speak of "regeneration by faith." The Bible never does this.

---

[12]Berkhof, 503.
[13]Berkhof, 503.
[14]Shedd, 509.
[15]Shedd, 530.

For Further Reading on Calvinism's View
of the Application of Salvation

Berkhof, Louis. *Systematic Theology.* Grand Rapids: Eerdmans, 1949 (pp. 225-251, 415-525).

Boettner, Loraine. *The Reformed Doctrine of Predestination.* Eerdmans, 1954 (pp. 61-82, 162-181).

Clark, Gordon. *Biblical Predestination.* Philadelphia: The Presbyterian and Reformed Publishing Company, 1969 (pp. 85-144).

Custance, Arthur. *The Sovereignty of Grace.* Grand Rapids: Baker, 1979 (pp. 91-130, 175-189, 359-364).

Shedd, William G. T. *Dogmatic Theology.* Grand Rapids: Zondervan, n.d. (vol. II, pp. 242-257, 490-552).

CHAPTER NINE

Salvation Applied in the Arminian View

As in the previous chapter, we are still concerned with two basic things—man's depravity and salvation's conditionality—and how these are involved in the way salvation is applied, or administered, to the individual in the grace of God. Only now we consider the Arminian position, especially where it may be the same as or in contrast with the Calvinistic view outlined in the previous chapter.

In summary, the Arminian agrees with the Calvinist about total depravity—although that is not true of all Arminians, and Calvinists think it is true of none—and disagrees about the conditionality of salvation. The problem of depraved man's inability to respond positively to the gospel is solved by what Arminius called "prevenient grace." And the *ordo salutis* begins with conversion: that is, with repentance and faith. This position is detailed in the following paragraphs.

Arminians and Total Depravity

For the Reformation Arminian view of depravity, one may simply review the section "Man After the Fall" in the preceding chapter. There the Calvinist's view of depravity was outlined, and the careful Arminian need not disagree with anything said there—although the *implications* drawn from those statements may differ.

To summarize:

1. Since the fall of Adam and Eve, all human beings inherit from the original parents a corrupt nature, as inclined toward evil now as Adam and Eve were toward good before the fall.

2. In consequence of this condition, man's will is no longer naturally free to choose God apart from the supernatural work of the Spirit of God.

3. Therefore, left to himself, no person either can or will accept the offer of salvation in the gospel and put saving faith in Christ.

4. This condition may rightly be called *total depravity*, in that it pervades every aspect of man's being, and *total inability*, in that it leaves him helpless to perform anything truly good in God's sight. As Watson expresses this: "The true Arminian, as fully as the Calvinist, admits the doctrine of the total depravity of human nature in consequence of the fall of our first parents"; he proceeds to express com-

plete agreement with the position of Calvin, namely: "Man is so totally overwhelmed, as with a deluge, that no part is free from sin, and
therefore whatever proceeds from him is accounted sin."[1]

Watson was, of course, a leading theologian of Wesley's following.
Calvinists often acknowledge that Wesleyans, unlike the seventeenth
century Arminians, believed in total depravity.[2] Paul Jewett recognizes that Wesley had such an "Augustinian" view of sin, and adds,
"Original sin was not simply a moral weakness for Wesley, as for the
classic Arminian, but a depravity that requires the grace of God for
salvation."[3] Wesley picked up on the Biblical use of the metaphor of
sleep as a description of man in his natural condition:

> His spiritual senses are not awake; they discern neither spiritual good
> nor evil. The eyes of his understanding are closed. . . . Hence, having no
> inlets for the knowledge of spiritual things, all the avenues of his soul
> being shut up, he is in gross, stupid ignorance of whatever he is most
> concerned to know.[4]

Again, speaking of the sinner, even after conviction has begun,
Wesley observes:

> Though he strive with all his might, he cannot conquer: sin is mightier
> than he. He would fain escape; but he is so fast in prison, that he can-
> not get forth. . . . Such is the freedom of his will; free only to evil; free to
> "drink iniquity like water"; to wander farther and farther from the living
> God, and do more "despite to the Spirit of grace."[5]

So much for Wesley. But the Calvinists are wrong about the original Arminians. Arminius and the first Remonstrants likewise held with
total depravity and its implications in respect to the need for grace.
Arminius himself said:

> In his *lapsed and sinful state*, man is not capable, of and by himself,
> either to think, to will, or to do that which is really good; but it is nec-

---

[1]Richard Watson, *Theological Institutes* (New York: Nelson and Phillips;, 1850), II:48.
[2]See Louis Berkhof, *Systematic Theology* (Grand Rapids: Eerdmans, 1949), 422, for
example.
[3]Paul K. Jewett, *Election and Predestination* (Grand Rapids: Eerdmans, 1985), 17.
[4]John Wesley, *Wesley's Standard Sermons,* ed. Edward H. Sugden (London: Epworth
Press, 1955-56), I:181-182.
[5]Wesley, I:188-189.

essary for him to be regenerated and renewed in his intellect, affections, or will, and in all his powers, by God in Christ through the Holy Spirit, that he may be qualified rightly to understand, esteem, conceive, will, and perform whatever is truly good.[6]

Elsewhere he bitingly reproves any who "think that man can do some portion of good by the powers of nature" as being "not far from Pelagianism."[7] And in yet another place, describing the fallen state, Arminius affirms:

> In this state, the free will of man towards the true good is not only wounded, maimed, infirm, bent, and weakened; but it is also imprisoned, destroyed, and lost. And its powers are not only debilitated and useless unless they be assisted by grace, but it has no powers whatever except such as are excited by Divine grace.[8]

A. Skevington Wood is therefore correct when he observes, "It is obvious that [Arminius'] outlook is to be distinguished from any Pelagian optimism regarding man's inherent capacity to achieve the ideal of goodness."[9] The Arminian Jack Cottrell insists that "the Bible does not picture man as totally depraved" and affirms that man "*is* able to respond to the gospel in faith."[10] I can agree with this in the sense that by *constitution* man has the ability to choose for good or evil. But *practically* speaking, given the seriousness of depravity, man's constitutional nature has been warped and God's grace must work before he can respond to the offer of salvation by faith. Thus while I differ with the implications Calvinists read into total depravity, and it certainly is not a Biblical term, I see no need for Arminians to deny that doctrine. Arminius himself certainly affirmed it.

In the previous chapter I mentioned, in passing, that guilt for the original sin and condemnation as a result both also passed to the entire human race from Adam, according to the Calvinist's view. As there, this matter need not occupy us at length in this chapter. The

---

[6] James Arminius, *The Writings of James Arminius* (three vols.), tr. James Nichols and W. R. Bagnall (Grand Rapids: Baker, 1956), I:252.

[7] Arminius, I:323.

[8] Arminius, I:526.

[9] A. Skevington Wood, "The Declaration of Sentiments: The Theological Testament of Arminius" (*Evangelical Quarterly* 65:2 [1993], 111-129), 123.

[10] Jack Cottrell, "Conditional Election," in *Grace Unlimited,* ed. Clark Pinnock (Minneapolis: Bethany Fellowship, 1975), 68.

subject has no direct bearing, at least, on the question of unregenerate man's ability to respond positively to the gospel offer, or on the
points of the *ordo salutis* at issue here.

It is sufficient to point out, then, that Arminians may well agree
that the guilt and condemnation of "original sin" passed on to the race
along with depravity of nature. True, not all Arminians have said this;
Richard Watson, for example, in his discussion of the results of the
fall, never affirms it, even though he speaks clearly about the depravity and the spiritual death of the human race that resulted from the
fall. Donald Lake emphasizes that Romans 5:12 "does not support the
conception that we are guilty for Adam's sin."[11] But this may well be
another of Lake's distortions of classical Arminianism.

There is every reason to conclude that Arminius himself and the
original Remonstrants taught that not only total depravity and spiritual death but also guilt and condemnation passed to all men from
Adam. The following clearly shows this.

> The whole of this sin [i.e.,"the first sin of the first man"], however, is not
> peculiar to our first parents, but is common to the entire race and to all
> their posterity, who, at the time when this sin was commited, were in
> their loins, and who have since descended from them by the natural
> mode of propagation, according to the primitive benediction. For in
> Adam 'all have sinned.' (Rom. v, 12.) Wherefore, whatever punishment
> was brought down upon our first parents, has likewise pervaded and
> yet pursues all their posterity. So that all men 'are by nature the children
> of wrath,' (Ephes. ii, 3,) obnoxious to condemnation, and to temporal as
> well as eternal death.[12]

Others agree with this conclusion: "Jacob Arminius . . . did, however, accept the basic premise of Augustinian teaching on original sin,
namely, that all of humanity were in Adam's loins when he sinned and
so share in his punishment. All are children of wrath until liberated by
Christ."[13] More than once Arminius affirmed, in no uncertain terms,
that "all men transgressed, in Adam, the law."[14]

---

[11]Donald M. Lake, "He Died for All: The Universal Dimensions of the Atonement," in
Grace Unlimited, ed. Clark Pinnock (Minneapolis: Bethany Fellowship, 1975), 34.

[12]Arminius, I:486.

[13]David L. Smith, *With Willful Intent: A Theology of Sin* (Wheaton, Ill.: Victor Books,
1994), 87.

[14]Arminius, III:178.

So have some other Reformation Arminians. Thomas Grantham, for example, wrote that

> . . . the sin of Mankind is either *Original* or *Actual.* The first is come upon all, even the very Infant State of Mankind lies under it; of whom that saying is true, *Rom. 5. They have not sinned after the similitude of Adam's transgression.* Yet Death reigning over them, proves the Transgression of *Adam* to be upon them.[15]

Again, "I do not deny Original Sin, for I know it is come upon all *Adam's* posterity, and Death passeth upon them, for that all have sinned in him."[16]

If Calvinists have difficulty agreeing among themselves whether this is so by natural or federal headship, we need not press that matter here either. However, I may say that Arminians are much more likely to see this as a result of natural headship. That would certainly appear to be the view of Arminius, as quoted above.

The Role of Pre-regenerating Grace

If for the Calvinist regeneration is the solution to the problem of depravity and inability, for the Arminian the solution is found in what Arminius called "prevenient grace" (or "preventing grace").

The Term

1. "Prevenient" or "preventing" reflect the now archaic English usage to mean *anticipating, going before, preceding.* This usage appears in the King James: for example in 1 Thessalonians 4:15: "we which are alive . . . shall not prevent them which are asleep," which means that we shall not precede them or get ahead of them. Compare Psalm 119:147, "I prevented the dawning of the morning," which means that the psalmist was awake before daybreak.

What Arminius meant by "prevenient grace" was that grace that precedes actual regeneration and which, except when finally resisted, inevitably leads on to regeneration. He was quick to observe that this "assistance of the Holy Spirit" is of such sufficiency "as to keep at the greatest possible distance from Pelagianism."[17]

---

[15]Thomas Grantham, *Christianismus Primitivus, or the Ancient Christian Religion* (London, 1678), II:76, 77 (italics his); cited by Matthew Pinson, "The Diversity of Arminian Soteriology" (unpublished paper), 4.

[16]Thomas Grantham, *The Controversie about Infants Church-Membership and Baptism, Epitomized in Two Treatises* (London, 1680), 14; cited by Pinson, 5.

[17]Arminius, I:300.

2. Given that this is an archaic usage, it will be far better if we call this by some other name. I have sometimes called it *enabling grace*, which aptly reflects its effects; but I equally like *pre-regenerating grace* and will usually use this term. This wording has the distinct advantage of closely connecting this work of the Holy Spirit with regeneration itself, where it belongs.

The Concept of Pre-regenerating Grace

1. By definition, pre-regenerating grace is that work of the Holy Spirit that "opens the heart" of the unregenerate (to use the words of Acts 16:14) to the truth of the gospel and enables them to respond positively in faith. Emphasizing this work is the theological "move," shall we say, that makes it possible for Arminians to insist, in all truthfulness, that "*in every case it is God who takes the initiative in salvation* and calls men to him, and works in their hearts by his Spirit . . . nor can anybody be saved without first being called by God."[18]

2. Theologically, this concept meets the need of the totally depraved sinner. As already acknowledged, the unregenerate person is totally unable to respond positively, by his natural will, to the offer of salvation contained in the gospel. Pre-regenerating grace simply means that the Spirit of God overcomes that inability by a direct work on the heart, a work that is adequate to enable the yet unregenerate person to understand the truth of the gospel, to desire God, and to exercise saving faith. As Arminius expressed it, when answering whether God can require faith from fallen man, man "cannot have [faith] of himself," and God can require it only because "he has determined to bestow on man sufficient grace by which he may believe."[19] Again, "It is very plain, from the Scriptures, that repentance and faith can not be exercised except by the gift of God. But the same Scripture and the nature of both gifts very clearly teaches that this bestowment is by the mode of persuasion."[20]

3. Scripturally, this concept is intended to express the truth found in passages like John 6:44: "No man can come to me, except the Father which hath sent me draw him." In this light, pre-regenerating grace may be called *drawing*. Or Acts 16:14: "Lydia . . . whose heart the Lord

---

[18] I. Howard Marshall, "Predestination in the New Testament," in *Grace Unlimited*, ed. Clark Pinnock (Minneapolis: Bethany Fellowship, 1975), 140.

[19] Arminius, I:383.

[20] Arminius, III:334.

opened, that she attended unto the things which were spoken of Paul": pre-regenerating grace may therefore be called *opening the heart.* Or John 16:8: "When [the Spirit] is come, he will reprove [or, convict] the world of sin, and of righteousness, and of judgment." In this sense, pre-regenerating grace may be called *conviction*—which is simply another form of the word "convincement."

The Elements of Pre-regenerating Grace

1. Conviction. As noted above, this means that the Spirit convinces the unregenerate person of the truth of the gospel. If the minds of the unregenerate are blinded (2 Corinthians 4:4) to the truth, this convincing work opens their eyes to see and understand it—essentially the same as "opening the heart" mentioned above, which let Lydia "attend" to the things she heard. This way the depraved sinner, otherwise unconvinced of any of this, is convinced of his sins and guilt, of his condemnation, of the fact that God's way is right, and of the fact that Christ has provided redemption for him if he will but accept the gift of God in faith.

2. Persuasion. While this word may not add much to what has been expressed as conviction, my purpose for using it is to emphasize that the conviction is not a merely sterile, intellectual convincement. The Spirit makes the truth appealing to the sinner. It draws him, woos him, puts the "bite" into conviction: "persuading the human will that it may be inclined to yield assent to those truths which are preached."[21] "By the internal persuasion of the Holy Spirit . . . He effects faith and binds Himself to give salvation to the believer."[22]

3. Enabling. It may also not be necessary to add this to conviction. Even so, there is a point to be made. By this gracious, pre-regenerating work, the Spirit enables the otherwise unable person to receive Christ by faith. For that matter, given that it is the blindness of a closed heart that prevents the depraved person from receiving the gospel offer in the first place, conviction of its truth may be all the enabling required. Or there may be a further work on the heart of the sinner required to effect this; we cannot fully explain all the mysterious workings of God's Spirit on the heart, for we do not understand all that well just how the understanding and will operate. Whatever is required, the Spirit makes saving faith possible.

---

[21]Arminius, I:301.
[22]Arminius, III:324.

Other Points About Pre-regenerating Grace

1. It is entirely gracious. Since there is nothing good in the depraved nature, the depraved person can do nothing to merit this work of grace. Arminius always insisted that he and his companions never excluded grace from the commencement of conversion, that they made this grace "to precede, to accompany, and to follow" salvation, and that without it "no good action whatever, can be produced by men."[23] Wood correctly insists that "[Arminius'] stress on prevenient, redeeming, and preserving grace makes it abundantly clear that it is on the basis of God's work in them and not their own that believers are elected."[24] William McDonald is both characterizing this kind of Arminianism and agreeing when he says, "God initiates and consummates the experience. He calls faith forth and graciously answers faith with the Spirit delivered within."[25]

2. It preserves the personal nature of God's dealings with men. As I have indicated in chapter 3, since God and men are both personal, this means that God deals with men in the mode of influence and response, not cause and effect. The latter is the mode of operation of machines, not persons.

3. It is so closely related to regeneration that it inevitably leads on to regeneration unless finally resisted. In this way the older divines spoke of "the motions of regeneration" and in so doing referred to the movements that initiate (but are not quite) regeneration. Thus Arminius referred to persons who "feel those motions of the Holy Spirit which belong either to preparation or to the very essence of regeneration, but who are not yet regenerate."[26]

4. It makes faith possible without making it necessary. In other words, it does not by itself guarantee the conversion of the sinner. While Calvinists would probably not discount any of the elements of pre-regenerating grace I have listed above (albeit perhaps including them in regeneration proper), the point of departure between Calvinists and Arminians here is simply this: Calvinists believe this work is performed only for the elect and that it is necessarily effectual; Arminians believe that this gracious work is performed for the elect and non-elect alike. Some who experience this pre-regenerating grace believe and are saved; others are brought to exactly the same

---

[23] Arminius, I:328.

[24] Wood, 122.

[25] William G. McDonald, "'. . . The Spirit of Grace' (Heb. 10:29)," in *Grace Unlimited,* ed. Clark Pinnock (Minneapolis: Bethany Fellowship, 1975), 84.

[26] Arminius, I:325.

point of possibility but reject the gospel and perish forever. To quote McDonald again, "One without God sleeps in the death of his sins, but when God's call awakens him, he can respond in faith, or he can resist the Spirit and go back to sleep in death."[27]

Arminius speaks of the persuasion wrought by this pre-regenerating grace as being two-fold. It is "sufficient" for all who experience it, in that "he, with whom it is employed, is able to consent, believe, and be converted." But it is "efficacious" only in the case of the one who "does consent and believe, and is converted."[28] In another place he strongly resists the confusion of the two and observes, "When God knocks, it is certain that the man can open, and consequently he has sufficient grace," supporting the argument of Bellarmine in referring to some who resisted God's grace in spite of the fact that "They had grace sufficient to enable them not to resist and even to yield to the Holy Spirit."[29] Thus Carl Bangs, for all his expertise on Arminius, is not quite accurate when he interprets Arminius to mean "Only he who does believe can believe."[30] In this he seems to be reading Arminius through Barthian eyes. His self-contradiction is evident when he acknowledges that Arminius taught that the unbeliever *refuses* God's saving grace. Arminius would have said, and did, that if one cannot believe he cannot refuse.[31]

5. It serves, by enabling, to reverse that much the bondage of the will. In accomplishing that, pre-regenerating grace preserves the basis on which God chooses to deal with men for salvation: namely, by their free choice. God desires that men freely and personally choose to submit to Him or rebel against Him. That is the way He has ordained for men, in His image, to act. Pre-regenerating grace, which enables the otherwise bound person to make that choice, serves therefore to uphold this method of dealing with men.

I pause just long enough to comment on "in His image." The possibility of faith, even though by the work of pre-regenerating grace, is found in the fact that man was created in the image of God. Gordon Clark—good Calvinist he—has it right when he observes that this "image of God" (which he stresses man *is*, not *has*) "was not destroyed by the fall."[32] In the image of God, man is personal and

---

[27]McDonald, 87.

[28]Arminius, III:335.

[29]Arminius, III:520, 521.

[30]Carl Bangs, Arminius: *A Study in the Dutch Reformation* (Nashville: Abingdon, 1971), 343.

[31]See Arminius, III:520, 521.

[32]Gordon Clark, *Faith and Saving Faith* (Jefferson, Md.: The Trinity Foundation, 1983), 113.

rational, severely affected by the fall but not destroyed. And so, once he understands truth—here by pre-regenerating grace—man can personally give assent to that truth. And in that assent is saving faith. But he can likewise personally reject that truth. And in that rejection is willful unbelief.

6. It requires the hearing of the gospel. Consequently this work of pre-regenerating grace is not *immediate* in the absolute sense, even though it is performed *directly* on the heart. But the Word is the instrument, the means used by the Spirit as a basis for the conviction, the persuasion, and the enabling. This observation accords with the concept of the power of the Word of God spoken of everywhere in the Scriptures, as in Hebrews 4:12 for example. Arminius' view on this is clear when, speaking of the persuasion involved in this pre-regenerating grace, he says, "This is effected by the word of God. But persuasion is effected, externally by the preaching of the word, internally by the operation, or rather the co-operation, of the Holy Spirit, tending to this result, that the word may be understood and apprehended by true faith."[33]

Apparently, this pre-regenerating grace is co-extensive with the intelligent hearing of the gospel. That much seems clear. But when we come to try to explain why some, when hearing the gospel, give more evidence of this conviction than others, we are not always able. Nor are we able to explain completely why the gospel is being preached to some and not to others. God has his reasons which we do not always perceive. I will not pursue this matter here.[34]

Calling and Pre-regenerating Grace

Given the nature of the description above, I am inclined to think that *calling* means essentially the same thing as pre-regenerating grace. This identification has several advantages.

• It serves to emphasize that salvation is always at the initiative of God, not man.

• It serves to make the call as universal as the gospel.

• It avoids the unhelpful distinction of the Calvinist between a sterile *external* call to the non-elect and an effective *internal* call to the elect. God's Spirit powerfully calls the non-elect by the gospel, even if they resist to their everlasting damnation.

---

[33] Arminius, III:334.
[34] Arminius, III:524, 525 has some helpful observations along these lines.

• It does not necessarily rule out a distinction between the call that is effective (or, efficacious) and the call that is not. But if we wish to maintain that distinction—and it seems helpful—it means that the final difference between the effective call and the one that is not is to be found in the free response of the one called. When the sinner, enabled by pre-regenerating grace, responds in repentance and faith, the call is thereby effective. But God has done no less—up to that point—for the person who determines to resist; the call is thereby not effective, although not for want of the Spirit's work.

I have already noted Arminius' distinction between the sufficiency of this pre-regenerating grace for some and its efficacy for others: "God uses many acts of His providence towards those, who are not predestinated, sufficient, indeed, for salvation, yet not efficacious."[35] Again he observes that "they are without excuse, who are all called by sufficient grace to repentance and faith."[36]

Arminius used essentially the same words when speaking of "vocation" as when speaking of "prevenient grace." Of the former he said, "This vocation is both external and internal," external in the proclamation of the word and internal by "the operation of the Holy Spirit illuminating and affecting the heart, that attention may be paid to those things which are spoken, and that credence may be given to the word."[37] Further, "Internal vocation is granted even to those who do not comply with the call. . . . In the very commencement of his conversion, man conducts himself in a purely passive manner; that is . . . he can do no other than receive it and feel it. But, when he feels grace affecting or inclining his mind and heart, he freely assents to it, so that he is able at the same time to withhold his assent."[38]

The Order of Salvation

Arminians have not been as concerned as Calvinistic theologians to provide a detailed *ordo salutis* or order of salvation. There is no good reason to avoid such a discussion, however. From what has already been indicated above, one can see that the Arminian order will be different:

---

[35]Arminius, III:276.
[36]Arminius, III:336.
[37]Arminius, II:105.
[38]Arminius, II:497-499. The entire section is instructive.

> calling = pre-regenerating grace
> conversion, including:
>   a. repentance
>   b. faith
> justification
> regeneration
> sanctification

Except that the Arminian will be unlikely to think it makes a great deal of difference which is logically first: justification or regeneration. We should probably insist that sanctification—even *initial* sanctification—is grounded in justification.

I have included pre-regenerating grace since, even though it does not *guarantee* the application of salvation (and is therefore technically distinct) it is *required* for it.

The logic of this arrangement is just as significant for Arminianism as that in the previous chapter for Calvinism. Especially important is the fact that this order makes salvation *conditional*. In other words, salvation is *by* faith rather than *to* faith. I will return to this matter below.

Furthermore, this *ordo salutis* allows no separation in time between conversion, justification, regeneration, and initial sanctification. They are *always* simultaneous. There is no possibility that one may receive regeneration and not be converted until later (or never) as in Calvinism. Nor is there any salvation apart from the Word.[39]

The Nature of Saving Faith

In the chapter to follow, I will treat the role of faith in the New Testament in considerable detail, pursuing several questions related to the nature of saving faith. For now, then, I will simply state some important observations about saving faith.

I affirm that according to Scripture salvation is by faith. The Calvinist, equally committed to being Scriptural, must repond that my "faith," however, is really a "work," and that therefore I am really affirming salvation by works. It is not enough, therefore, to discuss

---

[39]There are other facets of the salvation experience that can be included in the "order," including union with Christ, adoption, etc. It is beyond the scope of this work to pursue those details. For some of Arminius' observations about the order, see II:111ff, 229; III:18.

where faith belongs in the *ordo salutis*. One must also make sure that his understanding of the nature of faith is Scriptural.

To put this in the form of a question: If faith is a condition that *man* must meet in order to be saved, does that make salvation partly the work of man? Does faith, so conceived, become something man *does* (a "work") that in some way *merits* salvation? Berkhof thinks so: "The Arminians revealed a Romanizing tendency, when they conceived of faith as a meritorious work of man, on the basis of which he is accepted in favor by God."[40]

I will not attempt to justify all Arminians from such a charge; some appear to deserve it. Lake, for example, comes much too close to this when he approvingly quotes Paul Tillich's claim that "justification by faith means the acceptance of our acceptance."[41] But I will stoutly deny that I conceive faith in such a way, or that Arminius and the original Remonstrants did. It remains, however, for me to *demonstrate* that my denial is more than mere words.

Salvation by Faith, by Grace, and by Works

1. That salvation is by God's grace and not by man's works is a conclusion justly drawn from Scripture. It has stood the test of time, and not only among churches directly in what is called the Reformed tradition. This is so much the case that one must regard this dogma as essential to the Christian faith and the gospel. Arminius was often at pains to deny that faith results from our own strength, and to affirm that it is "produced in us by the free gift of God."[42] He avowed, "I ascribe to grace *the commencement, the continuance and the consummation of all good,* and to such an extent do I carry its influence, that a man, though already regenerate, can neither conceive, will, nor do any good at all."[43] (The contribution of passages like Romans 3:20—4:25; 9:30—10:13; Galatians 2:16; 3:2, 5; Ephesians 2:8, 9; and Philippians 3:9 to this will be discussed in the next chapter.)

2. Corollary to this, then, is this disjunction: "by faith" and "by works" are mutually exclusive—logically and Scripturally. "Faith" (rightly—that is, Scripturally—conceived) is not "works" and "works" is not "faith." The two words are not synonyms. Furthermore, in the very same passages that make this clear, it is clear that faith *as a condition* (not as a result) is being discussed: salvation *by* faith stands in

---

[40]Berkhof, 497.
[41]Lake, 44.
[42]Arminius, III:315.
[43]Arminius, I:253.

contrast to salvation *by* works. It would make no sense to contrast salvation *to* faith with salvation *by* works.

3. The Bible links salvation by faith and salvation by grace as com-
plementary. We do not have to rely on logical syllogisms for this: Paul
makes it plain in passages like Ephesians 2:8, 9; Romans 4:2-5; 10:3;
and especially Romans 4:16. (Again, see the following chapter for
detail.) Important then: so long as one means what the Bible means
by faith, salvation by faith is in perfect harmony with salvation by
grace, and precisely contradictory to salvation by works.

4. The nature of saving faith is such that it carries absolutely no
merit for the person thus believing. Biblically, faith stands in antithesis to works. The believer therefore gets no credit for faith; he is not
rewarded for believing. Faith is nothing more (or less) than *receiving
a gift*. It is therefore quite the opposite of earning, meriting, or deserving it. One may illustrate very simply: When I offer someone a gift, the
receiving carries no connotation of credit. Arminius may have had
something like this in mind when he emphasized that faith is not so
much the *instrument* (apparently, as a thing or quality) of justification
as an *act* which apprehends Christ on whose account righteousness
is imputed to the one believing.[44] Thus Wood is correct in concluding
that "What we have [in Arminius], however, is not a form of synergism
in which God's work and man's work cooperate, but rather a relationship in which God's will and work within man is [sic] welcomed in
an attitude of trust and submission."[45]

J. I. Packer insists, "Faith is a matter first and foremost of looking
outside and away from oneself to Christ and his cross as the sole
ground of present forgiveness and future hope."[46] Precisely! And so
long as faith is looking away from oneself to Christ for salvation, it is
by nature the opposite of merit. Faith is the holding out of *empty* hands
to God. It is saying, "I cannot save myself. I renounce all my vain efforts
and look to Him who gives salvation freely in Christ. I can do nothing,
and so I receive salvation from Him as a gift of grace." Faith is giving
up on one's works and submitting to the working of God.

5. Faith is, however, the personal attitude of the individual, reflecting that person's mind and will. Faith means that the person is believing, not that God (or Christ) is believing for him. Any number of New
Testament references to faith will confirm this:

---

[44]Arminius, I:363, 364.

[45]Wood, 124.

[46]J. I. Packer, *What Did the Cross Achieve?* (Theological Students Fellowship, n.d.,
booklet reprinted from Tyndale Bulletin 25 [1974]), 30.

Galatians 2:16	*We believed* in Jesus Christ in order to be justified.
Romans 4:3	*Abraham believed* in God and was reckoned righteous.
Romans 4:5	To the *one believing, his faith* is counted for righteousness.
Romans 4:24	is imputed . . . to *us who are believing.*
John 3:16	*Everyone who is believing* in Him has eternal life.
Luke 7:50	*Your faith* has saved you.
Romans 10:10	With the heart *one believes* unto righteousness.

Such a list might be extended indefinitely. Faith is personal, and the person who is regarded as believing is the human being exercising faith. Faith is not a "thing" possessed (on which merit might be grounded) but it is an active disposition of the mind and will that can be attributed to the person believing and to no one else—not even to God in that sense (see below). That human beings are persons, not machines, implies this. More important, the Scriptural language leaves us with no other choice.

For those needing it, I add that this is not changed by those passages that speak of "the faith *of* Jesus Christ," for example; Galatians 2:16 is the best of these—compare verse 20. In all such verses, the context makes clear that the Greek genitive, "of Jesus Christ," is being used objectively to mean the faith that has Him for its object. In Galatians 2:16 there can be no doubt: the subsequent statement "We put faith—a Greek aorist verb—in Christ" is deliberately made parallel to and explanatory of "the faith of Christ." Compare Mark 11:22, literally, "Have faith of God."

6. Is faith itself "counted" by God as though it were righteousness? In light of Romans 4:3-5 one hesitates to say No. Even so, in light of the rest of the New Testament, which so clearly eliminates all grounds for man to boast in salvation and attributes it wholly to the grace of God, I am satisfied that we must *not* say that "faith" is somehow looked at in such a way by God that He takes it as a substitute for and calls it righteousness.

Since I am confident that the Calvinist will agree that this is so, I will give but the briefest attention to Romans 4:3-5. My understanding of the former verse is that the Greek preposition *eis* is what we call the "predicate" use, serving as little more than a word carrier. In effect, then, the verse finally says, Abraham believed (put faith) in

God and righteousness was reckoned his. While faith thus clearly has a *conditional* role, faith itself is not counted to be righteousness by some equation. Verse 5 is not so easy, saying directly: "His faith is counted for (or, as) righteousness." I would suggest that Paul is using the kind of language short-cut we all use at times and means— expressed more fully—that God reckons a person's faith as, conditionally, the occasion (or means or instrument) for imputing the righteousness of Christ to him.

Arminius' own observations seem to parallel mine. After a somewhat confusing analysis—including a reference to things he himself had previously indicated, "not in a rigid manner," relative to Romans 4:3-5—he concludes:

> I believe that sinners are accounted righteous solely by the obedience of Christ; and that the righteousness of Christ is the only meritorious cause on account of which God pardons the sins of believers and reckons them as righteous as if they had perfectly fulfilled the law. But since God imputes the righteousness of Christ to none except believers, I conclude that, in this sense, it may be well and properly said, *To a man who believes, Faith is imputed for righteousness through grace,* because God has set forth his Son, Jesus Christ, to be a propitiation . . . through faith in his blood.[47]

Watson speaks in a similar vein:

> It is not quite correct . . . to say, that our faith in Christ is accepted in the place of personal obedience to the law, except, indeed, in this loose sense, that our faith in Christ as effectually exempts us from punishment, as if we had been personally obedient. The Scriptural doctrine is rather, that the death of Christ is accepted in the place of our personal punishment, on condition of our faith in him; and, that when faith in him is actually exerted, then comes in, on the part of God, the act of imputing, or reckoning righteousness to us; or, what is the same thing, accounting faith for righteousness, that is, pardoning our offences through faith, and treating us as the objects of his restored favor.[48]

---

[47]Arminius, I:264. Compare II:474 where he speaks in a similarly circuitous vein, that "faith is imputed to us for righteousness, on account of Christ and his righteousness. In this enunciation, faith is the object of imputation; but Christ and his obedience are the . . . meritorious cause of justification."

[48]Watson, II:242.

In other words, then, it can only indirectly and as a kind of short-hand be said that faith is counted for righteousness. And were it not for Romans 4:5, I would not say even that.

Faith as "the Gift of God"

Is faith, *per se*, the gift of God? In the previous chapter we have seen that Calvinism answers this question yes. Faith, as a gift, flows from regeneration when the seed of faith is implanted in the heart. We should not overlook, then, that this contradicts the concept of salvation by faith. Justification, as one part of the *ordo salutis* is by faith, but even that faith has been given as a gift that is a part of the larger province of the word "salvation." Thus salvation, at least regeneration, is *to*, not *by* faith, in the Calvinistic system. The implications of this will be the subject of inquiry in the next chapter.

Meanwhile, the idea that saving faith is the gift of God is essential to this way of thinking, and that is the question that needs resolving.

• *Scriptural evidence.* Only a few passages might be used to indicate that saving faith is the gift of God.

First Corinthians 12:9 lists faith as one of the gifts of the Spirit. But this is not saving faith. Instead, this "faith" is one of the *charismata* given to those who are already Christians. Furthermore, this particular gift of faith is given only to *some* Christians in the distribution of the gifts of the Spirit.

Galatians 5:22, 23 presents a similar situation. There faith appears among the nine-fold "fruit of the Spirit." Again, this cannot be saving faith since these are fruit produced in the lives of Christians. Indeed, many interpreters understand "faith" to mean *faithfulness* in this list, but we need not explore that matter here.

Ephesians 2:8, 9 is therefore the key passage: "*For by grace* [instrumental case, *tē chariti*, by the instrumentality of grace] *you have been saved* [periphrastic perfect, looking at the present condition that flows from the prior act] *through faith* [*dia* plus the genitive, intermediate agency]; *and this* [neuter *touto*] *not of you, the gift of God; not of works, in order that one may not boast.*

There are two reasons, one grammatical and one syntactical, for insisting that "this" does not refer back to "faith." Grammatically, "faith" is feminine and "this" is neuter. Only an unnatural stretching of the possibilities of Greek grammar can read "faith" as the antecedent of "this."

Syntactically, the fact (often overlooked) is that there are three complements of "this" which follow it:

(1) "this" (is) not of you,

(2) "this" (is) God's gift,

(3) "this" (is) not of works, lest anyone boast.

To read "faith" with "this" *might* make some kind of sense for the first two of these, but it will not work with the third: "this faith is not of works" would be nonsensical tautology in view of the fact that works is in contrast to faith already.

In Ephesians 2:8, 9, therefore, "this" has for its antecedent the entire preceding clause. This fits the "rules" of Greek grammar that called for a neuter pronoun to refer to a verbal idea, and it makes perfectly good sense in the context. "By grace you have been saved by faith: and this saving experience is not of you but is the gift of God, not of works lest any boast."

The Question of Meaning

What would it mean for saving faith to be the gift of God anyway? Would it mean that God, or Jesus, does the believing for the individual? We have seen already that this will not work.

Would it mean then that God's Spirit, internally, *makes* the person into a believer? Something like that, no doubt: God works believing within him against his will to disbelieve. By His own power (force?) He produces within him a frame of mind, a heart and will, that he did not have before. If we may use a "mechanical" analogy (which must inevitably fall short, of course), we may say that God "turns on" a "switch" that was "off."

Regardless how we express it, since faith is an attitude (or, disposition) or activity of the human person's mind and will, then to say that faith is the gift of God must mean that He, by supernatural intervention, directly (and without cooperation since up to the point of faith the person is a hostile unbeliever) produces the person's faith. He "turns" the person into a believer. (Or else, in the mind-set of Calvinism, the person will receive some kind of "credit" for doing the believing.) Frankly, this viewpoint utterly fails to take account of the pervasive Scriptural presentation that "blames" each unbeliever who hears for his unbelief and presents the believer as the one likewise responsible for the believing.

A word about the nature of saving faith is in order here. I have already, in discussing pre-regenerating grace, indicated that this work of the Spirit, using the Word, opens the closed heart of the sinner to the truth of the gospel in a persuasive and enabling way. Given his depravity, that work is absolutely necessary and must precede any positive disposition on the sinner's part. At that point, the sinner recognizes truth as truth. But saving faith is more than mere intellectual persuasion or convincement of truth. It requires a "decision," a positive commitment, a willful entrusting of one's circumstances and destiny into the hands of God in Christ. That is the act of the person, not of God, and that is the reason the Scriptures unanimously represent the person as responsible for faith or unbelief.

Faith as the Gift of God

Arminius freely represented faith as the gift of God and magnified the "acts of Divine grace" that "are required to produce faith in man."[49] He lists the divine decrees thus: "(1) It is my will to save believers. (2) On this man I will bestow faith and preserve him in it. (3) I will save this man." (Subsequently, he clarifies "bestow faith" as "administer the means for faith.")[50] In spite of all I have said above, then, I do not finally object to saying that faith is the gift of God.

But if that terminology is to be used, one must clarify exactly what it means, as follows:

1. The *capacity* to believe is from God.
2. The *possibility* of believing is from God.
3. The *content* of belief—the gospel truth—is from God.
4. The *persuasion* of truth which one believes is from God.
5. The *enabling* of the individual to believe is from God.

But the believing itself can finally be done by no one other than the person who is called on to believe the gospel, and that will to believe savingly is the free decision of the individual. If calling faith "the gift of God" is meant to depreciate that, then I must deny the terminology. Since it is not Biblical terminology in the first place, perhaps it is best to discard it.

Had it been important to indicate that salvation is to faith, that faith itself is part of the effects of salvation rather than a condition for salvation, one can think of numbers of ways the New Testament writers, and Jesus Himself, might have expressed that. Instead, as I hope to show in the following chapter, the New Testament everywhere presents faith as the condition for salvation that man must meet.

---

[49]Arminius, I:366.
[50]Arminius, I:387.

For Further Reading About the Arminian View
of the Application of Salvation

Arminius, James. *The Writings of James Arminius* (three vols.), tr. James Nichols and W. R. Bagnall. Grand Rapids: Baker, 1956 (vol. I, pp. 523-531).

Cox, Leo G. "Prevenient Grace, A Wesleyan View." *Journal of the Evangelical Theological Society*, 11:3 [1969] (pp. 143-149).

Forlines, F. Leroy. *Systematics.* Nasvhille: Randall House Publications, 1975 (pp. 149-173). [A colleague of this writer]

Miley, John. *Systematic Theology.* New York: Methodist Book Concern, 1892, 94 (vol. I, pp. 441-533; vol. II, pp. 241-253, 308-338, 505-524). [Later Arminianism as represented in Methodism]

Pope, W. B. *Compendium of Christian Theology.* Wesleyan-Methodist Book-Room, 1880 (vol. II, pp. 47-71, 358-385, 407-418).

Watson, Richard. *Theological Institutes.* New York: Nelson and Phillips, 1850 (vol. II, pp. 43-87, 207-283). [An important, early Wesleyan theologian]

CHAPTER TEN

The New Testament and Salvation By Faith

Once the Arminian agrees with the Calvinist about total depravity, the main issue remaining, in this section, is the conditionality of salvation. The issue reduces to the question, Is salvation by faith? Only a thoroughly "Biblical theology" answer will suffice.

Introduction: The Nature of the Question

Many Christians—at the "popular" level, anyway—would be surprised to find that there is a question whether salvation is by faith. In order to keep the introduction brief, I offer here the barest outline as to how the question arises. The previous chapters should have provided the detail.

Reflecting the logical consistency of Calvinism, many theologians would object to a simplistic statement that salvation is by faith. (1) Since election is unconditional (and must be so for God to be sovereign), it follows that salvation—in the broadest sense of the word—rests in the decree of God and not on the individual's faith. (2) Since the atonement was intended to save only the elect and is applied efficaciously to them by the gracious work of the Holy Spirit, it follows that salvation—still in the broad sense—is by atonement and grace rather than by faith. (3) Since man's depravity is so total that he is utterly dead and unable to respond to the gospel until regenerated, it follows that salvation—still the broad sense—is *to* faith rather than *by* faith.

If all this is true, can it be said that salvation is by faith? In a sense, yes: even the thoroughly committed Calvinist will insist that the words are legitimate. But in that case "salvation" is being used in a narrower sense. The Scripture is clear, and so is the Calvinist, that justification is by faith. As important and central as justification is, the word "salvation" is often used, by synecdoche, as though it were a synonym for justification. In that narrow sense, then, it can be said that salvation (justification) is by faith. In fact, however, "salvation" means more than justification. And when it is used in its fullest sense, it is essentially equal to *election*. We should make no mistake about this: if election is not by faith, then neither is salvation.

This must be understood, then, in the light of the Calvinist's *ordo salutis* discussed in chapter 8: (1) Regeneration is logically first.

(2) Following therefrom, conversion involves repentance and faith as gifts of God to the regenerate. (3) Justification, then, is a forensic action conditioned upon faith, which was itself the fruit of God's saving work of regeneration.

One can readily see, then, that "salvation" in its fullest sense includes regeneration, conversion, and justification (more, too, but this is adequate for now). None of this would be possible apart from regeneration, with all the rest growing out of that. Regeneration is not by faith, therefore salvation is not by faith. As Berkhof expresses it, "The seed of faith is implanted in man in regeneration. . . . It is only after God has implanted the seed of faith in the heart that man can exercise faith."[1]

Enough has been said to show why the question exists and the basic issues that are implicit in it. Once more, then: Is salvation by faith? What is the Biblically correct way to use the words?

The Meaning of "Salvation" When Conditioned on Faith

All parties agree that justification is by faith and that therefore it would be correct to say that "salvation" is by faith at least as a synecdoche; that is, if "salvation" is used in the narrow sense as a synonym for justification, then salvation is by faith.

The question, therefore, is whether the Bible connects "by faith" only with justification (or with "salvation" used in this narrow sense) or with "salvation" in the broad sense of the word as including regeneration or other aspects of the application of redemption to the individual. To put it another way, what exactly is it that the Bible says happens "by faith"?

The answer, based on a thorough examination of all New Testament passages that present faith as a condition, is that "by faith" is not limited to justification. Here are only some of the more important passages.

• Several passages present *the reception of the Holy Spirit* as "by faith."

1. Galatians 3 provides a good example. In verse 2 Paul makes clear (albeit by a rhetorical question) that the Galatians "received the Spirit by the hearing of faith." Verse 5 looks at this same fact from the apostle's side: he "ministered the Spirit" to them "by the hearing of faith."

---

[1]Louis Berkhof, *Systematic Theology* (Grand Rapids: Eerdmans, 1949), 503.

The "hearing" in this phrase looks at the dynamics involved in the preacher-listener encounter. Paul preached faith as the means of receiving the Spirit; they heard faith preached thus; they did just what they heard Paul say they should do and responded in faith.

This is equivalent, then, to saying that they received the Spirit "by faith" (*ek* with the ablative). Obviously this is not, by any figure of speech, as narrow as justification.

Verse 14 adds confirmation that Paul is describing what happens when one becomes a Christian: "in order that we might receive the promise of the Spirit through faith" (*dia* with the genitive). *Pneumatos*, here, is probably an appositional genitive; to render "the promised Spirit" is to say about the same thing. The point is that "the promise," in the New Testament, is often a technical term for the reception of the Holy Spirit; see Luke 24:49; Acts 1:4 (compare 11:15-18); 2:33, 38, 39; Ephesians 1:13 (where "the Holy Spirit of promise" is essentially equivalent to "the promise of the Spirit").

2. John 7:39 should perhaps be included here: "He said this about the Spirit, whom they who believed (aorist: put faith) in Him were about to receive." In view of the "dispensational" questions raised in interpreting this verse, too much need not be made of it. Even so, it appears to support the conclusion that faith is the condition for receiving the Spirit.

3. Ephesians 1:13 should certainly be included; it presents the same dynamics that were noted in Galatians 3. The order is: they heard the gospel, they responded by placing faith (aorist again) in Christ, they were "sealed" with the promised Spirit. The grammatical relationship between the response of faith and the sealing is tight: literally, "believing, you were sealed."

4. Peter's report on the events at Cornelius' house makes the same basic point: God gave to the Gentiles there the Holy Spirit, just as He did to Peter and the others in Jerusalem, when they put faith (aorist again) in the Lord Jesus Christ (Acts 11:17). There is room for doubt whether the participle "believing" (*pisteusasin*) modifies the "us" or the "them"—or both; either way, the point is the same and the grammatical connection is another tight one: "God gave to them as to us believing."

5. In Acts 15:7-9, at the Jerusalem Council, Peter recalls this same matter. Once again, precisely the same order is set forth as that found in Paul's treatment in Galatians 3 and Ephesians 1: Peter spoke, the Gentiles heard, they believed (still another aorist), and God gave them the Holy Spirit. Only here Peter adds another element as

explicative of what happened at the same moment: "(thus) purifying their hearts by faith" (using the instrumental-dative). We may understand "purifying their hearts" as a pregnant equivalent to the giving of the Spirit, or as an added element indicating the results—the cleansing work performed by the Spirit upon His reception. Either way (and the difference is not great), the meaning is certainly not the equivalent of justification in particular. The possession of the Spirit of life as salvation is meant.

• Some passages present *being sons/children of God* as "by faith."

1. As above, Galatians is a good place to start. In 3:26 we read that "you all are sons (*huioi*) of God by faith (*dia* with the genitive) in Christ Jesus." Obviously this is not "mere" justification but our relationship to God as full-fledged sons—adoption, in other words. The context of the passage makes this even clearer.

2. John 1:12 indicates essentially the same truth: becoming "children of God" is conditioned on faith, explained both as "believing in His name" and as "receiving Him." Here "children" is *tekna,* but it may be argued that the Johannine *teknon* is not radically different from the Pauline *huios.* If there is meant to be a difference, the *teknon* may refer to regeneration while the *huios* refers to adoption. Regardless, justification is certainly not in view.

3. First John 5:1 might be treated under a separate heading, but may as well be mentioned here: "Everyone who has faith that Jesus is the Christ has been born/begotten of God." It would be possible, of course, to take the faith here as a result, an identifying characteristic of those who have been regenerated; but that is not the most natural reading of the words. If, as seems more likely, the being born is seen as the result of the believing, then the point is that the new birth (regeneration), by which one becomes a child of God, is by faith.

• Some passages indicate that *resurrection from spiritual death* is "by faith."

1. Colossians 2:12 is one of these. Here the Christian is identified as one dead, buried, and raised to new life with Christ, as demonstrated in baptism and accomplished by the "inworking" of the God who raised Christ from the dead. Even so, this is said to have been "by faith" (*dia* with the genitive), and it is certainly not justification as such. This resurrection is, I would assume, regeneration. If not directly that, then union with Christ is directly involved and regeneration is implicit.

2. John 5:24 should be included under this heading, as well as under the one to follow. And now we see John (in the words of Jesus, of course) setting forth the same order that Paul and Peter (see above) have set forth: the spoken word, hearing, faith, and then: "has passed out of death into life." Without doubt, this is spiritual regeneration, resurrection from spiritual death, and it is specifically declared to follow faith.

3. We might treat John 12:46 as having the same meaning, even though spiritual darkness is the precise metaphor (rather than spiritual death). Using the aorist subjunctive with *hina*, in a clause of (realized) purpose, Jesus indicates that everyone with faith in Him no longer abides in spiritual darkness. Faith is the condition, and on that condition one has passed into the light—another way of saying the same thing as having passed from death to life. I do not see how anyone can doubt that regeneration (rather than justification, specifically) is meant.

• A number of passages state that *possession of eternal life* is "by faith."

1. Among these, in the Gospel of John, are John 3:36 and 6:40, 47. I suppose one might argue that possessing eternal life, in these verses, is—by a figure of speech—a "judicial" matter, rooted in justification. It seems far more likely to me that having eternal life, which is obviously more than a promise for the future but a present possession, is rooted in regeneration.

2. Consider also 1 Timothy 1:16: Paul regards his own experience as a pattern for anyone who will "believe in Him unto eternal life." Logically, in the *ordo salutis*, one has eternal life from the moment of regeneration.

• Finally, there are a number of passages that make *salvation* "by faith." These will not help decide the point of this chapter if they are using the word in the narrow sense as equivalent to justification. But if in fact—as seems the case—the context of these verses is such as to show that "salvation" is being used in the broader sense (inclusive of aspects of the *ordo salutis* other than justification), they will help.

1. Acts 16:31, for example, will probably not help us. The Philippian jailor is told, in response to his question, "Put faith (aorist) in the Lord Jesus and you will be saved." We do not have enough context to indicate the breadth of meaning in "saved"; still, there is really no good reason to think that Paul meant, specifically, justification as distinguished from the whole *ordo salutis*.

2. The same may be true of Mark 16:16 (whether it belongs in the original or not). Here, at least, the opposite of "saved" is "condemned," and that might easily be interpreted in an exclusively judicial sense.

3. First Corinthians 1:21, however, has more in the context that may clarify what Paul means when he says God is pleased "to save the ones believing." The immediate context contrasts this with those who, by wisdom, did not come to the knowledge of God. "Knowing God" is certainly broader than justification. In the wider context, being "saved" in verse 21 may well be defined by "You were (effectively) called into the fellowship of (being on common ground with, participation in) His Son Jesus Christ" (verse 9); or even by verse 30: "Of Him (God) are you in Christ." In context, then, Paul seems to be thinking about being in union with Christ and all the fruits of that union.

4. Consider also Ephesians 2:8, 9: "You have been saved by faith" (*dia* with the genitive). Considering the whole of Ephesians, with its treatment of all the spiritual riches possessed by being in Christ (1:3), it is patently unlikely that "saved" in 2:8 is meant in the narrow sense as equivalent to justification. More than that, the immediate context of chapter 2 makes this all the more unlikely: Paul is speaking specifically of the quickening of those dead in trespasses and sins, as verses 1, 5, 6 show. Here "salvation" is not being viewed from the point of justification at all but the deliverance of the unsaved from spiritual death and their fashioning as new creatures, ordained for good works. One could hardly find a better contextual description of, or set of words to elucidate, regeneration.

5. In view of the context of Romans, I will not attempt to make much of Romans 1:16 or 10:9, both saying that faith leads to "salvation." It is obvious that the predominant aspect of salvation discussed in Romans is justification; the presumption might therefore be that "salvation" in these verses is justification specifically. I will at least observe, however, that, since Paul can so readily speak of justification in Romans—using *dikaiosunē* and its cognates over and over again without apparently needing synonyms for the sake of variety—one might as logically think that when he uses "salvation" the change of words is deliberate.

6. Luke 8:12 should, however, be considered. There, in interpreting the parable of the sower, Jesus indicates (referring to the seed that fell by the way and never sprouted) that Satan takes away the word "lest they, believing (aorist), be saved." Perhaps it would be pos-

sible for the Calvinist to argue that this is entirely a reference to the possibility of conversion (including justification, specifically) that attends the gospel for the regenerated. But that would leave us with the intolerable view that Jesus means regenerated people whose conversion is successfully prevented by the Satanic hiding of the Word. While this is a negative sort of argument, it seems quite clear that conversion-justification, as narrowly distinguished from regeneration, cannot be the meaning of "saved" in this verse, since these persons never experienced salvation at all.

In conclusion, no one disputes the fact that justification, as such, is truly by faith. In view of the passages dealt with above, there should also be no disputing that "salvation" in its widest sense is also by faith. Regeneration and things rooted in regeneration are also said to be by faith. Furthermore, there is no reason to think that "by faith," when linked with these other aspects of salvation, including regeneration, means anything different from what it means when linked with justification specifically. That is, it bears the same *conditional* relationship in both linkings. One may compare, for example, the syntax and terminology Paul uses when declaring that justification is by faith in Galatians 2:16 with that which he uses when declaring that reception of the Spirit is by faith in Galatians 3:2, 5.

The Biblical Contrast Between Faith and Unbelief as the Dividing Line Between Being Saved and Being Lost

The meaning of "salvation by faith" will be clarified by pursuing the fact that the Bible presents faith and unbelief as the decisive difference between the saved and the lost.

John's Use of Faith

This is especially obvious in John's use of faith. While Paul especially contrasts faith with works, as two ways of seeking righteousness, John especially contrasts faith with unbelief as the watershed between the saved and the lost. Perhaps this explains why John's usage tends to be primarily verbal (using *pisteuō*), as compared to Paul's noun usage (*pistis*).

While this study could easily be developed into a lengthy presentation of Johannine theology, I mention here only a few of the more outstanding examples, in the barest outline form.

1. John 3:18, 36. Believing equals not being condemned and having eternal life. Not believing equals being condemned already, not seeing life, being under God's wrath.

2. John 5:24, 38. Believing equals having eternal life, not coming into condemnation, being passed from death to life. Not believing equals not having God's Word abiding in one, thus not having life.

3. John 6:35-47. Believing equals never thirsting, having everlasting life, being raised on the last day. Not believing equals death.

4. John 12:44-48. Believing equals not abiding in darkness and "seeing" the Father. Not believing equals abiding in darkness, being condemned in the last day.

5. This interplay actually underlies most of the discourses of Jesus in John and leads inexorably to the summary of John's own purposes, summed up in 20:31: "These are written that you may believe that Jesus is the Christ the Son of God and that, (by) believing, you may be having life in His name." This "life" is salvation in its broadest and best sense, and it is by believing. Those who do not possess it do not because of their unbelief—that is John's whole point.

Other New Testament Writers

John is not the only New Testament writer to make this point. A similar tracing of the theology of faith versus unbelief in Acts will reveal something quite similar. Belief versus unbelief (rejection) is, again, the watershed.

1. Thus, for example, Acts 28:24 characterizes results all through Paul's ministry: "Some believed the things being said, and some were unbelieving." Acts 17:4, 5 is typical: "Some of them believed, and consorted with Paul and Silas. . . . But the Jews which believed not. . . . "

2. As already noted, "belief," in this very sense, was the basis for the giving of the Holy Spirit (Acts 11:17; 15:7-9).

3. Thus, in Acts, the way a "Christian" or "disciple" is identified is, often, one "who believed" (16:1; 19:18, etc.) in distinction from the unsaved as "those who believed not." Indeed, being saved becomes "they believed" (13:12; 14:23; 17:12, etc.).

The Synoptics

The Synoptic Gospels do not speak of personal soteriology as much as John does, more often connecting faith with things like healings. Still, there is a definite parallelism between the language of faith as linked to healings and that same language as linked to forgiveness and salvation.

1. As but a few of many possible references, note Matthew 9:2 where Jesus healed the palsied man, brought by four, when He saw "their faith"; 9:22 when he said to the woman with the issue, "Your

faith has made you whole"; 9:29 to the blind men, "According to your faith be it"; Mark 10:52 where Bartimaeus is told, "Your faith has made you whole"; and Luke 17:19 where He said to the leper, "Your faith has made you whole." (In all of these it is clear both that the faith is the personal activity of the persons and that their faith was the condition for their healing.)

2. Now compare with these Luke 7:50 where the woman who washed Jesus' feet with her tears was not sick but *only* sinful and was told: "Your faith has saved you." The precise parallelism is obvious and apparently intentional.

If all other considerations show that faith is truly the condition required for salvation, the synoptics will certainly add confirmation.

The Relationship between Salvation by Faith, Salvation by Works, and Salvation by Grace

As already concluded in the previous chapter, the fact that salvation is by the grace of God and not by man's works is a conclusion justly and explicitly drawn from Scripture. The question, therefore, is: Does salvation by faith contradict salvation by grace? Does salvation by faith imply, in some subtle way, salvation by works. Scripture itself provides a clear answer: "By faith" is *not* "by works" but *is* "by grace."

Contrast Between Faith and Works as Condition

Paul is the New Testament writer who addresses this question at greatest length.

Romans 3:20–4:25 indicates what is at the heart of Paul's argument in all of Romans: faith, not works, is the condition for standing righteous before God. In 3:21, 22, righteousness is "apart from the law"; it is "by faith" (*dia* with the genitive). In 3:27, boasting is excluded—not by the "law" of works, but by the "law" of faith. In 3:28, justification is "by faith" (instrumental case, *pistei*) apart from the works of the law. In 4:2, 3, if Abraham were justified by works he might boast; instead, he "put faith" (aorist *episteusen*) in God and was accounted righteous. In 4:4, 5, for one who "works" any reward is reckoned by obligation, whereas for one believing his faith is reckoned for righteousness.

Romans 9:30—10:13 is at the heart of Paul's discussion of Israel's situation. In 9:32, Israel has not attained righteous standing before God because it was not sought by faith (*ek* with the ablative) but by works. In 10:5, 6, righteousness "of the (works of) the law" is directly contrasted with righteousness "of faith" (*ek* with the ablative).

Galatians 2:16 makes the contrast twice, stating it both in principle and experientially: justification is not by the works of the law but by faith. (And the role of faith is expressed three different ways: verbally, with *episteusamen*; by *dia* with the genitive; and by *ek* with the ablative.)

Galatians 3:2, 5 (already treated above) twice insists that the reception of the Spirit is by (the hearing of) faith and not by the works of the law.

Ephesians 2:8, 9 (also treated above) sets "through faith" in contrast to "of works" as the condition or instrument of salvation.

Philippians 3:9 contrasts self righteousness, which is of (the works of) the law, with the righteousness that is "of God" and "by faith" (expressed twice, once as *dia* with the genitive and once as *epi* with the locative or instrumental).

More passages could be cited, but these are adequate as a basis for an indisputable conclusion: "by faith" and "by works" are mutually exclusive. Faith (at least faith rightly conceived) is not works, and so "by faith" is not "by works." Logically or Scripturally, this disjunction holds up.

We should note, in passing, that such passages as these make clear that Paul means faith as a condition and not a result: salvation *by* faith and not salvation *to* faith. It would be nonsense to contrast salvation unto faith with salvation by works.

Faith and Grace As Complementary
Again, Paul's writings are the most helpful. What we find is that we do not need any logical syllogisms (as helpful as they might be); the Bible provides direct statements that "by faith" is in perfect accord with "by grace."

Romans 4:4, 5 (above) makes clear that reckoning with man on the basis of works would be by obligation, while reckoning with him as a man of faith is by grace.

Ephesians 2:8, 9 (above) explicitly states that salvation by faith is salvation by grace, in direct contrast to salvation by works.

Romans 4:2, 3 (and Eph. 2:8, 9) draws out the conclusion that salvation by faith eliminates man's boasting. And when man's boasting is excluded, that is clearly meant to exalt God's grace as unmerited favor; boasting implies merit.

Romans 10:3 makes salvation by faith (9:32) a matter of submitting to the righteousness God provides rather than attempting to establish one's own righteousness. The elimination of self righteousness establishes salvation by grace.

Most importantly, *Romans 4:16* expresses precisely what is involved in all these: "It is of faith (*ek* with the ablative) that it might be by grace (*kata* with the accusative)." "By faith," so far from contradicting grace, is precisely "according to grace." *It requires faith, and faith as a condition, in contrast to works, to establish grace as the basis for God's work of salvation.* On this point Paul is very clear.

Certain Conclusions

Certain conclusions are obviously justified, then.

1. Faith (whatever it is) is not works. To be sure, a "faith" wrongly understood to be something it isn't *might* be "works." But so long as one means what the Bible means by faith, the Bible itself is the basis for this absolute distinction.

2. Then salvation by faith is not salvation by works. One may deny salvation by faith on some other grounds, if he wishes (his view of depravity, for example, or his view of election), but the very thing he cannot do is deny it by equating it with salvation by works. Scripture prevents that equation. The very places we learn that salvation is not by works are the places we learn that it is by faith.

3. And salvation by faith is in perfect harmony with salvation by grace. Once again, it is the Scripture that teaches us this; indeed, salvation is by faith in order that it may be according to grace.

One may challenge the conclusions of this section by pointing out that several of the passages cited above deal with justification specifically ("salvation" in the narrow sense) rather than with salvation in the broader sense to include the whole *ordo salutis*. If so, the point has been missed. For one thing, not all of the passages cited deal narrowly with justification. But even if they did, the point is that they prove that, *in principle*, "by faith" complements "by grace" and contradicts "by works." And that principle will work equally well for salvation (broad) or for justification. If the earlier parts of this chapter have succeeded in showing that the Scriptures do not limit "by faith" to justification but apply it, in the same language, to other parts of the *ordo salutis*, then these conclusions apply to "salvation by faith" in the broadest possible meaning of that phrase.

Faith a Condition Not a Ground

Faith can be a condition for man to meet without being a meritorious cause or ground of salvation.

1. What we have seen, so far, makes clear that faith is the person's activity. And the rich variety of ways that the New Testament presents faith as a condition gives added weight to the idea that *the person meets the condition by believing.*

By rich variety I mean that we have seen faith presented by several grammatical constructions:

a. *dia* with the genitive (*dia pisteōs*): Romans 3:21, 22; Galatians 2:16; Ephesians 2:8, 9; etc. Here faith stands as the intermediate agent between the saved and the unsaved state.

b. *ek* with the ablative (*ek pisteōs*): Romans 10:5, 6; Galatians 3:2, 5; Colossians 2:12; etc. Here faith, as source, becomes the means by which salvation is received.

c. *instrumental case* (*pistei*): Romans 3:28; Acts 15:9; etc. Here faith is the instrument by means of which salvation is applied/appropriated.

d. *epi* with the locative (*epi tē pistei*: whether this is locative, instrumental, or dative may be debatable, but the point is not affected either way): Philippians 3:9 (apparently the only such occurrence). While this might be simple location, the more likely meaning is to suggest a basis or grounds. Kennedy suggests "founded on" faith.[2] Martin follows the Revised Standard Version in rendering "depends on" faith.[3]

e. *verbal expressions*—a considerable variety of them, in fact—that use the verb *pisteuō*: see the number cited above under "b."

2. As Berkhof insists, faith is not the *grounds* of our salvation:

> Scripture never says that we are justified . . . on account of (*dia* plus the accusative) faith. This means that faith is never represented as the ground of our justification. If this were the case, faith would have to be regarded as a meritorious work of man. And this would be the introduction of the doctrine of justification by works.[4]

I agree with him, without any hesitation—even though the use of *epi* with the locative in Philippians 3:9 may get fairly close to suggesting grounds. But we have seen in this study that belief versus unbelief provides the dividing line between being saved and being

---

[2]H. A. A. Kennedy, "The Epistle of Paul to the Philippians," in *The Expositor's Greek Testament* (Grand Rapids: Eerdmans, 1950), III:454.

[3]Ralph P. Martin, *The New Century Bible Commentary: Philippians* (Grand Rapids: Eerdmans, 1980), 133.

[4]Berkhof, 520, 521.

lost. That has brought us precisely to the point of saying that as surely as unbelief is the reason/cause that one remains condemned, so
surely faith is the reason/cause that one is saved.

True, this must not be thought of as "reason" or "cause" in the
sense of grounds—not in either case. This is not *meritorious* cause.
For condemnation, sin is the (de)meritorious cause; for justification,
the atoning work of Christ, applied by grace, is the meritorious cause.
But faith and unbelief certainly qualify, respectively, as the *instrumental* "cause"—although parting with the word "cause" is a far better
course.

3. Faith, as personal believing, is impossible apart from the gracious operation of the Holy Spirit. This provides another reason for
saying that faith itself carries no sense of merit. The Arminian position, as explained in the previous chapter, is that the sinner is so radically depraved that he cannot, of his own will and power, believe.
The enabling, pre-regenerating ("prevenient") gracious work of God's
Spirit to convince and persuade the sinner of the nature of his condition and of the truth of the gospel is required before faith. Only by
that work has the sinner ability to put faith in Christ.

For Further Reading on Salvation by Faith

Arminius, James. *The Writings of James Arminius* (three vols.), tr. James Nichols and W. R. Bagnall. Grand Rapids: Baker, 1956 (vol. I, pp. 355-369; vol. II, pp. 109-111; 499-501).

Forlines, F. Leroy. *Systematics*. Nashville: Randall House Publications, 1975, ch. 12, "The Condition of Salvation." [A colleague of this writer]

MacDonald, William G. " '. . . The Spirit of Grace' (Heb. 10:29)" in *Grace Unlimited*, ed. Clark H. Pinnock. Minneapolis: Bethany Fellowship, 1975 (ch. 4).

Watson, Richard. *Theological Institutes*. New York: Nelson and Phillips, 1850 (vol. II, pp. 234-253). [An important, early Wesleyan theologian]

PART FIVE

Perseverance in Salvation

Appropriately last among the points of tension between Calvinism and Arminianism is the question whether those who have been regenerated must necessarily persevere (or are preserved) or may apostatize and be lost. As we have noted in the first part of this work, Arminius himself and the original Remonstrants avoided a clear conclusion on this matter. But they raised the question. And the natural implications of the views at the heart of Arminianism, even in its early stages as a formal movement, tended to question whether Calvinism's assumption of necessary perseverance was truly Biblical.

Those tendencies indicated by the questions raised did not take long to reach fruition, and thus Calvinism and Arminianism have come to be traditionally divided on this issue.

Giving a brief historical introduction to the matter, Berkhof identifies five varieties of conviction:

1. Augustine taught that the "elect" could not fall away, but that some non-elected "regenerate" persons could.
2. Roman Catholic "Semi-Pelagianism" teaches that perseverance is dependent on the free-will obedience of the converted.
3. Lutheran theology emphasizes that perseverance is dependent on the regenerate person's continued activity of faith.
4. Arminianism holds that perseverance is dependent on the believers' will to believe and on their good works.

5. Calvinism, in contrast to all of these, insists that they whom God has regenerated can not fall away from that state and will certainly [read "necessarily"] persevere therein to final salvation.[1]

Whether Berkhof's definition of the Arminian view is correct on all counts should become clearer in the following chapters. It may be representative of some later Arminians, but I am sure that what he states was not true of Arminius or the original Remonstrants, or of many Arminians today, including this writer.

We turn now, in order, to the Calvinistic view, the Arminian view, and some important "Biblical theology" on the subject. I must observe, however, that not all who hold the popular doctrine called "eternal security" are really Calvinists. The position of these— whom I am calling "sub-Calvinists"[2]—will also be treated in the first of the three chapters to follow, and the nature of their views will be briefly explained.

---

[1] Louis Berkhof, *Systematic Theology* (Grand Rapids: Eerdmans, 1949), 545.
[2] I mean no opprobrium by this name: only that they are less than fully Calvinistic.

CHAPTER ELEVEN

Calvinism's Argument for Necessary Perseverance

The main ingredients of the Calvinistic view regarding perseverance can be outlined as follows.

Definition

As given on the preceding page, a good statement of the Calvinistic view requires two major clauses, one to indicate that those whom God has regenerated can not fall away from that state, and another to indicate that they will certainly persevere in that saved condition. Indeed, three main points are consciously involved in this definition.

1. Perseverance relates only to the *regenerated*, and to all of them. Calvinism does not make any distinction between the "elect" and the "regenerated." The whole number of each is the same. All the elect are regenerated; all the regenerated are elect.

This therefore distinguishes Calvinism from Augustine, who apparently thought that more are regenerated than elected, and that the non-elect regenerate will not persevere and be finally saved.

Arminius likewise appeared to show a willingness to make this distinction. He suggested, in his statements about election, that the elect are those whom God foresees as having saving faith and persevering therein. This would seem to mean that those who apostatize from faith were never elected.[3] (More about this in the next chapter.)

2. The view has a *negative* side. Regenerate persons can not become unregenerate. (As we will see later, those whom I call "sub-Calvinists" tend to emphasize this side and give little attention to the next point.)

3. The view has a *positive* side. They *will* certainly persevere. This means that the Holy Spirit will so continue to operate within the believer that the gracious work begun in regeneration will necessarily be brought to successful completion in sanctification.

Implications

Some of these are not always understood by Arminians.

---

[3]See, for example, James Arminius, *The Writings of James Arminius* (three vols.), tr. James Nichols and W. R. Bagnall (Grand Rapids: Baker, 1956), I:288.

1. This position does not affirm the sinlessness of the saved. Regenerate persons "may sometimes be overcome by evil and fall into sin."[4] This implication, of course, does not serve to distinguish Calvinists from Arminians—not even from those Wesleyan Arminians who teach perfectionism in one or another of its several forms.

2. This position does not affirm that people are saved in spite of evidence to the contrary. When Berkhof suggests the question, "Does the doctrine imply that one may be living in habitual and intentional sin, and yet be in a justified state?" he means the answer to be No.[5] Perseverance, according to Calvinism, means "perseverance in holiness."[6] (As we will see below, this is sometimes a difference between Calvinism and "sub-Calvinism.")

3. This position does not affirm perseverance apart from the *means* of perseverance; one must remember that in Calvinism the means are predestinated along with the ends.[7] Thus Calvinism does *not* teach "that God keeps us without constant watchfulness, diligence, and prayer on our part."[8] Even exhortations to persevere in the faith and warnings against apostasy are sincere and "are instrumental in keeping believers in the way of perseverance."[9]

I would pause long enough here to emphasize these last two points. Careful Calvinists agree wholeheartedly with those of us who emphasize that one whose life consistently indicates that he is under the dominion of sin has no grounds—not even in the doctrine of perseverance—for assurance of salvation. Many Arminians do not understand that this is so, in part because of that popular sub-Calvinism that I will refer to subsequently in this chapter.

In summary, Calvinism is not teaching perseverance in spite of wickedness. Instead, Calvinism teaches that God's Spirit so effectively works in the lives of the regenerate that they necessarily will, at least over the passage of time, manifest the fruits of regeneration.

---

[4]Loraine Boettner, *The Reformed Doctrine of Predestination* (Grand Rapids: Eerdmans, 1954), 187.

[5]Berkhof, 549.

[6]Berkhof, 548.

[7]W. G. T. Shedd, *Dogmatic Theology* (Grand Rapids: Zondervan reprint, n.d.), 557.

[8]Berkhof, 548.

[9]Berkhof, 548.

The Scriptural Argument for the Necessary Perseverance of the Saints

Scriptures claimed (by one or another Calvinist) to teach the certain perseverance of all the regenerate include (but are not limited to):

John 10:27-29 (Berkhof and Shedd)—"I give [my sheep] eternal life, and they shall never perish; neither shall anyone snatch them out of My hand."

Romans 11:29 (Berkhof and Shedd)—"For the gifts and calling of God are irrevocable."

Philippians 1:6 (Berkhof and Shedd)—"Being confident of this very thing, that He who has begun a good work in you will complete it until the day of Jesus Christ."

Second Thessalonians 3:3 (Berkhof)—"The Lord is faithful, who will establish you and guard you from the evil one."

Second Timothy 1:12; 4:18 (Berkhof)—"I know whom I have believed and am persuaded that He is able to keep what I have committed to Him until that Day." "And the Lord will deliver me from every evil work and preserve me for His heavenly kingdom."

1 Peter 1:5 (Shedd)—"Who are kept by the power of God through faith for salvation ready to be revealed in the last time."

Romans 8:29, 30, 35-39 (Boettner)—"Whom he foreknew, He also predestined to be conformed to the image of His Son. . . . Moreover whom He predestined, these He also called; whom He called, these He also justified; and whom He justified, these He also glorified."

Hebrews 10:14 (Boettner)—"For by one offering He has perfected forever those who are being sanctified."[10]

Explanations

The Scriptures that Arminians believe teach the possibility of apostasy are explained as follows:

1. Some of the passages that appear to describe apostasy are not referring to persons *really* regenerated but only to persons outwardly and superficially "converted." Berkhof speaks of their apparent saving faith as "a mere temporal faith . . . not rooted in regeneration."[11] This answer he uses for 1 Timothy 1:19, 20; 2 Timothy 2:17, 18; 2 Peter

---

[10]For use of these passages by the three Calvinist writers referred to, see Berkhof, 546, 547; Shedd, 556, 557; Boettner, 196-201.

[11]Berkhof, 549.

2:1, 2; and Hebrews 6:4-6. Shedd and Boettner also use it for 2 Peter 2:20, 21.[12]

2. Some of the passages describe only hypothetical situations and not real possibilities. These hypothetical observations are "made for the sake of illustrating or enforcing truth."[13] Shedd uses this answer for Hebrews 6:4-6 and Matthew 13:21, 22.

3. Positive exhortations to perseverance in faith and holiness and negative warnings against apostasy do appear in the Scriptures. However, they:

a. do *not* imply that apostasy really may happen; but instead

b. serve as means or instruments for keeping believers from apostasy;[14] and

c. are addressed to human beings from the human beings' subjective viewpoint, rather than from God's objective point of view;[15] Shedd adds that a believer in a state of assurance produced by the witness of the Holy Spirit does not need this warning.[16] Berkhof uses this answer for Matthew 24:12, 13; Colossians 1:23; Hebrews 2:1; 3:14; 6:11; 1 John 2:6. Shedd uses it also for 1 Timothy 6:12.

The Systematic Argument

As Boettner observes, "This doctrine does not stand alone, but is a necessary part of the Calvinistic system of theology."[17] The logic of this will be fully appreciated by any reader: if God has unconditionally elected those who are saved, sent Jesus to die efficaciously for them and them alone, and regenerates them without their conscious awareness and thus against their wills by an irresistibly gracious work, then it logically follows that He will necessarily bring to its final conclusion the work begun in them. For in no aspect of that work is salvation really conditional; any elements within it that are conditional (like justification by faith) are accomplished by conditions that God Himself supplies as part of the blessings of salvation by election.

Calvinistic Argument 1: The doctrine of unconditional election implies certain perseverance since election "is an election unto an end, that is, unto salvation."[18]

---

[12]Shedd, 558 (note); Boettner, 192.
[13]Shedd, 558.
[14]Berkhof 548; Shedd 557.
[15]Berkhof, 548.
[16]Shedd, 557.
[17]Boettner, 182.
[18]Berkhof, 547.

Arminian response: True, if unconditional election were proved, necessary perseverance would logically follow. One responds, therefore, in two ways.

1. Disproving the system as a whole, or any of its other key points (to which the earlier chapters of this work have been devoted) will mean that Calvinism's view of perseverance does *not* logically follow as a corollary.

2. Better yet, showing that the Scriptures teach conditional perseverance and the real possibility of apostasy serves both to establish the Arminian view and invalidate the Calvinistic system. We should remember that unconditional election effectively translates into unconditional salvation. The next two chapters will be devoted to this.

Calvinistic Argument 2: The doctrine of the "covenant of redemption" implies that God gave a certain number of "elect" to His Son in this covenant between the Father and the Son. The existence of such a "covenant" is clearly implied when Jesus referred both to promises and to a mission given to Him by the Father, as in John 5:30, 43; 6:38-40; 17:4-12. Among these covenant promises is the fact that the Father "gave" to Jesus certain people as His: namely, the elect. And the terms of agreement included His mission to atone for His people's sins. In fact, then, these covenant promises to the Son were conditioned only by Jesus' fulfillment of the terms of agreement between Him and the Father, which He completely fulfilled, and not on any such thing as the uncertain faithfulness of man.

Arminian response: This may be answered in more than one way.

1. In the first place, such discussion of a covenant between the Father and the Son ought to proceed, if at all, with great hesitation. Nowhere is there direct indication that such a covenant was made, and even more important is the fact that the terms of such a covenant are not revealed—especially not whether those promises were or were not condional.

Calvinists generally take the lead in insisting that the secret things belong to God, that His eternal counsels are not directly revealed. If there was such a covenant of redemption (and I do not object to the idea in principle), the *only* way we have of "reading" its terms respecting salvation is by reading in the New Testament how salvation is actually effected and applied. If, then, the New Testament makes clear that salvation really is conditional, then we dare not "read" the unrevealed terms of an implied covenant of redemption in such a way as to destroy that conditionality.

2. More briefly, this argument is in fact the same as the preceding argument, simply stated in a different set of terms. Both the concept and delineation of the terms of the "covenant of redemption" are expressed by Calvinists in ways that match the underlying concept of unconditional salvation. If election/salvation is unconditional, so is inclusion in the so-called "covenant of redemption." If the former is not, however, then neither is the latter.

Calvinistic Argument 3: The efficacy of the intercession of Christ implies certain perseverance, since His prayer for His people must certainly be answered. The single best recorded example of this intercession is to be found, of course, in the high-priestly prayer in John 17. There, among other things, Jesus prayed that all His believers would be one, be made perfect, be with Him, and behold His glory.

Berkhof also cites John 11:42, which expresses the principle: "I know that you always hear me"; and Hebrews 7:25: "He is able to save to the uttermost those who come to God through Him, since He ever lives to make intercession for them."[19]

Arminian response: If, as we believe, salvation is conditional and thus purposed by God for believers, then final salvation is for those who persevere in believing. Therefore, the intercessory prayers of Jesus are prayers for persons viewed as believers and requiring persistence in faith for the answer to the prayers is consistent with the efficacy of His prayers.

In reference to the great prayer in John 17, the implications for all this in verses 11, 12 are worth noting: "Holy Father, keep through Your name those whom You have given Me, that they may be one as We are. While I was with them in the world, I kept them in Your name. Those whom You gave Me I have kept; and none of them is lost except the son of perdition." The pronoun "them" can have as its antecedent nothing other than "those whom You gave me." This goes far to demonstrate (1) that "giving" them to Jesus does not guarantee their perseverance, since the son of perdition is clearly both among "them" and now lost, and (2) that His prayers for them were not therefore unconditionally efficacious—unless He had never prayed this for them before, which is patently unlikely.

---

[19]Berkhof, 547.

Calvinistic Argument 4: Union with Christ implies certain perseverance, since "It is impossible that they should again be removed from
the body."[20]

Arminian response: Why is it impossible? (One may ask this in
light of Romans 11:17-22 if for no other reason.) Such a statement is
nothing more than a "logical" affirmation, and one whose logic
remains unspecified at that.

In fact, the answer to this affirmation is simpler than that: it is precisely nothing more than a restatement of the position being argued,
not an argument for it, thus "begging the question." If salvation really
is conditional, then remaining in saving union with Christ is conditional: that is the very point we are arguing.

Calvinistic Argument 5: The nature of the Holy Spirit's work in the
heart implies certain perseverance, since He would most certainly
not desert such a work once begun.[21]

Arminian Response: The answer is exactly the same as that given
to the previous argument. First, why not? Statements that indicate
what God's Spirit "would not" do are always risky. Their very wording
reveals that they are drawing "logical" implications rather than citing
Scripture.

Again, then, the affirmation begs the question, being nothing more
than a restatement of the position being argued for rather than a new
argument to support or demonstrate the position. At the risk of repetition: if in fact salvation is really conditional rather than unconditional, as the Arminian contends, then the continued work of the Holy
Spirit toward the end purposed *for believers* is conditioned on their
continuing faith. This involves no contradiction of the purposes of
God, as the second section of this work has shown.

Calvinistic Argument 6: That the believer already possesses "eternal life" implies certain perseverance. As Berkhof rhetorically (and
sarcastically) asks: "Can we proceed on the assumption that eternal
life will not be everlasting?"[22] And in making this point he refers to
John 3:36; 5:24; 6:54. Even clearer is John 10:28: "I give them eternal
life, and they shall never perish."

---

[20]Berkhof, 547.
[21]Berkhof, 547, quotes Dabney.
[22]Berkhof, 548.

Arminian response: The *life* thus possessed—even though it may be more a matter of quality than duration—is certainly eternal. The *possession* of this life, however, is either conditional or unconditional. If the latter, then Calvinism is correct in its insistence on necessary perseverance. If the former, however, then the possession—being conditional—is not necessarily eternal.

Except for the attempt to draw implications from the word "eternal," this argument too is a restatement of the position being argued in different terms. But once we realize that the possession of eternal life is another way of stating salvation itself, then we realize that once again there is no other question involved here except whether that salvation is conditional or unconditional.

The verses cited in support of this argument are too important to leave with this brief response. I will return to them again in the following chapter and deal with them at greater length.

Calvinistic Argument 7: The efficacy of the atoning work of Christ implies certain perseverance, since His death actually, not just provisionally, accomplished the redemption of those for whom He died.

Arminian response: This is a restatement of an argument already dealt with, and answered, in the discussion of whether the atonement is limited or universal. See chapter 5, above, and the Arminian response to the Calvinist's third argument.

Calvinistic Argument 8: The possibility of confident assurance of salvation implies certain perseverance. If final salvation were not necessarily guaranteed, one could not have assurance of salvation.

Arminian response:

1. Assurance of salvation is, by nature, assurance that one "possesses" saving grace. That assurance, objectively, is not based on doctrine but on one's confidence in God to fulfill His Word. Given that He has committed Himself to save those who put faith in Him, assurance is directly related to faith. It is therefore co-extensive with saving faith, and this has no bearing on whether one may retract saving faith at some later date.

2. Furthermore, assurance of salvation results from the inner witness of the Holy Spirit which produces a subjective inner confidence. Consequently, assurance is not dependent on a confidence that one cannot apostatize in the future.

This may be the place to make a passing observation about those—especially sub-Calvinists who profess "eternal security"—who insist so strongly that they would have no assurance apart from believing that they can never again be lost. I submit that this is a misplaced assurance, an expression of confidence in a *doctrine*. For the Arminian, assurance is an expression of confidence in Jesus.

Calvinistic Argument 9: The fact that saving faith is a gift of God implies certain perseverance, since God would certainly not take back His gift.[23] See Romans 11:29, above.

Arminian response: I have argued, in the previous chapter, that faith is not *per se* the gift of God. If that is the case, this argument fails.

Calvinistic Argument 10: The fact that salvation is by grace alone implies certain perseverance since it means that salvation cannot be conditional in its beginning or continuation.

Arminian response: But that brings us back to what is at issue: namely, whether salvation is conditional or not. Arminians hold that salvation is, both in its beginning and in its continuation, conditional. Furthermore, in the previous section it has been proved, according to the New Testament, that salvation by faith is in no way contradictory to salvaton by grace. Indeed, according to Romans 4, salvation *must be by faith in order to be by grace*. To insist that continuation is by faith does no more contradict grace than to insist that it is received by faith in the beginning.

The Sub-Calvinist Argument for "Eternal Security"

There is a popular belief in unconditional security held by many (many Southern and Independent Baptists, for example) who think of themselves as Calvinists but really are not—as both Arminians and consistent Calvinists realize.

In fact, they typically believe in *conditional* rather than *unconditional* salvation—professing universal atonement, resistible grace, and conditional election. They are therefore Arminian in every point until it comes to the question of perseverance, more Arminian then than Calvinist. Many of them resist such observations, sometimes because they fail to understand the nature of true Calvinism and the absolute importance of each point of the system.

It is often, though not always, true that these "sub-Calvinists" (I am not aware that anyone else calls them that, and I mean no disrespect by the appellation) hold "eternal security" (as they like to

---

[23]Boettner, 183.

express it) somewhat differently. Many would affirm that the person once regenerated may return to a life indefinitely characterized by habitual and heinous sin and that this makes absolutely no difference at all insofar as security or assurance are concerned. In that way they differ dramatically from traditional Calvinism.

The sub-Calvinistic argument for unconditional perseverance may be both Scriptural and logical, sometimes identical with regular Calvinists' arguments, sometimes not.

1. The main Scriptures used will be essentially the same as those given above (page 189). Only, instead of linking those Scriptures with the other Calvinistic doctrines (like unconditional election, limited atonement, etc.), the sub-Calvinists will stress the *promises* contained in such passages. Then their confidence in unconditional perseverance is based on the fact that God will certainly not fail to keep any promise He has made, stated or implied.

There are many examples of such promises (especially in the Gospel of John) including:

John 10:28	I give them eternal life, and they shall never perish.
John 3:36	He who believes in the Son has everlasting life.
John 4:4	Whoever drinks of the water I give him will never thirst.
John 5:24	He who believes in God has everlasting life and shall not come into judgment.
John 6:54	He who eats and drinks of me has everlasting life and I will raise him up.

2. Logical arguments will be partly like, and partly unlike, the regular Calvinist's arguments already given.

a. The sub-Calvinists will not use those that draw from the other distinctive Calvinistic doctrines, as stated above. These deal with the plan and provision of salvation.

b. They will use arguments like those above that deal with the nature of salvation as applied. The basic point is that the nature of salvation is such as to rule out the possibility of apostasy. As Boettner (a true Calvinist, nonetheless) puts it, "No creature can change its nature. Nothing short of another supernatural act of God can reverse regeneration."[24] In brief, once a person is saved, he by nature will not ever desire to turn away from God.

---

[24]Boettner, 184.

3. The sub-Calvinists show a greater variety in using logical arguments than traditional Calvinists, as illustrated in the following.

a. One who has been born again can not be unborn.

b. God is not an "Indian giver": He will not forgive and then take back His forgiveness.

c. When a person is saved, he is forgiven for past, present, and future sins.

d. God will not allow a child of His, loved by Him, to perish.

e. One born again will not desire to depart from God.

f. If one could be removed from the body of Christ, His body would be maimed.

g. Even among human beings, one's child can never cease to be his child, regardless what he does.

Any number of similar logical arguments may be encountered. The more careful Calvinistic theologians do not tend to use such arguments, which generally express analogy with human experience in one way or another and do not directly state Scriptural teaching.

I have chosen not to respond to the sub-Calvinist arguments here. Some response will be outlined in the following chapter, which presents the Arminian view of conditional perseverance. I will observe here, however, that the attitude of a true Calvinist toward such sub-Calvinism, especially to its view that a persistent sinner can claim assurance of salvation, may be seen in the book, *Wrongly Dividing the Word of Truth*, by John H. Gerstner. He calls this viewpoint "spurious Calvinism" and tends to find the source of its heresy in dispensationalism. The headings within his chapter 7 read:

> Dispensational Total Depravity Is Not Total
> Dispensational Unconditional Election Is Not Unconditional
> Dispensational Denial of Limited Atonement Destroys the Possibility
>   of Calvinism
> Dispensational Irresistible Grace Is Not Irresistible
> Dispensational Perseverance of the Saints Is the Preservation
>   of the Sinner[25]

I find Gerstner's work intriguing, but remain uncertain whether he has made his case in blaming dispensationalism for all the problems

---

[25]John H. Gerstner, *Wrongly Dividing the Word of Truth* (Brentwood, Tenn.: Wolgemuth and Hyatt, 1991), vi.

(including that which is caused by the so-called "anti-Lordship" salvation view) he lays at its doorsteps. He is surely correct in attacking some of the hermeneutics of that school, but to speak further about this would take me too far afield.

For Further Reading on the
Calvinistic Doctrine of Perseverance

Berkhof, Louis. *Systematic Theology*. Grand Rapids: Eerdmans, 1949 (pp. 545-549).

Berkouwer, G. C. *Faith and Perseverance*. Grand Rapids: Eerdmans, 1958.

Boettner, Loraine. *The Reformed Doctrine of Predestination*. Grand Rapids: Eerdmans, 1954 (pp. 182-201).

Custance, Arthur. *The Sovereignty of Grace*. Grand Rapids: Baker, 1979 (pp. 191-224).

Shedd, William G. T. *Dogmatic Theology*. Grand Rapids: Zondervan, n.d. (vol. II, pp. 553-560).

CHAPTER TWELVE

Arminianism and
Conditional Perseverance

As noted in the introduction to this section, Arminius himself and the original Remonstrants did not clearly affirm that apostasy from regeneration is possible. Arminius' opinion on the subject can be captured in this relatively brief statement on the subject:

> My sentiments respecting the perseverance of the Saints are, that those persons who have been grafted into Christ by true faith, and have thus been made partakers of his life-giving Spirit, possess *sufficient powers* [or strength] to . . . gain the victory over those enemies—yet not without the assistance of the grace of the same Holy Spirit. . . . So that it is not possible for them, by any of the cunning craftiness or power of Satan, to be either seduced or dragged out of the hands of Christ. But I think it is useful and will be quite necessary in our first convention, to institute a diligent enquiry from the Scriptures, whether it is not possible for some individuals through negligence to desert the commencement of their existence in Christ, to cleave again to the present evil world, to decline from the sound doctrine which was once delivered to them, to lose a good conscience, and to cause Divine grace to be ineffectual.
>
> Though I here openly and ingenuously affirm, I never taught that a *true believer can either totally or finally fall away from the faith, and perish*; yet I will not conceal, that there are passages of Scripture which seem to me to wear this aspect; and those answers to them which I have been permitted to see, are not of such a kind as to approve themselves on all points to my understanding.[1]

From a historical perspective, Arminius insisted that the denial of such a possibility "was never, from the very times of the apostles down to the present day, accounted by the church as a catholic doctrine," and that the view that holds apostasy to be possible "has always had more supporters in the church."[2] And in his long "examination" of the treatise on predestination by William Perkins, he undertook to show that Perkins' arguments against the possibility of apos-

---

[1] James Arminius, *The Writings of James Arminius* (three vols.), tr. James Nichols and W. R. Bagnall (Grand Rapids: Baker, 1956), I:254.

[2] Arminius, II:502, 503.

tasy were not sufficient to make the case certain—even after he enters the discussion by remarking, "That true and saving faith may be, totally and finally, lost, I should not at once dare to say."[3]

The very fact that he and his followers raised this question, however, indicates that this view was sure to follow from the basic principle that salvation is conditional. Ever since that early period, then, when the issue was being examined again, Arminians have taught that those who are truly saved need to be warned against apostasy as a real and possible danger.

Key to this belief is the conviction that salvation is conditional. In that case, continuing to possess salvation is continuing to meet the Biblical condition of faith. It is true that Arminians of different times and places have presented the details of this view in different ways. Even so, this view most certainly does *not* require thinking that salvation (whether at first or subsequently) is by works in any sense.

The Arminian believes, with the Calvinist, that the Bible warns the regenerate against turning away from God: in other words, against apostasy. It seems clear to the Arminian, then, that the possibility of apostasy must therefore really exist.

Among matters that are debated by Arminians within their own ranks are such questions as the following.

• *Does the word "elect" include only those who persevere to final salvation, or does it include those who are regenerated and fall away?* Arminius himself defined election so as to favor the first of these two possibilities. In this way, he apparently agreed with Augustine, that the regenerate who apostatize are non-elect.[4] This issue may be as much a matter of terminology as anything else. It will not be pursued in this work.

• *Can apostasy be remedied?* In other words, can one who is regenerate and becomes unregenerate via apostasy be regenerated again? There have been Arminians on both sides of this question. Again, the details of this difference will not be explored at length in this work. I think it is clear that the answer is No, and some reasons for this will be indicated in the next chapter, as the message of the Book of Hebrews is expounded.

[3]Arminius, III:491ff.
[4]See Arminius' discussion in III:511, for example.

The Scriptural Argument for Conditional Perseverance

The Arminian is quick to urge that the issue whether a saved person may be lost should be settled not on systematic but on Biblical grounds. That is (as all would agree) the question: Does the Bible teach the possibility of apostasy?

New Testament Passages

New Testament passages teaching the possibility of apostasy include the following.

1. The Book of Hebrews as a whole. Warnings and exhortations relative to apostasy and perseverance are thematic throughout the book. Each main section has a hortatory "center" assuming the possibility of apostasy. These are:

- chs. 1, 2, with 2:1-4 at the heart;
- chs. 3, 4, with 3:7—4:2 at the heart;
- chs. 5-7, with 5:11—6:12 at the heart, especially 6:4-6;
- chs. 8-12, with 10:19-39 and 12:1-24 at the heart.

Especially do the sections 6:4-6 and 10:19-39 take this doctrine to its fullest and clearest development. Without expanding on this now, I will simply refer to the following chapter, which will explore the teaching of Hebrews on this subject in detail. As will be noted there, if one wishes to get the best Biblical material on any subject, he needs to consult the Bible where it is dealing directly with that subject, if this is possible. The book of Hebrews deals directly with perseverance and apostasy and provides the most important part of any Biblical discussion of the subject.[5]

2. Second Peter 2:18-22 is very similar to the passages that are at the heart of the Book of Hebrews. This will also be treated in the following chapter, although somewhat more briefly than Hebrews.

3. Other passages are often included in such a discussion as this, and will be mentioned here just briefly. My own approach to the subject is such that I do not tend to look for intimations of the possibility of apostasy everywhere in the New Testament, but instead to build the case on the passages that treat the matter directly. Following that, I am prepared for other intimations of the possibility when they arise. Among these are the following.

---

[5]I would also refer the reader to Grant R. Osborne,"Soteriology in the Epistle to the Hebrews," in *Grace Unlimited* (Minneapolis: Bethany Fellowship, 1975), 144-161.

a. First Timothy 1:18-20 and 2 Timothy 2:16-18 refer to some, by name, who evidently apostatized from the faith.

b. Colossians 1:21-23 presents final salvation as conditional upon continuing in faith.

c. First Peter 1:5 indicates that our keeping, like our original justification, while it is by the powerful work of God, is also by faith.

d. Galatians 5:1-4 warns about falling from grace and apparently implies that this had happened to false teachers troubling the Galatians.

e. First Thessalonians 3:5; Philippians 2:16; and Galatians 4:9-11 can be grouped together as places where Paul referred to the frightening possibility that his work (which produced true believers) would come to be vain.

f. First Corinthians 10:1-14 warns those who consider (apparently correctly) that they stand against falling, using Israel as a telling example.

Many will use other passages that vary in strength (and applicability) on this subject. I for one am willing to stake the doctrine on the teaching of Hebrews and 2 Peter and then let the other passages confirm what we learn there. If those two books teach that apostasy really is possible, and I am confident they do, then the Calvinist is mistaken on this doctrine.

Response to Calvinists' Scriptures

Response to Scriptures prized by Calvinists as teaching the necessary (for sub-Calvinists, unconditional) perseverance of the regenerate.

1. Those passages, especially in the Gospel of John, which contain strong *promises* of (final) salvation to believers and are therefore thought to imply necessary perseverance can not be used for that purpose lest they "prove too much." In other words, to say that those promises require the impossibility of a changed situation places too great a burden on the syntax of the statements. And this can quickly be seen by comparing similar promises, using the very same syntax, to unbelievers. For example:

John 5:24	*John 3:36*
He that believes . . .	He that believes not . . .
shall not	*shall not*
come into condemnation	see life.

Grammatically, if the first means that the condition of the believer *can not* be changed, then the second means that the condition of the unbeliever likewise *can not* be changed. In fact, neither passage is even speaking to that issue. The unbeliever can leave his unbelief, become a believer, and see life—thus escaping from the promise made to the unbeliever who continues in his unbelief. Likewise, the believer can leave his belief, become an unbeliever, and come into condemnation—thus escaping from the promise made to believers who continue in faith. Each promise applies with equal force to those who continue in the respective state described.

As a believer, I know that I will not come into condemnation and rejoice in the Lord's promise.

2. Furthermore, as additional clarification of this point, one must note that in the overwhelming majority of passages like these, the "believing" is consistently presented as a progressive action (present tense in Greek). Thus, for example:

John 3:36—"The one who *is believing* (present participle) has eternal life."

John 5:24—This is precisely the same as 3:36.

John 3:16—". . . that everyone who *is believing* (present participle) may *be having* (present subjunctive) eternal life." One notes that the "having" corresponds precisely with the "believing."

3. In some passages, even though the conditionality of salvation is not explicitly stated, that conditionality is implicit and to be assumed from the other passages which do teach it clearly. (Throughout Scripture, most of God's dealings with men assume this conditionality although it is sometimes and sometimes not stated.)

In this way John 10:27-29 is to be treated. The promise that "they shall never perish" is for those who are His sheep. It assumes that they remain His sheep. In fact, it is the same kind of promise as those mentioned above in point 1. Arminius observed, on this passage, that "unless the sheep are in the hands of the shepherd, they can not be safe against Satan," and went on to argue that if the sheep's defection precedes seizure by Satan the passage cannot be effectively used to prove unconditional safety.[6] (This passage also belongs in the category to follow.)

4. Some passages aim to assure us of our "security" from the forces that are against us. They do not mean to provide security

---

[6]Arminius, III:499.

against the consequences or possibilities of our own neglect, indifference, or unbelief.

As just noted, John 10:27-29 belongs in this category; the emphasis is that "no one is able to snatch them from My Father's hand." Satan himself cannot take us out of God's preservation.

So does Romans 8:35-39: none of the enemies listed in verses 38, 39 can separate us from God's love in Christ.

5. Passages that express confidence, for the writer or his readers, that "God will perfect the work He has begun" in them are expressing confidence in what God will do, *from His side*, assuming that the persons spoken about continue in faith.

This applies to Philippians 1:6 and 2 Thessalonians 3:3, for example, where Paul's readers are referred to; and to 2 Timothy 1:12; 4:18 where Paul refers to himself.

6. While it is true that 1 Peter 1:5 expresses confidence in God's power as the means of keeping, it also indicates in the same breath that faith is the condition the regenerate must meet for God's keeping power to be effectively applied to them. In fact this verse is stronger for the Arminian position than for that of the Calvinist.

7. Romans 8:29, 30 present the unbroken chain of calling-justification-glorification as the picture of what happens for those in whom God's purpose *is* fully accomplished, without even discussing the question whether any condition is required for any part of it to be accomplished. Regardless, "those whom He foreknew" still "conditions" the whole. See the treatment of this passage in chapter 4.

8. Romans 11:29 simply assures us that God is no "Indian giver" and cannot be thwarted in what He purposes to accomplish. Whatever else it may mean (which need not be pursued here), it is not in a context of personal-evangelical salvation as such.

The Systematic Argument

Generally speaking, Arminians do not rely so much on logical arguments as do Calvinists—that is, not in support of this particular doctrine. (Indeed, Arminians have not traditionally been as strong for systematic theology.) Even so, like the Calvinist, the Arminian will insist that the view that apostasy is possible makes sense when linked with other soteriological doctrines. If God truly desires that all be saved, and sent Christ to atone for the sins of all, and "draws" all who hear with intelligence thus restoring their "freedom" to believe or reject the gospel, and then saves only those who freely choose to believe, then it follows that salvation is conditional.

And if salvation is conditional, then it really is conditional. As Arminius expressed the basic truth, "[God] embraces no one in Christ, unless he is in Christ. But no one is in Christ, except by faith in Christ, which is the necessary means of our union with Christ. If any one falls from faith, he falls from that union, and consequently, from the favor of God by which he was previously embraced in Christ."[7] He goes on to caution that the regenerate cannot fall from being embraced in Christ "while they continue to be believers, because so long they are in Christ."[8]

All this means, simply, from the Arminian perspective, that one's possession of salvation is, at any time, conditioned on faith. In the final analysis, then, the Arminian can rely only on whether the Scripture teaches this.

Logical or not, the sub-Calvinists introduced in the preceding chapter apparently agree with Arminians on all the rest of the soteriological doctrines but disagree about perseverance. In other words, they seem to believe that salvation is conditional, but they do not follow through with insistence that it remains conditional after the initial experience of regeneration.

Both for consistent Calvinists and for Arminians, that position seems to be internally contradictory. For that reason, I do not desire to pursue treatment of that position at length. I will therefore suggest, just briefly, a few responses (in addition to those already given) to some of the sub-Calvinists' "logical" arguments briefly mentioned in the previous chapter.

1. Some of those arguments are based on analogy and do not stand up under closer examination. For example, if the apostasy of a true believer meant that Christ's "body" would be "maimed," one wonders whether it is deformed until the last person in history is saved. Christ's body is not a physical thing to be presented in such terms.

2. Some of the arguments are based on logical, rather than Biblical, statements about what God or a truly regenerate person *would* do, assuming that parallels with human experience can be applied. I readily want to believe that a regenerate person would not ever want to turn from God, in view of his new nature. But then I remember Adam and Eve, who did not even have a depraved nature to incline them toward sin within and fell by external temptation

---

[7]Arminius, III:498.
[8]Arminius, III:499.

alone. And then I am not so smug about what I am and am not capable of.

3. Some of the arguments are mere words. While I suppose it is true that one cannot be "unborn" (which intentionally paints a ridiculous picture) he can certainly *die*.

To repeat, then, all such arguments ultimately trace back to the underlying assumption that salvation is not conditional. If it is, all the things God or man "would" do flow from that. In the final analysis, God is no more unloving to condemn a former child of His than any other of His creatures. He loves them all, but His saving relationship to them is conditioned by faith.

Cautions About Developing a Doctrine of Apostasy

If the Bible teaches that apostasy from a truly regenerate state is possible, one must still be very cautious about expressing or formulating such a view. Here are some of the things to be careful about.

1. It is extremely important to express our view in such a way that faith, and not works, is the sole condition of salvation. We must not establish salvation by grace through faith with the right hand and take it away with the left.

The door out swings on the same hinges as the door in. In other words, the condition of salvation is always the same. As Arminius expressed this, it is "impossible for believers, as long as they remain believers, to decline from salvation."[9] If one gains access to saving grace by faith and not by works, he departs by unbelief and not by works. And, as saving faith has been defined in chapter 9, so its nature does not change once the person has been saved. It remains, as before, the holding out of empty hands to God to accept His free gift, the deliberate turning away from reliance in anything one can "do" and casting everything on what God, in Christ, has done.

"Saved by faith and kept by works" simply will not accord with Biblical teaching relative to the basis of salvation. That basis always remains the same.

2. In whatever ways the positive "works" of a believer are involved in perseverance, we must relate them to faith and not as conditions of continuing in salvation as such. Expressing this relationship precisely is sometimes difficult; the Bible itself does not always attempt

---

[9]Arminius, 1:281. For evidence and citations showing that Thomas Grantham also made this clear, see Matthew Pinson, "The Diversity of Arminian Soteriology" (unpublished paper), 12, 13.

to make sure we understand that such things are *not* "essential" to salvation.

One cannot doubt that faithfulness, right conduct, prayer, and obedience to God are required of Christians, or that they are important for the Christian's spiritual well-being—and thus eventually for his perseverance. Even so, these must apparently be understood as integrally related to the faith which is alone the condition of salvation. In other words, these "works"—if that is the right word—are evidences of faith (for the Christian, perhaps even means of strengthening or sustaining faith), but it is the faith and not the evidences of it that saves.

In that sense, we may even call them "essential," just as bearing apples is "essential" to an apple tree but manifests what the tree is instead of making the tree what it is.

3. Conversely (and equally difficult to express precisely sometimes), we must not make sinful acts, in themselves, the cause of falling from grace. Likewise we must not give the impression that every time a saved person sins he is lost and needs saving again. Furthermore we must not make the mistake of implying that saved people do not sin.

If faith is the condition for salvation, then unbelief is the "condition" for apostasy. Again then works have an important role, whether negatively or positively, but as evidences of faith and unbelief rather than as the fundamental condition of being saved or lost. As McKnight puts it, although somewhat awkwardly, "The only sin . . . capable of destroying a genuine believer's faith is the sin of apostasy."[10] Better to say that the retraction of faith is the only, final means of apostasy; apostasy is a willful retraction of faith.

Do Christians sin? Most assuredly so. Even Wesleyan Arminians who believe in some form of "entire sanctification" believe Christians sin. So do Calvinists, although the classical Calvinists do not encourage us to think that Christians go on indefinitely in lives characterized by sin. What, then, is the difference between the sins of a regenerate person and those of someone unregenerate?

While I am cautious enough to know that I cannot always examine the life of an individual and make a dogmatic judgment about his condition, I think I can *define* the fundamental difference involved. When an unsaved person sins, that sin represents what he really is by

---

[10]Scot McKnight, "The Warning Passages of Hebrews: A Formal Analysis and Theological Conclusions" (*Trinity Journal* 13NS [1992]), 55.

nature. When a regenerate person sins, that sin is a contradiction of what he really is, and he recognizes it as such. Consequently, in the loosely quoted words of 1 John 3:7, the regenerate person does not live in sin; the unregenerate person does. But in both cases the practice is *evidence* of the inner nature, not its cause.

We rejoice that God, who makes the only judgment that counts, knows perfectly the heart of each individual, whether genuine faith is there. We, on the other hand, can "judge" only by what can be seen on the outside, and that kind of judgment—even though it must often be made—may be wrong. In Biblical terms, then, we will rightly continue to regard any person whose life is characterized by sinful practice (regardless what he claims about "salvation") as having no grounds for assurance of salvation.

Does any of this mean that whenever I sin I must immediately doubt my salvation? No. And here we ought to be sure that our way of framing this doctrine provides for God's chastisement. According to Hebrews 12:3-15, God chastises His *children* when they sin, because He loves them as His children. This makes clear that one may do wrong and be chastised for it *as a child of God.*

4. Corollary to what has already been said, we must allow in our expression of this doctrine for the fact that the saving works of grace we receive are based on "union with Christ" and that union is established on meeting the condition of faith. I receive such soteriological blessings as justification—my righteous standing before God in the righteousness of Jesus Christ—by virtue of being "in Him."

If the righteousness of Christ is imputed to me "in Christ," then that status is mine so long as I am in Him. And if I am in Him by faith, then only by a forsaking of saving faith will I be "out of" Him—as crude as that sounds. (While this statement is "logically" expressed, I see no alternative to it when I grapple with the New Testament teaching about the meaning and condition of justification.)

One of the implications of this is, simply, that there is no state "in between" being saved and lost—no Protestant "purgatory" in this life or the next. Any given individual, at any time, is either in saving union with Christ or not. And if he is in Christ, he is by faith alone. Nor does physical death itself bring about any change in one's justified or unjustified state (although, of course, one's state might change very close to the point of death). At the same time, "dying in sin" is certainly a Biblical expression that refers to being lost.

5. It is important, therefore, for us who believe in the possibility of apostasy to teach assurance of salvation and the proper grounds

for that assurance. This viewpoint does not mean, for example, that one may not have assurance, or that one must go about as though walking on eggshells for fear of "losing" his salvation. Living in fear or with lack of assurance of salvation is neither God's will for His child nor in harmony with Biblical teaching.

Assurance, therefore, must be based on the Word of God which promises salvation to those who turn away from their works and put faith in Jesus Christ. Confirming that assurance for those who do this will be the inner testimony of the Spirit of God. Understanding that being accounted righteous before God depends on the righteousness of Christ imputed to the one in Him by faith should help the most timid believer have assurance of salvation.

At the same time, the Bible offers us no encouragement to provide assurance of salvation to those whose lives are characterized by sinful practice. Both traditional Calvinists and Arminians will agree with this.

6. Also important, we must express our view in such a way that apostasy is recognized as a serious and willful, decisive crisis. Apostasy is not what most people mean by "backsliding." It is not something that a true believer, regenerated by the Spirit of God, can do lightly and easily. One is not saved today, lost tomorrow, and saved again the day after.

So long as one continues to exercise saving faith, he has not committed apostasy. Indeed, it appears to be true that so long as one desires to be right with God in Christ he has not committed apostasy, but it is beyond my purpose here to explore that point.

Apostasy, apparently, can not be reversed and is final. As already noted, I will provide grounds for this view in the following chapter. At the same time, while apostasy is not easily arrived at, we ought not to say that it does not really happen. Both in the Bible and in the experiential observation of the church, cases of apostasy are *relatively* common.

7. It is equally important, therfore, for us to warn believers about the danger of apostasy and to exhort them to persevere in faith and good works, not as a means of frightening or troubling them but as a means of edifying them and nurturing their spiritual development, which is the one, sure, Biblical way of avoiding apostasy (2 Peter 3:17,18).

As already noted, the traditional Calvinist agrees that the New Testament itself does actually present such warnings and exhortations, and that these are in fact means of perseverance. It is obviously Biblical, therefore, to take up such warnings and exhortations. It is not so obviously Biblical, however, to teach believers that these are merely warnings against something that can not really happen. One wonders if these warnings and exhortations can have their intended effect if the presenter afterward assures his hearers that such apostasy is not a real possibility. Do any of those pastors who deny the possibility of apostasy warn their flock against it?

If not, that is most certainly not the Biblical way. Indeed, such warnings and exhortations have force precisely because they refer to a real danger. To convince believers that there is no possibility of apostasy is to negate the Biblical warning. I cannot avoid saying, therefore, that the Calvinist attempt to explain the Biblical warnings as means by which the perseverance is ensured is, finally, a sad travesty.

On the negative side, believers ought to be warned against those roads that might lead to apostasy. These will include tolerance of false doctrine, continued indulgence in sin, and rebelling against God's chastisement. Any of these may put one on a path that leads to the conscious and willful disbelief that is involved in "departing from the living God" (Hebrews 3:12).

On the positive side, believers ought to be exhorted and nurtured in spiritual development. As already noted, the entire epistle of 2 Peter presents this as the one way to be sure that one will not apostatize.

For Further Reading on the
Arminian Doctrine of Perseverance

Arminius, James. *The Writings of James Arminius* (three vols.), tr. James Nichols and W. R. Bagnall. Grand Rapids: Baker, 1956 (vol. I, pp. 252-255, 262-264, 278-282, 285-289; vol. II, pp. 499-501).

Duty, Guy. *If Ye Continue*. Minneapolis: Bethany Fellowship, 1966.

Forlines, F. Leroy. *Biblical Systematics*. Nashville: Randall House Publications, 1975 (pp. 207-230). [A colleague of this writer]

Marshall, I. Howard. *Kept By the Power of God*. Minneapolis: Bethany Fellowship, 1969.

Osborne, Grant. "Soteriology in the Epistle to the Hebrews" (ch. 8) and "Exegetical Notes on Calvinist Texts" (ch. 9), *Grace Unlimited*, ed. Clark H. Pinnock. Minneapolis: Bethany Fellowship, 1975. [Osborne does not seem to be as much in pursuit of novelty as do some of the other writers in this book, like Lake and Pinnock.]

Shank, Robert. *Life In the Son*. Springfield, Mo.: Westcott Publishers, 1960.

Watson, Richard. *Theological Institutes*. New York: Nelson and Phillips, 1850 (vol. II, pp. 295-301). [An important, early Wesleyan theologian]

CHAPTER THIRTEEN

Hebrews, Second Peter, and the Possibility of Apostasy

It seems clear to me that a truly Biblical or exegetical theology approach will sustain the doctrine I have set forth in the previous chapter. It is the purpose of this chapter to demonstrate this from Hebrews and Second Peter.

Hebrews 6:4-6

For those who believe in the possibility of personal apostasy, the Book of Hebrews as a whole and Hebrews 6:4-6 in particular is one of the most important passages involved in providing a Biblical basis for the view. The greater part of this chapter, therefore, is devoted to a thorough exegesis of this key passage in the context of the book and to treat questions about how it relates to the possibility that a truly regenerate person may "fall from grace."

Whether they can agree on this doctrine or not, all Christians should agree that our teaching on any subject ought to be based on what the Bible has to say rather than on traditional philosophical or theological arguments. My aim here, then, is to determine exactly what Hebrews 6:4-6 teaches.

The Context for the Passage

One of the requirements of good exegesis is to understand how a given passage fits into its context. In this case we should consider the general thrust of Hebrews as a whole. These three verses come in the midst of a book that has perseverance for its major theme.

We need not review the discussion about the original writer of Hebrews. The inspired text does not identify him or her.

Nor are we required to establish, for sure, the identity of the original audience. The inspired text does not tell us that either; the title "To the Hebrews" is a later addition.

Even so, the tradition that the "epistle" was written for Jewish Christians owes its strength to the obvious fact that all its teaching is presented against the backdrop of Jewish ritual. Kent is correct in saying, "Most conservatives would agree that the Hebrew-Christian

character of Hebrews is self-evident."[1] He explains the usual understanding of the first readers' situation at the time:

> A careful study of the five warning passages shows their problem to
> have been the very serious one of wavering before the temptation to
> leave the Christian movement and retire to the safer haven of Judaism.
> By such a move, they could avoid persecution from their Jewish kins-
> men, and also enjoy the legal protection which Judaism had from the
> government—a boon which Christians at this time [in the sixties] did
> not possess.[2]

Even if that conclusion were successfully challenged (and there
are some who would do so), the interpretation of the passage would
not be significantly affected. Whoever the original readers were, an
inductive study of Hebrews by itself makes clear that the readers
were considering defection and in need of exhortation to persevere in
the faith.

A Theme of Hebrews

One indication of the dominant motif in Hebrews is the frequent
occurrence of words urging the readers to *hold* to the faith. Several of
these reflect the Greek root *echō*. In 2:1, the King James says "We
ought to give the more earnest heed to the things which we have
heard." The word translated "give heed" is *prosechō*, meaning "hold
on to." In 3:6 we are said to make up Christ's house if we "hold fast"—
a good translation of *katechō*. The same word appears again in 3:14,
"We have become partakers of Christ if we *hold fast*; and in 10:23,
where we are exhorted to "hold fast." In 4:14 a different and even
more forceful word occurs, *krateō*, which means to cling to, seize,
grasp. We are urged there to "cling to" our profession—to hold on for
dear life.

Some writers have cited "let us go on" (6:1) as the key phrase of
Hebrews; Griffith Thomas even used this as the name for his commentary.[3] Shank has correctly observed that "let us hold fast" is much
more frequent and significant, far more deserving of status as the
theme of the book.[4]

---

[1]Homer A. Kent, *The Epistle to the Hebrews: A Commentary* (Grand Rapids: Baker,
1972), 23.

[2]Kent, 25.

[3]W. H. Griffith Thomas, *Let Us Go On* (Grand Rapids: Zondervan, 1944).

[4]Robert Shank, *Life in the Son* (Springfield, Mo.: Westcott Publishers, 1960), 233.

The Structure of Hebrews

More important than this recurring theme-phrase is the pattern of the contents of Hebrews. An exhortation to persevere is at the heart of every major section of the book.

Almost everyone will agree that Hebrews gives its consuming interest to convincing the readers that Christ and the New Covenant are (1) infinitely superior to all that went before and (2) final. This Christological center of interest is certainly the *doctrinal* passion of the book. But the *hortatory* concern is perseverance. Indeed, almost the only practical exhortation contained in the whole book, except for brief miscellaneous exhortations in the concluding chapter, is the exhortation to persevere. As Osborne observes, "The willful apostasy of some from the faith" is "the particular problem to which the epistle is addressed."[5]

This concern for perseverance, inseparably linked with warnings against apostasy, is therefore the dominant pastoral concern of Hebrews. It makes up the very warp and woof of it, the pattern about which all the cloth is woven. Even the teaching about the superiority and finality of revelation and religion in Christ serves as reenforcement for the repeated pleas to "hold fast to the faith." Guthrie comments, "The writer has no intention of writing a purely academic treatise, but aims throughout to emphasize the practical significance of the points he makes."[6] Marshall notes that the warning passages "are not parentheses . . . but form an integral part of the structure in which dogmatic theology and practical exhortations are intricately bound up together."[7]

Hebrews is not merely an "epistle" in the usual sense of the word. In form, it closes like one but does not begin like one. In content, it is more like a full-length sermon. Thus Buchanan's comment that Hebrews "is a homiletical midrash based on Ps 110."[8] (But this gives the "sermon" too narrow a scope.) The text and introduction to this sermon appear in 1:1, 2: God has spoken in various ways in the past, but has given His final and perfect word to us in His Son. The conclusion appears in 12:25-29: You must not refuse Him who speaks; if

---

[5]Grant R. Osborne, "Soteriology in the Epistle to the Hebrews," in *Grace Unlimited*, ed. Clark Pinnock (Minneapolis: Bethany Fellowship, 1975), 146.

[6]Donald Guthrie, *Hebrews*, Tyndale NT Commentaries (Downers Grove: Inter-Varsity, 1983), 81.

[7]I. Howard Marshall, *Kept By the Power of God* (Minneapolis: Bethany Fellowship, 1969), 139.

[8]George Wesley Buchanan, "To The Hebrews," *Anchor Bible* (New York: Doubleday, 1972), xix.

those who refused Him when He spoke in the past did not escape, much more we will not escape if we turn away from the one who is His final Word. This conclusion makes clear the point of the whole message, which 13:22 calls a "word of exhortation."

The first section of Hebrews (after the introduction in 1:1-5) is generally agreed to be chapters 1 and 2, which Westcott entitles "The Superiority of the Son, the Mediator of the New Revelation, to Angels."[9] At the heart of this is 2:1-4 (Kent's "First Warning Passage"). Verse 1 literally reads, "Because of this, it is necessary for us to be holding on all the more exceedingly to the things heard, lest haply we drift away (from them)." Even those who do not believe that personal apostasy is possible agree that the meaning really is, *lest we drift or slip away*: "The meaning of the word and its personal subject ("we") indicate not that something might drift away from us, but that 'we' might drift away from something."[10] The word was sometimes used for a boat that had slipped its moorings.

The second section is clearly chapters 3 and 4: "Moses, Joshua, Jesus—the Founders of the Old Economy and of the New."[11] At the heart of this is the passage 3:7—4:2 (Kent's "Second Warning Passage," which he extends to 4:13). There we read, literally: "Be on watch, brothers, lest haply there will be in anyone of you a wicked, unbelieving heart in departing from the living God" (3:12). "Departing" is the very Greek root that our English "apostasy" comes from (the verb *apostēnai*; the cognate noun is *apostasia*), "an unbelief which abandons hope."[12] The writer is saying, simply, "Brothers, be on guard against apostatizing from God."

Lenski notes that *unbelief* in Hebrews "is thus understood in the sense of once having believed in the living God and then having turned away from him."[13] Bruce compares "the action of the Israelites when they 'turned back in their hearts unto Egypt'. . . a gesture of outright apostasy, a complete break with God."[14] Guthrie sees in this "the greatest defection possible."[15]

---

[9]B. F. Westcott, *The Epistle to the Hebrews* (Grand Rapids: Eerdmans, 1955), xlviii.

[10]Kent, 47.

[11]Westcott, xlviii.

[12]*Theological Dictionary of the New Testament* (Grand Rapids: Eerdmans, 1972, hereafter identified as TDNT), I:513.

[13]R. C. H. Lenski, *The Interpretation of the Epistle to the Hebrews and The Epistle of James* (Minneapolis: Augsburg, 1966), 118.

[14]F. F. Bruce, *The Epistle to the Hebrews* (New International Commentary of the NT: Grand Rapids: Eerdmans, 1964), 66.

[15]Guthrie, 106.

We also read in this section, literally, "We have come to be partakers of Christ, if in fact we hold fast [the theme word discussed above] the beginning of our confidence firm unto the end" (3:14). Westcott comments, "That which has been stated as fact [that is, having become partakers of Christ] is now made conditional in its permanence on the maintenance of faith."[16]

The third and central section is chapters 5-7: "The High-priesthood of Christ, Universal and Sovereign."[17] At the heart of this is the extended exhortation of 5:11—6:12 (Kent's "Third Warning Passage," 5:11—6:20). Since this is the passage that contains 6:4-6, further comment is saved for the next part of this chapter.

The final section is chapters 8-12, although many interpreters prefer to make this into two sections, 8:1—10:18 and 10:19—12:29. If I were going to divide this into two main parts, I would divide at 11:1; then each of the teaching parts would be concluded with exhortation. But this matter does not need to occupy us here.

Regardless, there are two extended passages of exhortation woven into these five chapters. Kent's "Fourth Warning Passage" is 10:26-31; actually the exhortation extends from 10:10-39. Once again we are urged, literally, "Let us be holding fast [the theme word again] the confession of hope unwavering" (10:23). And to this is attached the terrible warning of verses 26-31: if we will to take back up our sinful ways, thus trampling under foot Christ's blood and doing insult to the Spirit, our punishment will be much worse than death without mercy as prescribed in the Mosaic economy.

Citing the favorite text for justification by faith, "The just shall live by faith," the writer adds (from the same source in the LXX), "but if he [the just one] draws back, my soul has no pleasure in him" (verse 38). Westcott correctly urges that it is altogether unwarranted to read the inserted "any man" of the King James as though this is someone other than "the just one."[18] The inspired writer of Hebrews is referring, specifically, to the "drawing back" of one justified by faith, leading to this pronouncement by God.

The final, extensive exhortation serves as the conclusion to the section and to the "sermon" as a whole and includes all of chapter 12 (although Kent includes, in his "Fifth Warning Passage," just 12:18-29). Here we are warned "lest anyone fall back from [Westcott: "implying

---

[16]Westcott, 85.
[17]Westcott, xlix.
[18]Westcott, 337.

a moral separation"[19]] the grace of God" (verse 15). The writer backs this up with the example of Esau as one for whom no place of repentance and restoration to what he had lost could be found. The serious conclusion, then, is that we will not escape if we "turn back from" the One who is, and who speaks, from heaven. Actually, the writer does not present this in a merely hypothetical manner; literally, the words are "we who are turning back from." He evidently regards the process of apostasy as having already begun and identifies himself with his people in this awful thing.

It is clear, then, that 6:4-6 is at the heart of a book that has the question of apostasy and perseverance at its very roots. The five warning passages tie the "sermon" together and reveal that its main thrust is to exhort the audience to hold fast to the faith they have placed in Christ lest apostasy occur, lest they forsake the very One God has revealed as providing, by His redemptive work, room for them to stand righteous before God. There is no sacrifice for sins, no provision for righteousness, outside Him.

Such is the context of 6:4-6, and it is clear that each of the five warning passages is clarified by the other warning passages. All five describe the same sin, include the same warning, and exhort the same audience. This fact has been conclusively demonstrated by Scot McKnight in a study that clearly establishes the meaning of each of these components by a "synthetic" comparison of the passages.[20]

The Text

To begin, here is my own more or less literal translation of the passage, arranged so that the reader can more clearly see the relationship of the clauses:

> For it is impossible for those
>> who were once-for-all enlightened
>> and who tasted of the heavenly free gift
>> and who became partakers of the Holy Spirit
>> and who tasted God's good word and the powers of
>>> the coming age
>> and who fell away
> to be being renewed again unto repentance,
> they crucifying again to/for themselves the Son of God and
>> exposing (Him) to public shame.

---

[19]Westcott, 406.
[20]Scot McKnight, "The Warning Passages of Hebrews: A Formal Analysis and Theological Conclusions" (*Trinity Journal* 13NS [1992]), 21-59.

The exegesis and interpretation of these words involve three key questions about the experience of the persons whom the writer is describing. (For the moment, this need not involve whether they had actually done all this or were simply candidates for it.)

Does the passage describe genuine Christians?

This question arises because some interpreters suggest that something less than genuine conversion is meant. The people that the writer of Hebrews describes are said to have experienced four positive things. The question, then, depends on the meaning of these four clauses, as follows.

1. They were once-for-all enlightened. This appears, by any reading, to refer to the spiritual enlightenment we associate with salvation. The verb *phōtizomai* means to give one light or bring him into light. The very same description appears again in 10:32, where also there is no reason to doubt that the writer consciously uses it to mean conversion. The Biblical background involved is the contrast between darkness and light and between those in the darkness and those in the light (cf. 2 Cor. 4:4).

The word translated "once," *hapax,* has the idea "once for all" or "once effectively." This same word occurs several times in Hebrews, and comparing them is instructive: 9:7, 26, 27, 28; 10:2; 12:26, 27. In all these places the word consciously implies something done once in a way that no repetition or addition is needed to complete it. Kent acknowledges that "The use of 'once for all' points to something complete, rather than partial or inadequate."[21]

2. They tasted of the heavenly free gift. Two points have sometimes been made against equating this with genuine salvation. One is the use of "taste," said by some to imply a partial rather than a full experience. But that objection reflects a modern English idiom rather than the way the ancient Greeks used *geuomai.* Even when referring to food, they could use this word for full-fledged eating, as in Acts 10:10. More important, they used this words metaphorically to mean "experience." Especially significant is the fact that the writer of Hebrews uses this very same word again in 2:9 to refer to Christ's "experiencing" death. No one would wish to say that He only partially or incompletely experienced death.

---

[21]Kent, 108.

The other objection is more technical: namely, that "taste" is followed here by a *genitive* object rather than by the accusative, and that the genitive case merely identifies what kind of thing it is while the accusative is the case of extent. The objectors say this means that the people referred to tasted *of* the gift rather than tasting to the full extent of experience.

Two things are wrong with this objection. First, while the genitive does not expressly speak of extent, it does not deny it. More important, the genitive is also the case used for the object in 2:9 where Christ tasted death! (See also on the fourth clause, below.)

The people being described, then, "experienced" the heavenly free-gift. Interpreters are not unanimous in identifying this "free gift," but the disagreement is more technical than substantial, and the general meaning is clear. The various interpreters suggest salvation, eternal life, forgiveness of sins, the Holy Spirit, or Christ Himself. Probably the best conclusion is that it means salvation and what goes with it: justification and eternal life in Christ, "salvation blessings."[22]

3. They became partakers of the Holy Spirit. Guthrie observes, "The idea of sharing the Holy Spirit is remarkable. This at once distinguishes the person from one who has no more than a nodding acquaintance with Christianity."[23] The word "partakers," metochoi, which means "to have together with," is apparently used by the writer of Hebrews exclusively to refer to Christians' common participation in things related to their salvation. In 3:1 we are "partakers" of the heavenly calling; in 3:14 "partakers" of Christ; and in 12:8 "partakers" of the discipline that distinguishes between true sons and bastards. Either of these three, or the one here, will by itself be adequate to identify such a "partaker" as a Christian.

To have the Holy Spirit, in common with other believers, is certainly to be a Christian. Receiving the gift of the Spirit, in the New Testament, is a regular way of stating what it means to become a Christian. Acts 2:38, 39 and Galatians 3:14 are just two of many examples.

4. They tasted God's good word and the powers of the coming age. We meet "taste" again; see above on the second clause. If any doubt should remain about the fact that the genitive object was used in the clause above, this one will remove that doubt. The object is accusative here.

---

[22]Osborne, 149.
[23]Guthrie, 142.

Those described have "experienced" God's good word. This means that they have experienced the goodness that God has spoken of. God has spoken good to those who put faith in Him, and these have experienced that good. As Kent puts it, this is "experiencing the word of God in the gospel and finding it good."[24] Compare 1 Peter 2:3.

Furthermore, they have "experienced" the powers of the coming age. "Powers," *dunameis*, often means "miracles" (as in 2:4). In its broadest sense, that is the idea here: supernatural workings. Manifestations of Divine power do not have their origin in this present age. All the mighty works of God are from the age to come, "other-world power" as Lenski expresses it.[25] But Christians, though still living in the present age, have already begun to experience the supernatural workings characteristic of the age to come. This includes more than we need to discuss here, but regeneration and the gift of the Spirit are the initial powerful works of the age to come that all Christians have in common.

Osborne points out that "the age to come" is important in the eschatology of Hebrews, where "Eschatology becomes a part of soteriology" and so this phrase implies a foretaste of "kingdom blessings."[26] J. Behm, discussing all the "taste" clauses in the verse, says they describe "vividly the reality of personal experiences of salvation enjoyed by Christians at conversion."[27]

Of these four clauses as a whole, then, we may say that one would be hard put to find a better description of genuine regeneration and conversion. Either of them will stand by itself in this respect. The four together provide one of the finest statements about salvation, from its experiential side, that appears anywhere in the Scriptures.

Among those who apparently agree with the position taken here is Scot McKnight, who calls these "phenomenological-true believers," by which he means that they are genuine believers at present, in every way observable. The writer of Hebrews perceives them so. But they might or might not persevere in that faith. If they do, their faith is "saving" faith in the eyes of the writer of Hebrews, since he uses "salvation" to mean *final* salvation. Meanwhile, theirs is the condition of *all* believers in the present life.[28]

---

[24]Kent, 109.
[25]Lenski, 184.
[26]Osborne, 148,149.
[27]TDNT, I:676.
[28]McKnight, 24, 25.

I must criticize McKnight's terminology in what is otherwise an outstanding monograph. Although he justifies this as a way of being true to the use of words like faith and salvation in Hebrews, I think he is at fault on several counts. (1) He seems not to realize how jarring are statements like, "This expression gives us even more evidence for contending that these readers were, at the phenomenological level, converts to Jesus Christ."[29] In fact, the statement would sound more like the writer of Hebrews if "at the phenomenological level" were omitted. (2) The "phenomenological" qualifier casts doubt on the genuineness of their Christianity, even though McKnight makes clear that he does not intend this, affirming that those referred to are "Christian" and "regenerate," and that the faith of *all* Christians is "phenomenological-true."[30] (3) It is confusing to use terms in ways different from their customary use. Nor does it soften the underlying disagreement with Calvinism—not that I suppose McKnight intended it to. (4) While *we* may not be able to judge the genuineness of faith on just an observable basis, God is not thus limited and the divine inspiration of the writer of Hebrews would apparently guarantee the genuineness of the faith of those he describes as genuine. In other words, then, there is finally no difference between a "phenomenological-true believer" and a "true believer" in the Book of Hebrews.

Does the passage describe apostasy from salvation?

The answer to this question resides in the meaning of the clause which the King James renders, "If they shall fall away."

There is not much dispute about the meaning of the words. In light of the impossibility of repentance attached (to be discussed below), most interpreters readily accept that to "fall away" as used here leaves a person outside a saving relationship with Christ.[31]

"Fall away" is *parapiptō*, and this is the verb's only appearance in the New Testament. It occurs in the LXX in passages that also refer to apostasy, as Ezekiel 18:24. As Kent says, though he does not believe apostasy is possible, the words mean "complete and final repudiation of Christ (as in 10:26, 27)" and describe "those who are regenerated and then repudiate Christ and forsake Him."[32] The "falling away" is

---

[29]McKnight, 47.
[30]McKnight, 49.
[31]An exception is T. K. Oberholtzer in a series, "The Warning Passages of Hebrews," in *Bibliotheca Sacra* 145,146 (1988-89).
[32]Kent, 110.

defection from the experience described in the four positive clauses that precede.

That is what apostasy means. In light of the contents of the entire Book of Hebrews, as outlined above, the "falling away" is obviously synonymous with "drifting away" (2:1), "departing from [literally, apostatizing from] the living God" (3:12), "drawing back" (10:38), and "turning away from the One from heaven" (12:25). McKnight convincingly shows that the one "sin" of apostasy is in view throughout Hebrews.[33]

Some interpreters, perhaps unfamiliar with the Greek original, misunderstand the relationship of the clauses. They readily acknowledge that the first four, positive clauses describe a truly regenerate state. Then they add, using the King James wording, that such regenerate persons as these, *if* they should fall away, could not possibly be renewed to repentance. One notes the emphasis on the "if." In fact, they say, this is a purely hypothetical addition; the truly regenerate cannot really "fall away."

But the grammar of the original will not permit this reading. The fifth clause cannot be made a merely hypothetical attachment to an otherwise real set of circumstances. The literal translation I gave earlier shows this in English. In Greek the grammar is equally clear. We have *five equal, coordinate, aorist-tense participles* in a series. The persons described have done all five things equally: they were enlightened, experienced the gift of God, became partakers of the Holy Spirit, experienced God's good word and the miraculous works of the age to come, and fell away.

That is exactly the way the Greek reads. I assume the King James translators introduced the "if" to make the long sentence smoother and more readable, at the same time omitting the Greek *kai* ("and"). Kent recognizes what is involved: "Grammatically there is no warrant for treating the last [participle] in the series any differently from the others."[34] The NASB gives an especially clear and accurate translation: "In the case of those who have once been enlightened . . . and then have fallen away, it is impossible to renew them again to repentance." (Even the "then" is unnecessary and not in the original.)

---

[33]McKnight, 39, 40.
[34]Kent, 108.

What is the nature of the impossibility referred to?

Of those who have experienced the five things listed, the writer says that it is not possible to be renewing them again to repentance. This affirmation is very strong. For emphasis the word "impossible" is moved up to the front of the whole sentence.

Two things are involved in this impossibility, although they cannot be separated. First, one must consider *what* is impossible. It is "renewal to repentance," which makes clear that they had repented earlier. Repentance is a thorough-going change of heart, mind, and will. Now that the falling away has taken place, repentance from that apostate unbelief is not possible. All this seems fairly obvious from the words themselves.

Repentance has already been introduced into the immediate context. In verses 1-3 the writer has said that we ought, in our experience, to let ourselves be carried along toward maturity rather than putting down again (among other things) the foundation of "repentance from dead works." For, he adds in verses 4-6, the person who is converted and falls away cannot be renewed unto repentance. Clearly, then, the same repentance is meant: the repentance from dead works that comes at conversion.

The association of "repentance" with a warning against apostasy in 12:15-17 strengthens this understanding. The warning "lest anyone fall back from the grace of God" is linked to the case of Esau for whom "a place (opportunity) of repentance was not found"—one that would enable him to receive the inheritance he had so tragically traded away.

The second consideration is *why* there is no possibility for repentance. The explanation is contained in the words (in the King James), "seeing they crucify to themselves the Son of God afresh, and put him to an open shame." The translators supplied "seeing"; the literal words are, "(they) re-crucifying to (or, for) themselves the Son of God and exposing (Him) to public shame." The cross, in Roman times, was an object of special shame. Apostates are "identified with those whose hatred of Christ led them to exhibit him as an object of contempt on a hated Roman gibbet."[35] Arminius faced William Perkins' objection to the possibility of apostasy on the grounds that "entire defection from true faith would require a second ingrafting, if indeed he, who falls away, shall be saved." One line of his response was, "It is not absolutely necessary that he, who falls away, should be again

---

[35]Guthrie, 144.

ingrafted; indeed some will say, from Heb. vi and x, that one, who wholly falls away from the true faith, can not be restored by repentance."[36] It is not clear whether this would have been the view of Arminius himself. It is clear that Thomas Grantham, the early General Baptist theologian, agreed that apostasy is "an 'irrevocable Estate' from which the apostate can never return."[37]

A very few interpreters would argue that this is not a *reason* at all and that the KJV translators made a poor choice of words when they used "seeing." The technicalities of the grammar are that these are circumstantial participles, which leaves it to the interpreter to determine from the context just what *kind* of circumstances are meant. Thus Shank offers his opinion that these are circumstances of *time* and not of cause (as in KJV). He would therefore translate thus: "It is impossible to renew them again to repentance so long as they are crucifying . . . and publicly shaming Him."[38]

Such a view leads to the conclusion that the apostasy described here can be remedied, that repentance from apostasy back to God is not finally impossible after all, so that the writer of Hebrews only means a temporary impossibility. Westcott (even though he, unlike Shank, takes the participles as causal) believes that the passage teaches apostasy and that the apostasy can be remedied: "The moral cause of the impossibility which has been affirmed . . . is an active, continuous hostility to Christ in the souls of such men."[39] He therefore limits the impossibility to *human* agency and sugests that *divine* agency *can* accomplish in such a case a restoration from death to life (technically not another new birth).[40] I agree with Marshall that "The passage gives us no right to assert that there may be a special intervention of God to restore those whom men cannot restore."[41]

Very few interpreters will accept that the apostasy described here can be remedied. There are several good arguments against it. For one thing, the clause simply does not fit as a temporal clause. It "feels right" only as causal and the interpreters and translators are nearly

---

[36]James Arminius, *The Writings of James Arminius,* tr. James Nichols and W. R. Bagnall (Grand Rapids: Baker, 1956), III:494.

[37]Matthew Pinson, "The Diversity of Arminian Soteriology" (unpublished paper), 13, citing Thomas Grantham, *Christianismus Primitivus, or the Ancient Christian Religion* (London: Francis Smith, 1678), II:154.

[38]Shank, 318.

[39]Westcott, 151.

[40]Westcott, 150, 165.

[41]Marshall, 142.

unanimous in rendering it, "It is impossible . . . *because* ("seeing") they are re-crucifying Him."

For another thing, the emphasis on the *impossible*, as noted above, makes more sense if this is a real (and not just a merely human) impossibility. Shank's interpretation winds up saying that it is impossible to renew them to repentance so long as they persist in their attitude of rejection—which is not much of a point since it is always impossible to bring anyone to repentance so long as he persists in rejection: "a truism hardly worth putting into words."[42] This almost amounts to saying that it is impossible to bring such a person to repentance so long as he persists in an attitude that makes it impossible to bring him to repentance; and that is pure tautology. Westcott's way of putting it is not quite that weak. What he is saying is that it is impossible for *men* to bring this person back to repentance because of his active, on-going hostility to Christ. But that does not do justice to the sentence either; it is always impossible for men to produce repentance without Divine agency.

Yet another thing: one must do justice to the point of verses 7, 8. The "for" in verse 7 attaches these two verses to verses 4-6 as a reason, given in the form of an illustration. Thus the impossibility of verses 4-6 lies not merely in the attitude of the apostate but also in the judgment of God. The land in the illustration is "reprobate land"[43]—*adokimos* (as in 1 Cor. 9:27, "castaway").

Finally, one more reason for regarding the apostasy of verses 4-6 as final is found in the other passages about apostasy in Hebrews, as listed earlier in this article. Thus 2:1-4 asks how we shall escape if we "drift away" from this great salvation, implying that there is no escape. The passage beginning at 3:7 backs up its warning against apostasy by reminding us of the Israelites to whom God swore that they would not enter the promised rest. In 12:25, again, the warning is that we will not escape if we turn away from Him.

Especially does 10:26-39 shed light on the serious finality of apostasy. This passage warns that God will take no pleasure in the one who draws back (verse 38). Bruce speaks of this as "the divine displeasure which will rest upon him."[44] The passage also provides us with the true reason for the impossibility: for the one who wills to return to sin, thus treading under foot the blood of Christ's sacrifice

---

[42]Bruce, 124.
[43]Bruce, 125.
[44]Bruce, 274.

for sin and insulting the Spirit of grace, there "remaineth no more sacrifice for sins." Christ's blood is the only atonement for sin. Having
experienced and then rejected that, the apostate has nowhere else to
turn. The re-crucifying and public exposure of Christ in 6:6 clearly
refers to the same thing as the treading under foot and counting the
atoning blood an unholy thing in 10:29.

For all these reasons, then, it seems clear that the apostasy of
these verses is a final and irreversible apostasy.

Other Readings of the Text

Briefly, and in summary fashion, notice should be taken of the
views of those who disagree with the position taken here, whether
Calvinists or sub-Calvinists. Among those who do not believe that
personal apostasy from saving faith is possible, there are two main
ways of explaining the meaning of Hebrews 6:4-6.

Denial of Regeneration

The first is to say that the people described here were not meant
to be pictured as truly regenerate. As Wuest expresses this view, the
"apostasy" referred to in Hebrews is "the act of an unsaved
Jew . . . renouncing his professed faith in Messiah."[45] Bruce compares
these to people "immunized against a disease by being inoculated
with a mild form of it . . . something which, for the time being, looks
so like the real thing that it is genuinely mistaken for it.[46] Morris compares Simon Magus, quoting Acts 8:13, that he "believed and was baptized. And he followed Philip everywhere." Then he notes, "This is as
definite as anything in Hebrews 6."[47] (In fact, *everything* in Hebrews
6:4, 5 is more definite than that!)

This approach has already been answered above and need not be
discussed at length again. (One wishes to say that such exegesis
serves the Calvinist's need to negate the Arminian view; one wonders,
however, if it serves equally well as a basis for warning persons who
are in such danger.) The fact is that the four positive participles
describe, in the clearest way possible, genuine conversion. Even Kent
has it precisely right when he says that he "doubts whether the same
description if found elsewhere would ever be explained by these

---

[45]Kenneth S. Wuest, "Hebrews Six in the Greek New Testament" (*Bibliotheca Sacra*
119 [1962]), 46.

[46]Bruce, 118, 119.

[47]Leon Morris, *Hebrews*, Bible Study Commentary (Grand Rapids: Zondervan,
1983), 59.

interpreters in any way other than full regeneration."[48] Nicole, after offering Calvinistic explanations of the fact that these apostates had earlier "repented," acknowledges that "neither of these explanations appears entirely free of difficulty, although one may prefer to have recourse to them rather than to be forced to the conclusion that regenerate individuals may be lost."[49] Good for his honesty, bad for his exegetical objectivity!

Hypothetical Warning

The other approach is to say that the writer is dealing only with a hypothetical situation. I have noted earlier that it simply will not do to regard the first four participles as real and then treat the fifth as hypothetical. But some interpreters treat the entire description as hypothetical. In other words, they say that the passage really describes a truly regenerate person who commits apostasy. But, they say, such a case is hypothetical and cannot really occur.

This is Kent's view. He suggests that "The author has described a supposed case, assuming for the moment the presuppositions of some of his confused and wavering readers."[50] In other words, assuming that the readers as true Christians were being tempted to forsake Christianity and return to Judaism, the writer is showing them the folly of their consideration by saying that a person who was truly saved and forsook Christ could never again be saved. "True believers (seeing what an awful consequence apostasy would have, if it were possible) would be warned by this statement to remain firm (and from the human standpoint the warnings of Scripture are a means to ensure the perseverance of the saints)."[51]

Kent quotes Westcott for this explanation: "The case is hypothetical. There is nothing to show that the conditions of fatal apostasy had been fulfilled, still less that they had been fulfilled in the case of any of these addressed. Indeed the contrary is assumed: vv. 9ff."[52] But he is clearly mistaken in his reading of Westcott, who means something else entirely by "hypothetical." Westcott only means that the writer of Hebrews assumes that his readers had not yet apostatized,

---

[48]Kent, 112.

[49]Roger Nicole, "Some Comments on Hebrews 6:4-6 and the Doctrine of the Perseverance of God with the Saints," in *Current Issues in Biblical and Patristic Interpretation*, ed. G. Hawthorne (Grand Rapids: Eerdmans, 1975), 361.

[50]Kent, 113.

[51]Kent, 113.

[52]Westcott, 165.

not that they *could* not. Westcott believes apostasy is a *real* possibility. Guthrie understands Westcott more correctly: "The writer appears to be reflecting on a hypothetical case, although in the nature of the whole argument it must be supposed that it was a real possibility."[53]

In that sense, one may agree that the writer of Hebrews is not necessarily describing people who had already committed apostasy, as 6:9 implies. At the same time, I am confident that the passage describes apostasy as a real possibility, even if an extreme case. For the writer to describe the awful consequences that would result if people were saved and apostatized finally carries no warning value at all if it cannot happen. As Morris puts it, "Unless he is speaking of a real possibility his warning means nothing."[54] In the previous chapter I have commented on the fact that theologians who do not believe apostasy is possible do not warn believers against it!

Furthermore, the grammar of the passage is against reading it as a merely hypothetical construction. The Greeks had several ways to present hypothetical propositions: the subjunctive mode, the optative mode, even the imperfect of the indicative mode (as in 11:15, for example). But aorist participles, used as they are in this sentence, simply do not convey hypothesis. I have counted 77 other instances of the aorist participle in Hebrews, and not one of them is hypothetical—unless one counts these in 6:4-6 and those in 10:29 where the grammar and theology are the same as here.

If we look not at the participles but at the main clause, the writer is forthrightly saying that "It is impossible to renew [these] to repentance"—not that it *would* be impossible to renew them under given circumstances. The construction is exactly the same as in 6:18 (It is impossible for God to lie); 10:4 (It is impossible for the blood of bulls and goats to take away sin); and 11:6 (It is impossible to please God without faith).

In every way then the writer is saying in a straightforward manner that it is not possible to renew to repentance persons who have done the five things he lists. This warning, considered by itself or in association with the repeated warnings of the entire book, is so effective just because this apostasy is possible and recovery impossible. (Once more, I recommend the NASB translation of these verses.)

Having considered how the text is read by those who do not believe apostasy is possible, I should add for completeness that those

---

[53]Guthrie, 145.
[54]Morris, 59.

who believe apostasy is possible but can be remedied also read the text in a way different from that which I have supported in this chapter. I have already mentioned the (somewhat different) views of Shank and Westcott to this effect and need not repeat the discussion above. I would only note that the other uses of "impossible" in Hebrews (6:18; 10:4; 11:6, as cited just above) add weight to the view that the word does not refer to a "temporary" impossibility but to something impossible by its very nature. Guthrie comments, "The statements are all absolutes."[55] McKnight, after comparing all the warning passages, concludes, "In such a context 'impossible' is to be understood as 'God will not work in them any longer so it is impossible for them to be restored'."[56]

Conclusion

As I have noted elsewhere, one ought to derive doctrine about any subject from a passage that treats that subject directly. Hebrews 6:4-6 and the entire book seem too clear to dispute: personal apostasy from a truly regenerate condition really is possible and recovery from it impossible.

This apostasy is therefore much more serious than what most people mean by "backsliding." Since salvation is first and always by faith, this apostasy involves a willful defection from the saving knowledge of Christ, a final retraction of faith from Him in whom alone is provision for forgiveness of sins. The apostate forsakes the cross where he found redemption: "By renouncing Christ they put themselves in the position of those who, deliberately refusing His claim to be the Son of God, had Him crucified and exposed to public shame."[57]

I should probably add that such an apostate, apparently, will not desire to find forgiveness in Christ. That is precisely what he has turned away from. Those who sincerely desire forgiveness and fellowship with God have not committed apostasy. "Those who worry over whether they have committed this sin show thereby that they have not commited it. . . . Apostasy in Hebrews lead[s] . . . to pride in one's sinful defiance of God's will."[58]

I should also add that my purpose has not included developing the practical implications of this teaching. As a summary of such implications, Osborne's observations will do well: "The only remedy [against the danger of apostasy] is a constant perseverance in the

---

[55]Guthrie, 141.
[56]McKnight, 33 (note 39).
[57]Bruce, 124.
[58]McKnight, 42, 43.

faith, and a continual growth to Christian maturity."[59] Also to be noted is that the writer of Hebrews "calls his readers to assist each other by mutual exhortation on their pilgrimage journey."[60] See 3:13; 10:24f; 12:12f; 13:17.

2 Peter 2:18-22

For reasons of space and repetition I will not attempt so thorough a treatment of this passage as I have for Hebrews, above. Even so, it is clear to me from a careful study of the entire epistle (in even greater detail than for Hebrews) that the same kind of analysis yields the same kind of results.

Considerations of context, for example, are similarly important and indicative. The danger of apostasy is before Peter[61] throughout and is explicitly referred to in 1:8, 9 and 3:17, thus being like bookends for this brief library about the importance of spiritual growth as fortification against the apostasy of false doctrine. The passage before us provides the heart of why Peter is warning his readers so sternly.

Here is a working translation of the passage:

> For, uttering over-swollen (words) of emptiness, they [the false teachers described in the preceding verses] lure, in lusts of the flesh with wanton excesses, those who really (or, just now) escaped from the ones living in error, promising them freedom, they themselves being slaves of corruption; for by what a person has been overcome, by this he has been enslaved. For if, (after) escaping the pollutions of the world by the knowledge of our Lord and Savior Jesus Christ, they have been overcome by being again entangled with these (pollutions), there has come to pass for them "the last things worse than the first." For it were better for them not to have come to the knowledge of the way of righteousness than, (after) coming to knowledge, to turn back from the holy commandment delivered to them. There has happened to them that of the true proverb, "A dog returning to its vomit," and "A sow washed for a wallowing in the mire."

---

[59]Osborne, 153.

[60]Marshall, 153.

[61]I assume Simon Peter to be the inspired writer of this letter. For a defense of this view and a presentation of other introductory matters, see Robert E. Picirilli, "Commentary on the Books of 1 and 2 Peter" in *The Randall House Bible Commentary: James, 1,2 Peter and Jude* (Nashville: Randall House Publications, 1992), 217-227.

A preliminary question concerns the identity of the "they" in verse 20, who are identified as the apostates: Are these the false teachers, or their intended victims? In view of the fact that Peter will deal with this as an apostasy that has already occurred, I am satisfied that he is identifying the false teachers as the apostates. However, as Bauckham observes, "The false teachers are in the state of definite apostasy described in verses 20-22; their followers are doubtless in severe danger of joining them."[62] For our purposes here, however, it makes no difference which group Peter regards as apostates or in danger of apostasy.

The main "movements" of the passage can be indicated in a relatively simple outline:

> *verses 18, 19*   the attempts of the false teachers to lure
>   believers astray;
> *verses 20, 21*   the apostasy which they exemplify;
> *verse 22*   an illustrative analogy.

The key verses to consider, in discussing apostasy, therefore, are verses 20, 21. Without taking time to analyze everything leading up to them, then, I will proceed to the major questions involved.[63]

1. That these whom Peter regards as apostates had a genuine Christian experience is seen in at least three ways.

First, they "got clean away" from the pollutions of the world, which recalls 1:4. The aorist *apophugontes* (verse 20 and in 1:4) harks back to the time of their conversion.

Second, they accomplished this escape "by the knowledge of the Lord and Savior, Jesus Christ." My special study of Peter's use of *epignōsis* leaves me in no doubt that he uses this compound for knowledge consciously as a way of representing the saving knowledge of Christ one gains at conversion.[64]

Third, they "have come to know the way of righteousness." The verb "have come to know" is cognate to the noun *epignōsis* just referred to, and is used with the same meaning. That it is perfect tense focuses on the state of knowledge that followed the initiation therein. The "way of righteousness" is obviously the same as "the way of truth" in verse 2 and "the straight way" in verse 15.

---

[62]Richard J. Bauckham, *Word Biblical Commentary: Jude, 2 Peter* (Waco: Word, 1983), 277.

[63]For a more thorough treatment, see Picirilli, "Commentary," 285-292.

[64]Robert E. Picirilli, "The Meaning of 'Epignōsis'" (*Evangelical Quarterly* 47:2 [1975]), 85-93.

As I have observed, above, in reference to the four expressions used in Hebrews 6:4-6, it would be hard to find a better description of what it means to become a Christian. Bauckham, after comparing the words here with those used in 1:3, 4, concludes that they are similar because "this is the vocabulary in which our author expresses the essential content of Christianity."[65]

2. The apostasy which Peter ascribes to these and warns his readers against is found in two expressions, each standing in sharp contrast to the experience just described.

First, they "have been overcome by being again entangled with these (pollutions)." And this after their escape from those very pollutions! In light of verse 19b, this being overcome is being re-enslaved. Clearly, these apostates have returned to the practice of the fleshly wickedness that previously defiled them.

Nor does the fact that this is introduced with an "if" mitigate this conclusion. This is a first class condition in Greek, the "if" of reality which might as well be translated "since." Even Kistemaker, a thorough-going Calvinist, acknowledges that the ones referred to were once "orthodox Christians" who "escaped the world's defilements"— and then hurries to make these "orthodox Christians" orthodox in external profession and lifestyle only.[66] He apparently does not realize how self-contradictory this sounds, or how unlike Peter's more obvious meaning.

Second, they have come to the place where they "turn back from the holy commandment delivered to them." And this after having come to know the way of righteousness! The "holy commandment" may be "the moral law of the gospel,"[67] or the whole range of gospel truth,[68] or better "Christianity as a whole way of life."[69] It was "delivered to them" when the gospel was preached to them and its implications taught. It is a holy commandment because it sets people apart as God's and teaches them a way of life appropriate for saints.

3. The seriousness of this apostasy Peter indicates in two expressions and a proverb.

---

[65]Bauckham, 276.

[66]Simon J. Kistemaker, *New Testament Commentary: Peter and Jude* (Grand Rapids: Baker, 1987), 311, 312.

[67]Henry Alford, *The Greek Testament*, vol. 4 (Cambridge: Deighton, Bell and Co., 1871), 411.

[68]R. C. H. Lenski, *The Interpretation of the Epistles of St. Peter, St. John, and St. Jude* (Columbus, Ohio: Brethren Book Concern, 1938), 340.

[69]J. N. D. Kelly, *A Commentary on the Epistles of Peter and Jude* (Grand Rapids: Baker, 1981 reprint), 350.

First, "the last things have come to be worse for them than the first." No doubt Peter is alluding to Jesus' words in Matthew 12:45 and sees that principle fulfilled in the experience of these apostates. They are in worse condition than before they came to the saving knowledge described above.

Second, "it were better for them not to have come to know the way of righteousness." This is an incredibly startling thing: can *anything* be worse than never having come to the saving knowledge of the way of the Lord? As Kelly notes, apostates are worse off than unconverted unbelievers "because they have rejected the light."[70] And if our study, above, of Hebrews has led us to the right conclusions, we understand even better why Peter puts this so strongly. An apostate cannot be recovered; a never converted unbeliever can.

Third, Peter illustrates with a two-fold proverbial saying (or with two proverbial sayings). That the idea proverbially represented "has happened" to the apostates means that the proverbs fit their situation. Like a dog that comes back to lick up the spoiled vomit that sickened him in the first place, like a sow that gets a bath and goes back to the mud from which she had been cleansed, these apostates return to the enslaving, polluting wickedness from which they had been delivered.

Those who attempt to mitigate Peter's teaching by suggesting that the real nature of the sow or the dog had not been changed, and that this implies that these apostate false teachers were never regenerated, are pressing the illustrations beyond what they are intended to convey. Indeed, the proverbs must be interpreted by the clearer words that precede them and not the other way around. The previous paragraph expresses precisely what the proverbs are intended to convey.

In conclusion, it is clear that Peter is describing a real apostasy from genuine Christianity. I will not pursue the passage further and respond to Calvinistic interpretations since this would be essentially repetition of my response to the Calvinistic interpretations of Hebrews, above.

---

[70]Kelly, 349.

For Further Reading About
the Biblical Teaching on Apostasy

Marshall, I. H. *Kept By the Power of God*. Minneapolis: Bethany
Fellowship, 1969.

McKnight, Scot. "The Warning Passages of Hebrews: A Formal
Analysis and Theological Conclusions," in *Trinity Journal* 13NS
(1992), 21-59.

Osborne, Grant R. "Soteriology in the Epistle to the Hebrews," in
Grace Unlimited, ed. Clark Pinnock. Grand Rapids: Bethany
Fellowship, 1975, 144-166.

Shank, Robert. *Life in the Son*. Springfield, Mo.: Westcott Publishers,
1960. [Shank's views are not entirely parallel to those of this
writer.]

Afterword

When one comes to the end of a lengthy presentation, he tends to ask himself whether he can finish without appearing to be too abrupt and whether there is some overall pattern to what he has said, one that can be summed up in a few sentences or paragraphs.

I have been occupied with many issues in the preceding pages. Can they be incorporated in one? I think they can, and that the issue, finally, is whether salvation is by faith. Indeed the issue has not frequently enough been expressed in those terms. It is that simple, and it is that complex, and that is where the focus needs to be.

We must make no mistake on this: the traditional Calvinist position is that salvation is not by faith, and the various elements in the theology of salvation make this clear. When the Calvinist looks back into eternity to explore God's plan, he sees salvation by election without regard to any decision by man. Having made such a decision, God sends Christ to ransom those chosen and those only. When it comes their time, in human history, to experience that redemption, God's Spirit first regenerates them so that He can give them the faith He requires. Certainly the summary is overly simplified, but it is accurate; and the preceding chapters serve to deliver us from the oversimplification.

The Reformation Arminian shares some of the same basic, Biblical principles: man is a totally depraved sinner, naturally unable even to accept God's gracious offer; salvation must therefore be wholly by grace and not by works and God's all-inclusive plan for His creation must be, will be certainly achieved. Even so, salvation is by faith. God constituted man with moral agency and wills for him to have freedom of choice; therefore any person who exercises choice for good or evil is, as such, fulfilling God's will. Seeing man's plight as fallen, He determined to provide redemption for all human beings and to apply it to any and all who will receive it by faith. This provision He made in the atoning work of Christ. He likewise determined that as the gospel of this redemption goes forth so will the Spirit of God by pre-regenerating grace enable man to exercise the faith He requires. Thus all salvation blessings, whether regeneration or justification, are by faith, not by works, and are therefore entirely gracious. Once saved by faith, the believer is kept through faith.

The Arminian position, of course, is that the latter is the Scriptural view. God's "secret" will regarding salvation is nothing other than the will He has revealed in the Bible, and that will is to save all who believe. Long live the Reformation cry: *by grace alone, by faith alone, by Christ alone.*

Scripture Index

(pages in **bold italic** represent more extensive
treatment of the passages indicated)

Index of Selected Subjects

(pages in *bold italic* represent more extensive
treatment of the subjects indicated)

Index of Citations from Arminius

(arranged by subject)

Index of Citations from Other Authors

**Teacher, Leader, Shepherd:
The New Testament Pastor
By Robert E. Picirilli
$12.99
ISBN 0892655690**

Teacher, Leader, Shepherd: The New Testament Pastor focuses on an understanding of what the Bible has to say to or about the pastor and his ministry. The author gives a solid treatment of the New Testament passages, which speak specifically, whether directly or indirectly, to the role of the pastor.

"I have a feeling that our first need is to lay a solid foundation for our concept of the pastor's role by setting forth what the Lord Himself has to say about it. Even the veteran pastor can benefit from such a study. Every candidate for a pastoral ministry will, I trust, find this work to be informing and challenging, helping to point his understanding in the right direction."

-Robert E. Picirilli

randall house

**To order call
800-877-7030
or visit
www.RandallHouse.com**

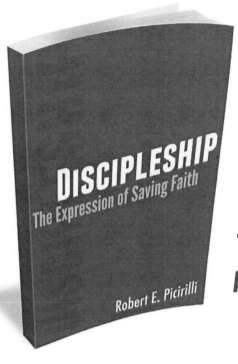